The Social Psychology
of Group Cohesiveness

The Social Psychology of Group Cohesiveness

From Attraction to Social Identity

MICHAEL A. HOGG

Department of Psychology
University of Queensland

NEW YORK UNIVERSITY PRESS
Washington Square, New York

First published in the USA in 1992 by
NEW YORK UNIVERSITY PRESS
Washington Square
New York, NY 10003

Library of Congress Cataloging-in-Publication Data

Hogg, Michael A., 1954–
    The social psychology of group cohesiveness : From attraction to
social identity / Michael A. Hogg.
        p.   cm.
    Includes bibliographical references (p.   ) and indexes.
    ISBN 0-8147-3499-5
    1. Small groups.   2. Group identity.   3. Social interaction.
4. Solidarity.   5. Interpersonal attraction.   I. Title.
HM133.H56   1992
302.3'4–dc20   92–22551
                                                              CIP

For my mother and Marion

Contents

Preface and acknowledgements

It has always intrigued me that being a member of a group can have such dramatic effects upon how you perceive and feel about yourself and others. In a group you can experience a unique sense of belonging and identity, accompanied by powerful positive feelings towards your fellow members. There is unity of purpose, uniformity of conduct and attitude, and a shared sense of invulnerability. Together these constitute that powerful sense of group solidarity and cohesion which we all experience from time to time: for example as members of sports teams, work groups, cultural or ethnic groups, national groups, and so forth. It is this sense of solidarity and cohesion that is the subject matter of this book.

I could have placed *group solidarity* or *group cohesion* in the title, but instead I opted for *group cohesiveness*, as this is the term most often used by social psychologists. It is also the name of the scientific concept that has been employed for over forty years to explain the social psychology of group solidarity. Since this is a book about the social psychology of group cohesiveness, it seemed appropriate to have group cohesiveness in the title.

The book explores in detail how social psychology explains group solidarity through the scientific concept of group cohesiveness. An important objective is to document, systematize and integrate the critical literature on group cohesiveness. Reconceptualizations and alternative perspectives are described, and evaluated against the claim that the original concept is limited because it ultimately reduces group processes conceptually to interpersonal processes. In later chapters a social identity and self-categorization perspective is described and evaluated in some detail, as I feel that it goes some way towards satisfactorily addressing many of the limitations and concerns of other formulations, and provides the most promising direction for future developments. I like to think of this book as an odyssey in which we proceed from traditional, theoretically problematic, largely attraction-based concep-tualizations of group cohesiveness to a new, theoretically more powerful, social identity and self-categorization-based conceptualization: hence the subtitle, *From attraction to social identity*.

The book is concerned with how we do – and how, perhaps, we ought to – conceptualize or theorize group cohesiveness, rather than with data. Relevant empirical findings and studies are, of course, summarized or described, but the emphasis is on a comprehensive and detailed discussion of how cohesiveness can be explained. So, the book is intended to appeal to anyone with an interest in the social psychological explanation of group cohesiveness, and more broadly with an interest in group processes. Social identity theory and self-categorization theory (e.g. Hogg and Abrams, 1988; Tajfel and Turner, 1979; Turner, 1982, 1985; Turner, Hogg, Oakes, Reicher and Wetherell, 1987) figure prominently, in later chapters, as a proposed new direction in the conceptualization of cohesiveness. Anyone with an interest in these theories will find that the book constitutes an extension of self-categorization theory to the explanation of attraction phenomena in and between groups.

My academic interest in group solidarity and cohesiveness began in 1978 when, under John Turner's supervision, I embarked on my doctoral studies at the University of Bristol. There appeared to be a number of limitations to the traditional group cohesiveness concept that rendered it problematic as an explanation of psychological group formation and group solidarity. A more cognitive model based on the process of self-categorization, and embraced by social identity theory, seemed more useful. I have pursued this idea ever since.

While I was working on cohesiveness, Stephen Reicher, Margaret Wetherell and Penny Oakes were investigating the cognitive bases of collective behaviour, conformity, group polarization, and identity salience. We were working with John Turner as a highly cohesive group on the development of self-categorization theory. Together we published this work in 1987 as *Rediscovering the Social Group: A self-categorization theory*. My first acknowledgement is an enormous intellectual debt to this small group, and to the wider group of social psychologists who were at Bristol University in the late 1970s and early 1980s: Henri Tajfel, Howard Giles, Philip Smith, John Colvin, Nick Pidgeon, Karen Henwood, Susan Condor. It was a very special place at a very special time.

A unique debt is of course owed to John Turner, without whose support, encouragement and inspiration I would never have begun. let alone continued, investigating group cohesiveness. Another special intellectual debt is to Dominic Abrams, who has been my close colleague over the years. We have collaborated on numerous ventures pursuing the development of social identity theory.

The general background to this book is a continuing research programme into group cohesiveness that has been funded since 1988 through research grants from the Australian Research Council. Without their support there would never have been a book at all. A special thanks goes to Elizabeth

Hardie, who worked as a research associate and close collaborator on the project for three years while I was at the University of Melbourne, and to Kate Reynolds, who is currently working as a research assistant on the project here at the University of Queensland.

This book was conceived, planned and researched while I was on sabbatical at the University of California, Los Angeles, in 1990. I would like to thank Marilynn Brewer for hosting the visit, and the University of California's Education Abroad Program for helping to fund it. Harvester Wheatsheaf kindly agreed to publish the book. For this I am grateful to Farrell Burnett, who, in her editorial capacity, has provided invaluable advice and copious enthusiastic encouragement.

In these days of the hegemony of social cognition, when one might be forgiven for sometimes thinking that no one studies group processes any more, it can be a lonely business researching group cohesiveness. Group cohesiveness is, after all, originally a 'small-group' concept. So I was relieved to discover that every summer a small group of dedicated researchers migrated to Bibb Latané's summer house on North Carolina's Outer Banks for the annual Nags Head Conference on Groups, Networks and Organizations. Those meetings from 1987 through 1990 were particularly valuable in the development of my ideas on group cohesiveness. They also produced some memorable illustrations of group solidarity: particularly on the volleyball court.

Finally, I have some specific people I would like to thank: Marilynn Brewer, Itesh Sachdev and Lucy Johnston for reading and commenting on an early draft of the manuscript; Dick Moreland, Kip Williams and Art Beaman for comments and ideas relating to specific topics in the book; Kate Reynolds for helping to assemble some of the literature; and Wendy Nelson for word processing. Last of all, but definitely not least, a very special thank you to my wife Bee. Not only did she daily risk life and limb reviewing literature in the earthquake-prone research library at UCLA, but she has also ridden the vicissitudes of book writing with patience and understanding. I am grateful for her support and encouragement.

Michael A. Hogg.
Brisbane, January 1992

Chapter 1

Introduction

This is a book about the social psychology of group cohesiveness. Specifically, it is about how social psychology has conceptualized group cohesiveness in the past, how it conceptualizes it now, and how, perhaps, it ought to conceptualize it in the future. 'Cohesiveness' is the descriptive and technical term used by social psychologists to refer to the essential property of social groups that is captured in common parlance by a wide range of other expressions, such as solidarity, cohesion, comradeship, team spirit, group atmosphere, unity, 'oneness', 'we-ness', 'groupness', and belongingness.

Any proper discussion of cohesiveness is inextricable from more general discussion of the social group, group formation, group processes, and relations between groups. Potentially, then, the discussion of cohesiveness can encompass a significant portion of social psychology. One aim of this introductory chapter is to establish the intended scope of the book, and the relationship between its subject matter and other areas of social psychological enquiry. There is also an overview and rationale of the structure of the book and the content of chapters.

Social groups

Social groups occupy much of our day-to-day life. We work in groups, we socialize in groups, we play in groups, and we represent our views and attitudes through groups. Groups also largely determine the people we are, and the sorts of lives we live. Selection panels, juries, committees and government bodies influence what we do, where we live, and how we live. The groups to which we belong determine what language we speak, what accent we have, what attitudes we hold, what cultural practices we adopt, what education we receive, what level of prosperity we enjoy, and ultimately who we are. Even the groups to which we do not belong, either by choice or by exclusion, have a profound impact on our lives. In this overwhelming matrix of group influences, the domain of the autonomous, independent, unique self may be very limited indeed.

For example, consider some of my activities yesterday. At the office I attended a thirty- or forty-member academic committee meeting, followed by a small six-person *ad hoc* committee meeting, followed by a colloquium meeting of the social psychology group. Later in the evening I met up with a small group of friends at a riverside bar. These are face-to-face interactive groups, some of which were more fun than others. But other groups also impinged on my activities. Before going out for the evening, I, along with many millions of Australians, watched live television coverage of the final Rugby League test between Australia and our arch-rivals from across the Tasman, New Zealand.

During the day, while driving to and from the office, I observed speed limits, and traffic signals. I didn't do this purely for my own preservation – often I could, for example, have ignored traffic signals with no risk whatsoever to myself or others. I observed these rules because I am a member of the community of Australian road users, and thus define my activities on the road in terms of the norms and standards (formalized through legislation in this case) that this group has evolved over the years. Finally, my current major activity is writing this book, and this is in itself a reflection of being a member of a group: the group of academics. If I was not a member of this group, I would have been unlikely to occupy my day in this way.

Groups differ in all sorts of respects. Some have a large number of members (a nation, a sex), while others are small (a committee, a family); some are relatively short-lived (a group of friends, a jury), while some endure for thousands of years (an ethnic group, a religion); some are concentrated (a road crew, a selection committee), others dispersed (radio 'hams', academics); some are highly structured and organized (an army, a flight crew), others more informally organized (a supporters' club, a community action group); some have highly specific purposes (an assembly line, an environmental protest group), others are more general (a tribal group, a teenage 'gang'); some are relatively autocratic (an army, a police force), others relatively democratic (a university department, a commune); and so on.

Any social group can thus be described in terms of an almost limitless array of features that highlight similarities to and differences from other groups. These can be very general features, such as membership size (a religion versus a committee), but they can also be very specific features, such as group practices and beliefs (Catholics versus Muslims, Liberals versus Conservatives, Masai versus Kikuyu). However, this enormous variety of groups could be reduced by selecting a limited number of significant dimensions in order to produce a restricted taxonomy of groups. Social psychologists have tended to focus more on group size, group 'atmosphere', task structure and leadership structure than on other dimensions.

Irrespective of how one classifies a group in terms of some sort of descriptive taxonomy, all groups – religions, ethnic groups, teams, committees, gangs, and so forth – vary in cohesiveness. Cohesiveness is a general property of all groups, irrespective of their size, dispersion, longevity, leadership structure, purpose, and so on. Not only can we describe and compare groups in terms of their overall cohesiveness, but we can also focus upon the individual group member and try to understand the psychological process responsible for producing varying degrees of cohesiveness. It is this latter process that is the focus of this book. As we shall see, these two levels of cohesiveness are often confounded in social psychological explanations of cohesiveness. More precisely, perhaps, it is the way one is theoretically translated into the other that can be problematic.

Groups pervade every aspect of our lives. They are both the background to our existence and the focus of our day-to-day activities. I have painted a picture in which individual human beings are actually socially constituted by the groups to which they belong – where every group membership, past and present, leaves an indelible mark. There is, then, a real sense in,which people appear to be unique, only because they each have a unique biography of group memberships. However, although we acknowledge commonalities (e.g. a common language) mediated by shared group membership (e.g. ethnolinguistic group), subjectively we consider ourselves to be unique entities. And so, in our lives we continually seek close interpersonal relationships (friends, partners, rivals) in which subjective individuality can be confirmed, proclaimed and developed. Usually we do this within the framework of group memberships: for example, we often develop friendships with people we see on a day-to-day basis at work.

This raises the questions of what constitutes a group, psychologically, and how, if at all, group relationships are different to interpersonal relationships. These are vexed questions for social psychologists because the jury is still out over the fundamental social psychological issue of whether there is a psychological discontinuity between group processes and group relationships, on the one hand, and interpersonal processes and interpersonal relationships on the other. The jury may remain out, as probable verdicts reflect entrenched metatheoretical and ideological interests. Psychologically orientated social psychologists who embrace a metatheory of individualism (e.g. Floyd Allport, 1924) would promote a 'no difference' verdict, while more sociologically orientated social psychologists who embrace a non-reductionist metatheory (e.g. Tajfel, 1981a) would promote a 'difference' verdict. This issue is the metatheoretical thread running through this book.

In the meantime, however, how can a group be distinguished from a mere aggregate of individuals? The answer depends on how one defines a group, social psychologically. For some social psychologists, many of the groups I used as illustrations above might perhaps not be considered groups at all.

Studying the social group

There are almost as many definitions of the social group as there are social psychologists who research social groups. However, these definitions tend to reflect researchers' different research emphases. So, for example, Johnson and Johnson (1987, pp. 4–7) identify seven separate emphases. The group is:

1. A collection of individuals who are interacting with one another – e.g. Bonner (1959, p. 4), Homans (1950, p. 1), Stogdill (1959, p. 18);
2. A social unit consisting of two or more persons who perceive themselves as belonging to a group – e.g. Bales (1950, p. 33), Smith (1945, p. 227);
3. A collection of individuals who are interdependent – e.g. Cartwright and Zander (1968, p. 46), Fiedler (1967, p. 6), Lewin (1951, p. 146);
4. A collection of individuals who join together to achieve a goal – e.g. Deutsch (1959, p. 136), Mills (1967, p. 2);
5. A collection of individuals who are trying to satisfy some need through their joint association – e.g. Bass (1960, p. 39), Cattell (1951, p. 167);
6. A collection of individuals whose interactions are structured by a set of roles and norms – e.g. McDavid and Harari (1968, p. 237), Sherif and Sherif (1956, p. 144);
7. A collection of individuals who influence each other – e.g. Shaw (1976, p. 11).

Johnson and Johnson's definition incorporates all these emphases: 'A group is two or more individuals in face-to-face interaction, each aware of his or her membership in the group, each aware of the others who belong to the group, and each aware of their positive interdependence as they strive to achieve mutual goals' (1987, p. 8). The reader will notice that this definition, and many of the 'emphases' in the previous paragraph, either cannot encompass large groups and/or do not distinguish between interpersonal and group relationships. This constitutes a relatively accurate portrayal of the social psychology of group processes. It is generally restricted, explicitly or implicitly, to small, face-to-face, short-lived, interactive, task-orientated groups. In addition, 'group processes' generally does not mean *group* processes, but interpersonal processes among more than two people. The concept of group cohesiveness was developed and sustained within these parameters.

One consequence of this tradition in social psychology is that the study of group phenomena is dispersed among relatively independent research topic areas that do not often communicate readily with one another. For example, research into cohesiveness, conformity, obedience, leadership, prejudice, intergroup conflict, social identity, categorization processes, stereotyping, and so forth, all deal with group processes, but there is only minimal integration. In general, researchers often see themselves as – for example – social cognition, intergroup relations, or small-group-processes people rather than group researchers. They go to different meetings, publish in different places, read different literatures and generally engage in intergroup rivalry! There are, of course, a number of notable exceptions, but the general description is, I think, fairly accurate. This means that while phenomenon-specific short-range explanations abound (e.g. social impact [Latané, 1981], deindividuation [Diener, 1980]) it is difficult to encounter systematic global theories of the social group.

This is a great pity, as the social group is a quintessentially social psychological phenomenon. Marx, in his sociological theory of history and social change, found a need for a psychological analysis of the individual class member (e.g. Marx, [1844] 1963). Freud, in his psychological analysis of the individual unconscious, found a need for a social analysis of the relationship between the individual unconscious and group life (Freud, 1922). Both these great theorists were essentially striving for a social psychology of the group – a social psychology that lay in the interstice between their respective theories of society and the individual. Others, specifically the Frankfurt School, have tried explicitly to link Freud's psychological analysis with Marx's sociological analysis, and thus generate a social psychology of the group (see Billig, 1976, for a critical discussion).

An important aim of this book is to approach the analysis of group cohesiveness from a perspective that is unrestricted by the parameters of its 'small-groups' metatheory. Indeed, it is this metatheoretical constraint which, I feel, is responsible for many of the limitations of the social psychology of group cohesiveness. An alternative perspective involves a metatheory that self-consciously avoids explaining group phenomena exclusively in terms of interpersonal processes, but rather distinguishes group processes from interpersonal processes and does not explain one in terms of the other. Group processes are conceptualized in terms of processes that are unique to groups, but are common to all groups, irrespective of size, dispersion, and so forth.

This perspective is embodied in social identity theory and self-categorization theory. These are self-consciously non-reductionist theories of the social group that encompass the form and content of the whole range of inter- and intragroup behaviours (conformity, cohesiveness, stereotyping, norms, prejudice, discrimination, intergroup conflict, and so forth). They are overlapping theories that articulate with one another: self-categorization theory is a more recent and more specific development of the older and wider social identity theory (cf. Hogg and McGarty, 1990).

A great deal has been published on social identity theory and self-categorization theory. Apart from numerous articles and chapters, there are a number of specific books. Most recently, there is Hogg and Abrams's (1988) integrative text (*Social Identifications: A social psychology of intergroup relations and group processes*), Abrams and Hogg's (1990a) edited book (*Social Identity Theory: Constructive and critical advances*), Turner, Hogg, Oakes, Reicher and

Wetherell's (1987) major theoretical statement of self-categorization theory (*Rediscovering the Social Group: A self-categorization theory*), and Turner's (1991) social influence text (*Social Influence*) which, although it is not a social identity or self-categorization book, adopts a self-categorization perspective. In addition, there are four older edited books: Tajfel (1978, 1981a, 1982a), and Turner and Giles (1981).

This book is not another social identity or self-categorization book, though these theories are covered in two chapters, and the critique of reductionism that frames these theories is a major theme running throughout. One chapter surveys basic principles and develops, in detail, a self-categorization theory of group cohesiveness. The other examines and assesses this formulation against empirical evidence, related concepts and meta-theoretical considerations. The bulk of the book, however, reviews, examines and critically assesses the traditional concept of group cohesiveness, and alternative formulations.

Group cohesiveness

Many people trace the explosive expansion of experimental social psychology to the study of group dynamics at the Research Center for Group Dynamics in the 1940s (Cartwright, 1979; Festinger, 1980; Marrow, 1969). The agenda was to theorize about the actions, thoughts and feelings of interacting people in small groups such as neighbourhoods, housing programmes, sororities, sports teams, military units, decision-making groups, and work groups. Researchers sought to develop a systematic theory to explain how groups change the attitudes, beliefs, norms and behaviours of their members (e.g. Coch and French, 1948; Lewin, 1943; Pennington, Harary and Bass, 1958; Radke and Klisurich, 1947), and to identify variables influencing group productivity, performance, morale, and communication structure.

Group cohesiveness was initially a mainly descriptive term with no consensual or formal definition. However, in 1950 Festinger, Schachter and Back produced a formal statement. Group cohesiveness now became a key theoretical construct, intended not only to describe the 'groupness' of individuals constituting an interactive small group, but to theorize about underlying psychological processes. In other words, as a psychological theory, it was intended to be able to account for the group level of cohesiveness in terms of the operation of individual psychological processes.

However, it was no easy matter to achieve this goal. In fact, the problematic of how to account satisfactorily for the group-level phenomenon of cohesiveness in terms of psychological processes that are isolated within the head of the individual has plagued the study of cohesiveness for its entire half-century history. Although it makes perfect sense to describe a group in terms of its cohesiveness, it is not so meaningful to do so at the individual level. One can sensibly say that a group is more or less cohesive, but not that an individual is more or less cohesive. An assessment of the concept of group cohesiveness is in many ways an evaluation of its success in addressing this very issue.

This is what the book is about: how can one explain group cohesiveness social psychologically, without sociologizing or psychologizing the explanation, and without restricting oneself to a narrow range of groups or group phenomena? I am concerned mainly with explanations, concepts, theories and metatheory, rather than the documentation of empirical findings. As regards group cohesiveness, empirical reviews abound elsewhere: Blumberg, Hare, Kent and Davies (1983); Carron (1980); Cartwright (1968); Crosbie (1975); Drescher, Burlingame and Fuhriman (1985); Evans and Jarvis (1980); Kellerman (1981); Levine and Moreland (1990); Lott and Lott (1965); McGrath and Kravitz (1982); Shaw (1976); Zander (1979).

The fact that some variable 'X' affects cohesiveness, or that cohesiveness in turn affects 'X', is difficult to appreciate if the precise nature of cohesiveness is not understood or properly specified. This sentiment is shared by Zander, who, in dealing with cohesiveness in his 1979 review of group processes, warned that 'in the absence of a reliable method for measuring cohesiveness . . . or a reliable procedure for creating it . . . , one cannot be sure to what phenomena investigators are attending when they examine its origins or effects' (p. 433). I hope to show that the traditional concept of cohesiveness (and the traditional perspective on cohesiveness) is sufficiently flawed to render the concept a sealed black box.

This book

This book is about the social psychology of group cohesiveness. It describes the development of the scientific concept of group cohesiveness, shows how it has been changed and how it has been used over the years, and exposes the fundamental and often implicit processes that underlie the concept. Conceptual limitations are documented, described in detail, and subsumed by a general critique of reductionism. Alternative formulations are described and evaluated, and the relationship between group cohesiveness and other group processes is highlighted. A social identity and self-categorization approach is proposed, and specifically applied to the reconceptualization of the attraction component of cohesiveness. This model is assessed against related concepts, alternative formulations and empirical tests. Some prospects for the future, and some new ways to interpret old phenomena, are alluded to.

The book is concerned with understanding how properly to conceptualize group cohesiveness, rather than providing a comprehensive review of research findings. Empirical research is described only where it has direct bearing on understanding conceptualization. Elsewhere relevant research is simply summarized, or the reader is referred to other reviews. One of the novel aspects of this book is that it represents a badly needed systematic and critical assessment of the concept of group cohesiveness from the perspective of 'mainstream' social psychology. This assessment directly produces a systematic alternative approach that is grounded in a non-reductionist conceptualization of the social group – a reconceptualization that is as relevant for large groups as small, and connects with the entire array of other group behaviours at both inter- and intragroup level.

The history and problems of group cohesiveness are shared by much of social psychology. Likewise, group-solidarity phenomena can encompass an enormous portion of social psychology. So in many ways this book is not only about group cohesiveness but also about social psychology, social psychological theories, and doing social psychology. In keeping it to a manageable size I have attempted to include all and only those areas that are most relevant to the main argument. However, I will no doubt have excluded some areas and points that others may feel ought to have been included.

One exclusion that may require justification is the area of psychotherapeutic and psychoanalytic group research. These areas invoke the notion of group cohesiveness quite heavily in their case studies of small therapy groups (see Kellerman, 1981). I have not actually omitted this area entirely (see Chapter 2), but I have not become involved in detailed discussion or comprehensive coverage. There are three main reasons: (1) this literature generally does not use the term cohesiveness in the same way as does social psychology; (2) a proper discussion of this literature would have required an entire chapter; and (3) I personally believe that there is little to be gained by the social psychology of group processes from the psychoanalytic literature – see Billig's (1976) classic critique of psychoanalytic and Freudian perspectives on group processes and intergroup relations.

I have written this book to be read from cover to cover. However, I have packaged individual chapters to be self-contained to some extent so that readers can focus in on specific parts. To help in this, each chapter has a brief introductory and concluding summary that surveys the main points, and locates the chapter in the overall logic of the book. There are eight chapters, including this one. Chapter 2 contextualizes the concept of group cohesiveness in early experimental and pre-experimental social psychology of group solidarity, and shows how the concept has been simplified since 1950 so that group cohesiveness is explained largely in terms of interpersonal attraction. The latter part of the chapter describes how this type of perspective on group cohesiveness represents a much wider model of the social group that underlies, with differing emphases, many of the major social psychological models of the group.

Following this characterization of the traditional theory of group cohesiveness, Chapter 3 goes on to summarize traditional research methods and findings concerning group cohesiveness. In describing what we know and what we are not so sure about, special attention is given to contradictory, inconclusive and novel findings. This is not intended to be a comprehensive review or overview. The aim is simply to illustrate the type of research that has been done, and the findings that have been obtained. Since it is also necessary to consider the practical or applied utility of the concept of group cohesiveness, the other major aim of this chapter is to describe the various different scales that have been – and still are – used to measure the cohesiveness of groups.

Chapter 4 describes how group cohesiveness has suffered diminishing popularity in mainstream social psychology. This is attributed to historical trends in social psychology, and to specific problems with the concept (problems that are shared by other areas of social psychology). The bulk of the chapter is dedicated to a detailed exposition of limitations of the group cohesiveness concept. Traditional criticisms question the concept but not the metatheory, while radical criticisms are framed by a critique of the reductionist metatheory.

Attempts to address these limitations are described and evaluated in Chapter 5. One problem with cohesiveness is that it is largely tied to attraction phenomena in small groups. There are, however, many other facets of group behaviour that have been researched, and may cast light on cohesiveness. Of these, conformity and deindividuation are perhaps two of the most important. Chapter 5 also discusses the process of group socialization.

Because of its emphasis on interpersonal factors, group cohesiveness lacks an intergroup dimension. Social identity theory, in contrast, is a theory of intergroup relations which – principally through self-categorization theory – analyzes intragroup phenomena in the context of intergroup relations. Chapter 6 describes social identity theory and self-categorization theory, shows how these theories can explain social influence in groups, and provides some comment on the measurement of social identity. An important part of this chapter is a detailed explanation of how the process of self-categorization can produce group-level attraction phenomena that are conceptually independent of interpersonal attraction. The chapter also develops principles for a self-categorization theory of group cohesiveness.

Chapter 7 evaluates this new model of group cohesiveness. It is related to the other reconceptualizations presented in Chapter 5, and to related concepts in the social cognition, intergroup relations, and interpersonal attraction and relationships literatures. It is also evaluated against its metatheoretical aims. A major part of the chapter is dedicated to a description of relevant empirical evidence.

Chapter 8 presents some concluding comments about group cohesiveness, and outlines some prospects for the future. It illustrates ways in which a self-categorization perspective on group cohesiveness furnishes new insights for the explanation of some established group phenomena, and how it can address a much wider range of group contexts than can traditional formulations. One aim is to show how the reconceptualization presented in Chapter 6 may help to explain phenomena that have been problematic for a traditional cohesiveness approach. Specifically, there is a critical discussion of groupthink, a discussion of the group performance/cohesiveness relationship, and a discussion of social loafing and motivation losses in groups. Another aim is to show how such an approach equips us with concepts that are equally at home in explaining large-scale solidarity phenomena (e.g. ethnolinguistic solidarity) and small-group solidarity phenomena.

I have written this book because I feel that it is timely. Since the early 1950s social psychology has made enormous advances, yet the concept of group cohesiveness – which, in dealing with the essence of being a group, addresses a fundamental social psychological issue – has remained relatively unchanged. There have been no systematic and cumulative social psychological attempts to overhaul the concept in the light of our advanced understanding of intergroup behaviour, social cognition, reductionism, and the social group.

I hope that this book provides a framework for others to research group cohesiveness and cohesiveness phenomena with some awareness of the limitations of a reductionist model, and some recognition of the possible advantages of a self-categorization formulation. It would be valuable for social psychology to examine critically the concept of cohesiveness for its own sake, rather than simply to invoke or employ it uncritically. I hope that this book reinvigorates basic research into group cohesiveness.

Chapter 2

The concept of group cohesiveness

The scientific concept of group cohesiveness emerged from the burgeoning experimental social psychological study of group processes in the 1940s and 1950s. Previously, others had, of course, thought about the solidarity, cohesiveness and formation of groups. Some of these pre-experimental endeavours are important, as they provide the background against which later ideas were formed. In this chapter some influential pre-experimental social psychological views on the solidarity, cohesiveness, and formation of groups are described. I go on to document early experimental social psychological ideas about cohesiveness that culminated in a formal statement in 1950, and then show how the concept has been altered over the years. The chapter concludes with a detailed characterization of the real nature of the concept, how it reflects a general social psychological model of the social group, and how it differs from or is similar to other related ideas about the social group.

Pre-experimental perspectives

Contemporary social psychology is indelibly marked with the ideas and metatheories of some of its early non-experimental forebears. For the social psychology of group processes, perhaps the most important of these include Gustave LeBon, Sigmund Freud, and William McDougall. In this section, a few words are also said about the early work of Donald Campbell: not that this work is really 'pre-experimental', but it is more appropriately described here than elsewhere.

LeBon

LeBon (1908, 1913) lived through a period of French history characterized by great social unrest: the revolution of 1848 and the Paris Commune of 1871.

He believed that French society was in danger of complete disintegration and that salvation lay in rigid social stratification with the ruling political elite equipped to control the masses. This ideological stance led LeBon to mount a 'sustained attack upon collective protest' (Reicher, 1987, p. 174). He observed and read accounts of the great revolutionary crowds of the time, so vividly described by Emile Zola (in *Germinal* and *La Débâcle*) and Victor Hugo (*Les Misérables*), and was horrified by the primitive, base and ghastly behaviour of the crowd, and the way in which 'the sentiments and ideas of all the persons in the gathering take one and the same direction, and their conscious personality vanishes' (1908, pp. 23–4). LeBon believed that 'by the mere fact that he forms part of an organized crowd, a man descends several rungs in the ladder of civilization. Isolated, he may be a cultivated individual; in a crowd, he is a barbarian – that is, a creature acting by instinct' (1908, p. 12). Crowds produce these effects (i.e. primitive and homogeneous behaviour), LeBon believed, because (1) members are anonymous and thus lose personal responsibility for their actions; (2) ideas and sentiments spread rapidly and unpredictably through a process of contagion; and (3) unconscious antisocial motives are released through suggestion (a process akin to hypnosis). (See Figure 2.1.)

For LeBon, then, the solidarity of the crowd is a matter of its uniformity of action, which is due largely to anonymity and contagion, with suggestibility ensuring that the behaviour will be antisocial. LeBon's ideas were popular with mid-twentieth-century dictators (e.g. Mussolini), and have influenced recent social psychological treatments of collective behaviour (e.g. Zimbardo's [1970], discussion of deindividuation). Perhaps most significantly, they were the basis of Freud's group psychology. Freud formalized many of LeBon's descriptive terms to construct a general theory of the social group – LeBon was concerned only with collective behaviour.

Freud

Freud's basic insight was that much of human behaviour is produced by primitive motives (mainly associated with primary biological functions) that are repressed and rendered unconscious through the course of infantile interaction with parents. The complexity of Freud's thinking, not to mention myriad modifications made by Freud and his followers, allows only a thumbnail sketch to be provided here of his theory of group formation, solidarity and cohesiveness – originally published in 1921 as *Group Psychology and the Analysis of the Ego*.

Freud believed that young children have a strong sexual yearning for their opposite-sex parent, which is thwarted by the competitive presence of the same-sex parent. Thus, the same-sex parent is simultaneously loved as a primary caretaker and hated as a sexual rival: the classic Oedipus complex (or

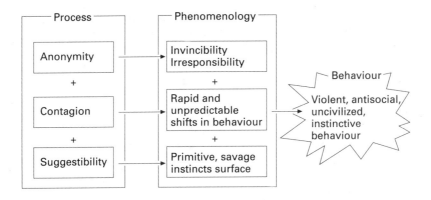

Figure 2.1 *LeBon's model of the crowd*

Electra complex for females). The complex is resolved by identifying with the same-sex parent, though Freud's analysis is primarily concerned with the resolution of the Oedipus complex. The process of identification involves introjection (internalization) of the father as the ego ideal (a set of strict standards and codes of behaviour that are difficult to match). In this way the child 'becomes' the father and thus 'possesses' the mother while at the same time retaining love for the father. Freud believed that all father figures are strong authoritative leaders, and thus that the original identification with the father is generalized to all leaders – a process called primary identification.

Primary identification explains loyalty and attachment to the leader, as well as the high degree of psychic similarity that exists in groups. In fact, Freud deemed a group to comprise 'a number of individuals who have put one and the same object in the place of their ego ideal and have consequently identified themselves with one another in their ego' (1921, p. 116). He believed that group members are bound not only to the group leader but also to fellow group members 'by intense emotional ties' (1921, p. 95), which represent the social bonds of groups. Although he introduced the notion of secondary identification to explain this social bond among members, the underlying process was left imprecisely defined – only vaguely hinting at a process related, perhaps, to empathy.

Freud's ideas have been enormously influential in social psychology – in particular in theories of aggression and prejudice (e.g. Adorno, Frenkel-Brunswik, Levinson and Sanford's [1950] authoritarian personality theory, and Dollard, Doob, Miller, Mowrer and Sears's [1939] frustration–aggression hypothesis), but also in small-group dynamics (e.g. Bion, 1961). There are excellent critiques of Freudian explanations of group processes and intergroup relations (e.g. Billig, 1976), but it is beyond the scope of this book to summarize them. There are, however, some glaring limitations of Freud's analysis of group solidarity, which must be mentioned here.

Freud's theory is one which, unlike LeBon's, deals with groups of all sorts, and is not restricted to crowds. However, Freud felt that an important distinction ought to be made between groups with leaders, and groups without leaders — the latter being considered psychologically impoverished. Freud's theory is relevant only to the former — he did not elaborate or pursue his passing suggestion that 'we should consider whether an idea, an abstraction, may not take the place of the leader' (1922, p. 32). Freud then, can offer an explanation of only one type of group. At this juncture it should be noted that Freud's distinction between groups with and groups without leaders emerges in different guises elsewhere: for example, Bion's (1961) 'work groups' and 'basic-assumption groups', and McDougall's (1921) 'organized' and 'unorganized' groups.

Another problem with Freud's formulation is that the basis of group solidarity is in resolution of the Oedipus complex — a uniquely male phenomenon. How, then, can females form groups? If the Electra complex is exactly analogous to the Oedipus complex, men and women would identify only with same-sex groups. If there are differences between the two complexes, as Freud occasionally claims, where is his separate theory of group solidarity for women? Finally, the existence and strength of social bonds among group members, the essence of solidarity and cohesion, is inadequately explicated with reference to the vague notion of secondary identification.

McDougall

The third major pre-experimental theorist is William McDougall (1908, 1921). McDougall believed that the role of social psychology was 'to display the reciprocal influences of the individual and the society in which he plays his part', and that 'we can only understand the life of individuals and the life of societies, if we consider them always in relation to one another'. The role of collective or group psychology was 'to study the mental life of societies of all kinds' in order to develop general principles of group life and to document their expression in specific societies and groups (1921, p. 6).

McDougall's group psychology appears in his classic book *The Group Mind* (1921). He believed that 'the group . . . is more than the sum of the individuals, [and] has its own life, proceeding according to laws of group life, which are not the laws of individual life' (p. 13). McDougall argued that if social aggregates have a collective mental life that is not the sum of the mental lives of its members, then it has a collective mind or collective soul: a *group mind*. The focal paradox for McDougall — reflecting on the work of others, such as LeBon on the crowd — was that:

participation in group life degrades the individual, assimilating his mental processes to those of the crowd, whose brutality, inconstancy, and unreasoning impulsiveness have been the theme of many writers; yet only by participation in group life does man become fully man, only so does he rise above the level of the savage. (p. 20)

McDougall sought a theory that would account for similarities and differences in the behaviour of the 'unorganized crowd' at one extreme, and more highly organized groups such as a church or army, at the other.

For McDougall the fundamental conditions for collective mental life were 'a common object of mental activity, a common mode of feeling in regard to it, and some degree of reciprocal influence between the members of the group' (p. 23). He felt that the crowd possessed these features in their most elementary and simple form, and was therefore a good place to start his analysis. McDougall's characterization of the nature of crowd behaviour was identical to that of LeBon:

> excessively emotional, impulsive, violent, fickle, inconsistent, irresolute and extreme in action, displaying only the coarser emotions and the less refined sentiments; extremely suggestible, careless in deliberation, hasty in judgement, incapable of any but the simpler and imperfect forms of reasoning; easily swayed and led, lacking in self-consciousness, devoid of self-respect and of sense of responsibility, and apt to be carried away by the consciousness of its own force, so that it tends to produce all the manifestations we have learnt to expect of any irresponsible and absolute power. (1921, p. 45)

McDougall's explanation was in terms of instinctive primary emotions, 'primitive sympathy', depersonalization, and loss of personal responsibility. He argued that the most widespread instinctive emotions are the simple primitive ones (e.g. fear, anger). Any given aggregate will be highly homogeneous regarding these emotions, but heterogeneous regarding more subtle complex emotions that are less widely shared. Stimuli eliciting the former, the primitive simple emotions, will cause a strong consensual reaction, while stimuli eliciting the latter, the more developed complex emotions, will cause only a few individuals to react. Primary emotions spread and strengthen very rapidly in a crowd as each member's expression of the emotion acts as a further stimulus to others: there is an irresistible snowball effect that McDougall dubbed 'primitive sympathy'. The spread and amplification of these emotions are not easily modulated, as individuals feel depersonalized and have a lowered sense of personal responsibility.

McDougall believed that the unorganized crowd does not possess a group mind. For a group mind to emerge a number of other factors are involved, the most important being: (1) continuity of existence regarding members and/or specific roles; (2) emergence of traditions, customs, and habits; (3) organization of the group with respect to differentiation and specialization of functions; and perhaps most importantly, (4) group self-consciousness –

members have an idea in their mind of the group, what it represents, how it functions, and how it is structured.

McDougall considered groups to differ in group self-consciousness, from its lowest level in unorganized crowds to its highest in organized groups. Associated with group self-consciousness was a sentiment of attachment to the group, with the two together representing the *group spirit* or *esprit de corps*. McDougall believed that the group spirit — we could equally well call it group cohesiveness or solidarity — 'involving knowledge of the group as such, some idea of the group, and some sentiment of devotion or attachment to the group, is . . . the essential condition of all developed collective life, and of all effective collective action' (1921, p. 66). 'The development of the group spirit consists in two essential processes, namely, the acquisition of knowledge of the group and the formation of some sentiment of attachment to the group' (p. 86). Group self-consciousness alone is not sufficient for group solidarity; positive group sentiment, 'almost inevitably one of attachment' (*ibid.*), is also needed. McDougall is quite explicit in identifying this sentiment as comprising liking, trust, pride, and/or respect. The origin of the sentiment is in self-regard (self-regarding sentiments are extended to the group), and the target of the sentiment is the group as a knowledge structure, not necessarily specific group members.

McDougall's work is important because his attempt to construct a social psychology of groups was ambitious, and thus contains many of the major themes, controversies, hopes and disappointments that have punctuated the history of subsequent attempts. He was a Gestaltist with a belief that group behaviour required its own level of analysis, distinct from individual psychology or interpersonal processes, yet he rested heavily on the idea of instinctive emotions. His notion of group mind, though appealing, is nevertheless vague and intangible. The process of social influence responsible for the spread of emotions is simply named as 'primitive sympathy' and is not really explicated; nor is the mechanism whereby group self-consciousness is formed. It is interesting, in the light of subsequent developments, to note that McDougall introduced the notion of 'attachment' to explain solidarity and cohesiveness, but that he avoided reducing it merely to interpersonal attachment.

Perhaps McDougall's major 'fault' is simply that he introduced a number of ideas before their time: over half a century of social psychology was necessary in order finally to unpack some of his insights. In any event, with Floyd Allport's famous and far-reaching dictum that 'there is no psychology of groups which is not essentially and entirely a psychology of individuals' (1924, p. 4), his characterization of the crowd as 'a number of persons within stimulating distance of one another' (*ibid.*, p. 5), and his view that 'the actions of all *are* nothing more than the sum of the actions of each taken separately' (*ibid.*, original emphasis), the prevailing sentiment swung unrelentingly in favour of attempts to explain group processes in terms of properties of individuals and their interpersonal relationships. Nevertheless, some of the concerns that fired McDougall have surfaced from time to time – for example in Sherif's (1936) study of social norms, Asch's (1952) approach to social psychology, Campbell's (1958) discussion of 'entitativity', and more recently Tajfel and Turner and colleagues' work on social identity and self-categorization (e.g. Hogg and Abrams, 1988; Turner and Oakes, 1986).

Campbell

Although it is not really representative of a 'pre-experimental' perspective, Donald Campbell's (1958) discussion of entitativity is dealt with more appropriately here, following on from McDougall, than in the next section on early experimental social psychology. Campbell coined the term 'entitativity' to describe 'the degree of having the nature of an entity, of having real existence' (1958, p. 17). Rejecting the view that the group is a nominal fallacy, he argued that just as people have little difficulty perceiving physical objects as entities (e.g. an aggregate of rock particles is imbued with reality as a single object: a stone), they also, under certain circumstances, perceive aggregates of people as single entities. For Campbell, entitativity is determined by Gestalt principles of general perception: primarily perceived common fate and similarity of elements, but also, to a lesser extent, proximity of elements and permeability of boundaries.

Thus, a social aggregate is perceived and reacted to as an entity to the extent that its elements (people) are similar, have a common fate, and are close to one another, and its boundary is relatively impermeable. Entitativity refers to the degree of perceived groupness, solidarity, or cohesiveness of a social aggregate. Unlike McDougall, Campbell did not extend his analysis to introduce any notion of interindividual attachment. It is a more purely cognitive/perceptual analysis that resonates rather well with some elements of much more recent social-cognitive treatments of the social group, such as self-categorization theory (Turner *et al.*, 1987; see Chapter 6).

Early experimental social psychology

Floyd Allport's individualistic prescription for the analysis of the group coincided with an important and far-reaching change in methodological emphasis – from observational and ethnographic to experimental method – in social psychology. The term 'cohesiveness' now increasingly entered into the vocabulary of research on groups.

The term had already been introduced in the 1930s and 1940s, before Festinger, Schachter and Back's formal statement on group cohesiveness was published in 1950. This early work was largely unsystematic and merely described how individuals tend to 'stick together' in groups. For example, Moreno and Jennings defined cohesiveness as 'the forces holding the individuals within the groupings in which they are' (1937, p. 371; see also Moreno, 1934); and French (1941, p. 370) noted that the group exists as a balance between cohesion and 'disruptive forces'. Other similar descriptions were proposed by Deutsch (1949a, b), Homans (1950), and Krech and Crutchfield (1948). Contemporary work still characterizes group cohesion in much the same way: for example, as 'the tendency to stick together and remain united . . . [or as] . . . the construct used to represent the strength of the social bond within the group' (Carron, 1982, p. 124).

The early 1950s witnessed a concerted effort, initiated by Festinger and his University of Michigan colleagues at the Research Center for Group Dymanics, to construct a systematic theory of group cohesiveness. The initial theoretical context of this work was – not surprisingly – Lewin's (1936, 1948, 1952) field theory approach to psychology. Lewin, often portrayed as the father of experimental social psychology, had – and continues to have – an enormous influence on social psychology (Cartwright, 1979; Deutsch, 1968; Deutsch and Krauss, 1965; Festinger, 1980; Marrow, 1969).

Lewin believed subjective reality to be the totality of the psychological events experienced by the individual (called the 'life space' or 'field'), patterned into distinct regions (or points) of experience. Specific needs or goals, ranging from fundamental physiological ones such as hunger to complex socially constructed ones such as writing a novel, cause a state of psychic tension in the relevant region of the field. This imbues it with a positive or negative valence that locomotes the individual (psychologically) to that region of the field which can achieve tension reduction. The human organism is powerfully driven to reduce psychic tension in order to reinstate equilibrium between regions of the life space. After the early 1940s Lewin did not further develop his theory of the person. His insights are, however, clearly evident in subsequent theories of cognitive consistency (see Abelson, Aronson, McGuire, Newcomb, Rosenberg and Tannenbaum, 1968).

Lewin turned his attention to groups. Just as his thinking about the person emphasized dynamics, so did his thinking about groups: thus was born the area of group dynamics. For Lewin:

> The essence of a group is not the similarity or dissimilarity of its members, but their interdependence. A group can be characterized as a 'dynamical whole'; this means that a change in the state of any subpart changes the state of any other subpart. The degree of interdependence of the subparts of members of the group varies all the way from a loose 'mass' to a compact unit. It depends, among other factors, upon the size, organization, and intimacy of the group. (1948, p. 84)

This quotation captures remarkably well the way in which Lewin drew a theoretical parallel between dynamic interdependence among points in the life space and dynamic interdependence among members of the group. This was no mere descriptive analogy. He considered the latter to be represented in the life space of the individual member – in this way the group could affect the behaviour of the individual member.

Lewin first mentioned cohesiveness in a 1943 publication (see Lewin, 1952, p. 162). No formal definition was offered: the term was used largely in an ordinary everyday sense. At times, however, its usage suggests that Lewin may have been relating it to – or perhaps using it as a shorthand for – the degree of group interdependence. In turn, this interdependence is viewed in terms of forces of attraction and repulsion that hold the group together or tear it asunder.

Floyd Allport (1962), though not particularly sympathetic to Lewin's approach, provides a useful interpretation and summary of the role attributed to cohesiveness in Lewinian theory. Forces in the group field derive from a number of sources: solidarity or cohesion heads a list which also includes group goals, place of residence, competition or cooperation, type of leadership, social atmospheres, social climates, and the importance of an issue to the group. These forces produce group locomotions or 'social outcomes' which include attitudes, performance, amount of communication, discussion directed at changing the opinions of dissidents, conflicts, acceptance or rejection of individuals as members, and the adoption of common standards. Cohesiveness is thus an important *cause* of a range of measurable group behaviours.

Festinger, Schachter and Back ===

It was Festinger, Schachter and Back (1950) who finally formalized a theory of group cohesiveness. They felt that it was a central concept in the explanation of group dynamics, and therefore in need of formal theoretical statement. For example, Schachter, Ellertson, McBride and Gregory wrote: 'Cohesiveness as a concept . . . represents an attempt to formalize or simply verbalize the key group phenomena of membership continuity – the "cement" binding together group members and maintaining their relationships to one another' (1951, p. 229). It is well worthwhile to look in some detail at Festinger, Schachter and Back's classic work, as it has significantly influenced – one might even say determined – the subsequent course taken by all research on group cohesiveness.

Festinger and colleagues set out to investigate how face-to-face, small, informal social groups exert pressure upon their members to adhere to group standards (norms). Equipped with a collection of intuitions, and more or less established 'facts', they collected observational, interview and questionnaire data from a field study of group formation and functioning in two new housing projects, called Westgate and Westgate West, established in 1946 for married veterans enrolled at the Massachusetts Institute of Technology. For Festinger and colleagues, a particularly appealing feature of this arrangement was that participants moved into the housing project simultaneously, did not originally know one another, and were 'randomly' assigned to houses/ apartments. The major finding was that ecological factors, in particular residential proximity, were the major determinants of friendship or group (the terms are generally used interchangeably – e.g. 1950, p. 57) formation. Festinger and colleagues also studied the development of organized groups, specifically a tenants' organization, from these *ad hoc* groups, and communication processes associated with adherence to group standards.

From their investigations, a formal 'theory of group structure and group standards' (1950, p. 151) was developed. It was loosely based on – or rather, formed within the intellectual context of – Lewin's field theory. Group structure was defined as 'the pattern of connections among different parts of the group' (p. 152), where 'parts' means people, and 'connections' means friendships – for example: 'the process of making a friendship (establishing a connection)' (p. 153). At Westgate these connections/friendships were determined by similarity and residential proximity, such that 'ecological factors determine not only specific friendships but the composition of groups' (p. 58). In fact, Festinger *et al.* quite explicitly define the group as a 'number of interacting and sociometrically connected people' (p. 58).

Festinger *et al.* believed that 'the formation of friendships is, of course, related to the formation of informal social groups' (1950, p. 160), but were careful to warn that 'a collection of individuals with a relatively high number of sociometric linkages among them may constitute . . . a psychological group, or may merely constitute a series of friendship relationships with no real unification of the group as a whole' (p. 99). So, although some psychological distinction is suspected to exist between networks of friendships and social groups, a very close empirical relationship between the two is admitted. 'It is highly likely, of course, that . . . friendship relations among a number of people will in time make for the development of a cohesive group' (p. 99), and 'informal social groups . . . are a more or less cohesive pattern of friendship relations among a number of people' (p. 160).

The concept of cohesiveness appears to hold the key not only to group solidarity as a variable property of a group, but also to psychological group formation as a binary event. Festinger *et al.*'s definition of cohesiveness, which reverberates down the decades, is: 'We shall call the total field of forces which act on members to remain in the group the "cohesiveness" of that group' (1950, p. 164). Festinger *et al.* suggest, as regards describing the group as a whole, that 'perhaps cohesiveness may best be related to the average magnitude of this force in all parts of the group' (*ibid.*).

Cohesiveness is influenced by two classes of factors (see Figure 2.2): (1)

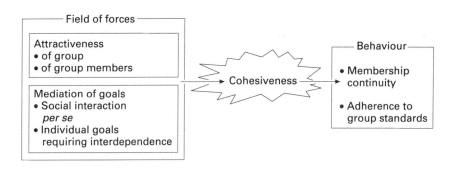

Figure 2.2 *Festinger, Schachter and Back's theory of group cohesiveness*

'the attractiveness of the group — the extent to which the group is a goal in and of itself and has valence. A group can have such positive valence for various reasons. The positive valence of an informal social group, however, will be mostly affected by the extent to which one has satisfactory relationships and friendships with other members of the group' (1950, p. 165). So there is a positive relationship between social structure and cohesiveness: the better the structure (i.e. the more friendships) the greater the cohesiveness; (2) 'the extent to which the group mediates goals which are important for the members' (*ibid.*). The goals referred to are of two sorts: social interaction itself and specific individual goals which require, for their achievement, interdependent or cooperative interaction with others.

The relationship between cohesiveness and friendship is sometimes quite explicit, for example: 'the more cohesive the group, that is, the more friendship ties there are within the group . . .' (1950, p. 175). There is also an explicit recognition that groups are rewarding and produce attraction. Festinger and colleagues believed that groups can exert influence over their members because of 'gratifications available only as a result of memberships' (p. 3). They list friendships, companionships, warmth and pleasure of close emotional ties, prestige, social status, approval of others, and group goals as factors that 'add to the attractiveness of the group' (*ibid.*).

Operationally, Festinger and colleagues, confronted by the daunting task of operationalizing 'the total field' of forces acting on the individual, simply relied on the single question 'What three people in Westgate or Westgate West do you see most of socially?' (1950, p. 37) in order to measure not only patterns of friendship but also cohesiveness (see p. 91). The proportion of ingroup friendship choices relative to the total number of friendship choices was taken as the index of group cohesiveness. So, for example, a 10-person group for which 18 of the 30 nominated friends were ingroup members would be more cohesive than a 10-person group for which only 16 choices were ingroupers.

Festinger *et al.*'s theory was developed on the basis of – and perhaps in order to explain – a particular type of group: the small, face-to-face informal group characterized by interpersonal friendships. It may be at least partly for this reason that friendships are given such a high profile in the analysis. It is, however, important to recognize that Festinger and colleagues themselves do not provide any such explicit caveat. They present their theory as a theory of group formation and cohesiveness, without explicitly specifying any limits of applicability or generalizability. It is a theory of groups, and the equation of cohesiveness with interpersonal friendship and attraction rings out loud and clear.

Transformation of the concept

Festinger *et al.*'s (1950) operationalization of group cohesiveness was very promptly criticized as inadequate (Gross and Martin, 1952). To simplify the task of integrating an unspecified number of different forces, Gross and Martin suggested measuring the resultant of the total field of forces – a strategy which had already been suggested in 1950 by Festinger in a subtle alteration of the definition of cohesiveness to 'the resultant of all the forces acting on members of a group to remain in the group' (Festinger, 1950, p. 274).

Gross and Martin's alternative definition of cohesiveness as 'the resistance of a group to disruptive forces' (1952, p. 553), and van Bergen and Koekebakker's suggestion of 'the degree of unification of the group field' (1959, p. 85) both proved as operationally cumbersome as Festinger *et al.*'s 'total field of forces' (but see Brawley, Carron and Widmeyer, 1988).

Now that the complexities of 'the total field' had been done away with, cohesiveness was defined in terms of attraction to the group. Back defined cohesiveness as 'the attraction of membership in a group for its members' (1951, p. 9); Libo as 'the attraction of the group for its members' (1953, p. 1; see also Frank, 1957, p. 54); Israel as 'attraction to the group' (1956, p. 25); and van Bergen and Koekebakker (1959) as 'attraction-to-group'. Cartwright concluded from his comprehensive review of group cohesiveness that 'most investigators have equated the term cohesiveness with "attraction to the group"' (1968, p. 92). Mudrack concurred by observing that most research adopts 'a variant of the attraction-to-group definition' (1989a, p. 43); and Carron noted that in sport psychology the operationalization of cohesiveness has been 'unidimensional in the sense that the focus has been on some form of attraction' (1982, p. 125).

Mudrack (1989a) has pointed out that the subtle shift of definitional emphasis from 'the total field' to 'the resultant' opened the way for a conceptualization of the cohesiveness of the group as a whole in terms of the sum or average of the forces upon the individuals within the group. Taken in conjunction with the 'attraction-to-group' formulation of cohesiveness at the individual level, this has resulted in a conceptualization of the cohesiveness of the group as a whole in terms of the 'average of the individual members' attraction to the group' (Roark and Sharah, 1989, p. 62), 'the pooled effect or average of individual members' attraction-to-group' (Israel, 1956, p. 25), or 'measuring the levels of attraction of individual group members and averaging them' (Evans and Jarvis, 1980, p. 359). Cartwright's (1968) review confirmed that summation or averaging across members are the dominant procedures for producing an index of cohesiveness at the group level (cf. McGrath, 1978; Wheeless, Wheeless and Dickson-Markman, 1982).

Although group cohesiveness, as attraction to the group, can be influenced by the attractiveness of the group's activities, goals, atmosphere, defining features, etc., the attractiveness of the group members, and the degree to which the group mediates achievement of important individual goals (cf. Festinger *et al.*, 1950), the conceptual and empirical emphasis is usually on the attractiveness of the group members: that is, interpersonal attraction (e.g. Back, 1951; Berkowitz, 1954; Downing, 1958; Fisher, 1973; Knowles and Brickner, 1981; McGrath, 1978; Newcomb, 1953; Nixon, 1976; Pepitone and Reichling, 1955; Wheeless *et al.*, 1982; Wolf, 1979).

Shaw (1974) felt that by far the most powerful determinant of attractiveness of the group is the attraction of one person to another. When a given individual is attracted to the members of a group, then he or she is likely to find the group attractive and to desire membership of it. In another publication, Shaw (1976) considers group cohesiveness to be an interpersonal relationship: 'One such interpersonal relationship is the degree to which the members of the group are attracted to each other, or the degree to which the group coheres or "hangs together". This aspect of the group is usually referred to as group cohesiveness' (p. 197).

Perhaps the most explicit statement of group cohesiveness as interpersonal attraction is B.E. Lott's definition of cohesiveness as 'that group property which is inferred from the number and strength of mutual positive attitudes among the members of a group . . . [where] . . . the primary condition for the development of mutual positive attitudes among group members will be seen to be the attainment of goals or the receipt of rewards in one another's presence' (1961, p. 279; see also Lott and Lott, 1965). Consistent with Carron's analysis of sport groups (cohesion is 'the adhesive property of groups' [1980, p. 234]), Schachter *et al.* feel that interpersonal attraction is 'the "cement" binding together group members' (1951, p. 229), and Gruber and Gray feel that it is the 'adhesive property of a group' (1981, p. 21), while Bonner argues that 'without at least a minimal attraction of members to each other a group cannot exist at all' (1959, p. 66). Cohesiveness traditionally seems to mean 'bonded, mutually attracted, cemented' (Budge, 1981, p. 11).

Empirical and conceptual reviews (e.g. Cartwright, 1968; Lott and Lott, 1965; McGrath and Kravitz, 1982; Zander, 1979) confirm that group cohesiveness is widely treated as equivalent to interpersonal attraction. For example, in their review of cohesiveness research in group-therapy contexts, Bednar, Weet, Evensen, Lanier and Melnick concluded that 'cohesiveness is usually defined as interpersonal trust, attraction, and involvement' (1974, p. 155). Drescher *et al.* reviewed research between 1965 and 1985 on cohesiveness in therapy, encounter and analogue groups, concluding that the predominant measures are 'self-report measures of attraction to group or other members, attitudes toward group, or degree of investment in the group's purpose' (1985, p. 16).

Forsyth concluded, in his group dynamics text, that at the 'individualistic level, cohesiveness refers to the member's attraction to other group members, whether this attraction is based on liking, respect, or trust' (1983, p. 349), and elsewhere I have argued that 'although the concept of group cohesiveness permits and encourages different operationalizations . . . overwhelmingly it has been operationalized as, and identified theoretically with, attraction between group members, i.e. interpersonal attraction' (Hogg, 1987, p. 90; see also Hogg and Abrams, 1988, pp. 92–115).

Floyd Allport, in pursuing his argument that the group is merely a nominal fallacy, poses the question: 'When the group dynamicist speaks of "attraction of the group for the individual" does he not mean just the attraction of the individuals for one another?' (1962, p. 23). Allport feels that the answer must be yes, because 'if individuals are all drawn toward one another [they are] ipso facto drawn to the group' (pp. 23–4). If the answer were no, and attraction is meant to refer to some complex of interrelationships or common interests, then, Allport believes, 'we shall . . . probably have to recite a whole nexus of meanings . . . so complex as to make the notion of attraction to the group too inexplicit to serve as an experimental variable' (p. 24).

The social cohesion model

Group cohesiveness is a formal theory of group solidarity and psychological group formation that appears to treat interpersonal attraction as the generative process. Although this interpretation is often explicit, it is also frequently implicit: lying only a short distance beneath the surface. In these implicit formulations it is often unclear what process, apart from interpersonal attraction, is actually being invoked. The *formal* theory of group cohesiveness may be only the tip of the iceberg as regards general social psychological conceptualizations of the social group, and explanations of specific group phenomena. For example, in Chapter 8 I show how Janis's (1972) notion of groupthink represents a model of deficient group decision-making produced by interpersonal attraction.

The idea of group cohesiveness embraces a distinctive model of the social group, the 'social cohesion' model (see Hogg, 1987; Hogg and Abrams, 1988; Turner, 1982, 1984, for discussion). This model tends to liken the group to a molecule in which individual atoms are people and interatomic forces are interpersonal attraction (e.g. Kellerman, 1981; Raven and Rubin, 1983, p. 405). (In turn, this represents a manifestation of the wider tendency in social science to adopt physical or biological metaphors as models of social processes, documented by Pepitone, 1981.) The social cohesion model attributes the emergence of 'interatomic' forces of interpersonal attraction to the multitude of factors that are known to determine liking, including cooperative interdependence to achieve shared goals, attitude similarity, physical proximity, common fate, shared threat/a common enemy, being liked or approved of by the other, attractive personality traits, and success on group tasks (Lott and Lott, 1965). It is taken for granted that one is attracted to or likes people who are 'rewarding', and that a 'reward' is some action, attitude or attribute of oneself or another that satisfies a need (desire, drive, motive, etc.). Thus it follows that a collection of people come together to form a group, spontaneously or deliberately, to the degree that they have needs capable of mutual satisfaction and in this sense are *dependent* upon one another.

Turner *et al.* (1987) have identified the fundamental hypothesis as being the belief that people who depend upon each other (which need not be an exclusive dependence) to satisfy one or more of their needs, and who achieve or expect to achieve satisfactions from their association, develop feelings of mutual attraction and hence become a group. This is schematically portrayed in Figure 2.3 as a general framework of the social cohesion model. It is

Figure 2.3 *General framework of the social cohesion model*

important, however, to be quite clear that this is a general framework which contextualizes, or locates, conceptualizations of the social group. Different theorists and different theories emphasize different aspects and linkages portrayed in the model. Although some theorists are more explicit than others as regards the importance of interdependence as the key to association, there is wide acceptance of the Gestalt assumption that the 'wholeness' of the group, despite what may be very different 'parts' (i.e. members), reflects the interdependence of those 'parts'. Differences between theorists are largely to do with how explicit an emphasis is placed on interdependence, what antecedents or aspects of interdependence are stressed, and whether or not interpersonal attraction is credited explicitly with a direct role. Even where a researcher makes no mention of interpersonal attraction as important for group formation or solidarity, stressing instead some kind of interdependence or other relation between people, the idea will often be implied in their understanding of the effects of interdependence. To substantiate these points, let us look briefly at a selection of important treatments of the social group (see Figure 2.4).

In general, theories of the group can be divided into two camps: those emphasizing explicit interindividual interdependence (e.g. Lewin, Sherif,

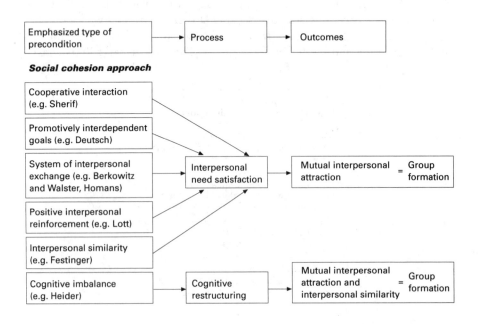

Figure 2.4 *Some different social psychological perspectives on how groups form. (This figure is modified, by permission of Routledge, from Figure 5.1 in Hogg and Abrams (1988, p. 100).)*

Deutsch) and those emphasizing interindividual similarity (e.g. Festinger, Heider) as the basis of attraction. As we have already seen, Lewin believed that the 'essence of a group is not the similarity or dissimilarity of its members, but their interdependence. A group can be characterized as a "dynamical whole"' (1948, p. 84). Cohesiveness (as mutual forces of attraction within the group) was considered a fundamental property of groups (Lewin, 1952, p. 162) that covaried with interdependence, and related to need satisfaction. The implication is that need satisfaction is the motive for interdependence, and the more complete the latter, the greater the need satisfaction and the greater the group's cohesiveness.

The Sherifs consider that cooperative interdependence in the pursuit of shared goals which cannot be achieved by an individual alone results in the establishment of a well-defined group structure (i.e. role relationships and shared rules of conduct), and it is this that distinguishes a group from a mere aggregate of individuals (Sherif, 1967; Sherif and Sherif, 1969; cf. McDougall, 1921). Psychologically speaking, however, the crucial process is repeated positive interindividual interaction: group formation proceeds 'from interaction among unrelated individuals to the stabilization of role-status relations and norms' (Sherif and Sherif, 1969, p. 132). Mutual need satisfaction through cooperative interaction imbues group members with positive valence and so makes the group attractive and encourages members to remain within it. Although M. Sherif believes that there is more to group formation than the development of spontaneous personal friendships (Sherif, 1967), his theory nevertheless rests upon the implicit idea that individual members become attractive (and the group therefore cohesive) to the degree that they contribute, through interindividual interaction, to the attainment of one's goals.

Deutsch's (1949a, 1973) analysis is extremely similar, except that the emphasis is on goals rather than activity. Goals that can be achieved only through cooperation between individuals are 'promotively interdependent', and an individual 'will acquire positive valence . . . [become attractive] if . . . seen to be promotively related to need satisfaction' (Deutsch, 1949a, p. 138); that is, an individual will 'accept, like or reward' (*ibid.*) another's actions which achieve promotively interdependent goals, and this in turn will generalize to liking for the actor (p. 146). It is clear that the promotive interdependence of individuals is believed to create attraction between them through need satisfaction. It is also clear, therefore, that interpersonal attraction is at the heart of the group as a psychological entity, since the psychological group comprises individuals who 'perceive themselves as pursuing promotively interdependent goals' and whose cohesiveness is determined by 'the strength of goals perceived to be promotively interdependent and . . . the degree of perceived interdependence' (p. 150). The basic message is that interpersonal attraction is the psychological force responsible for group belongingness, and that its emergence can be traced to mutual need satisfaction through cooperation for promotively interdependent goals.

There is an ambiguity in the Lewinian and Sherifian approaches to interdependence and interpersonal attraction that is well reflected in the views of Cartwright and Zander (1968). On the one hand, the stress on the group as a dynamic system of interdependent members strongly implies that there are properties of the group as a whole, such as cohesiveness, which cannot be simply reduced to interpersonal attraction, but on the other hand there is a theoretical failure to explain how attraction to the *group* could be generated by any process that does not ultimately boil down to inter*personal* attraction. Thus, Cartwright and Zander subscribe to the interdependence theory of the group, are explicit in their recognition of the role of cohesiveness, and seek to restrain the tendency to identify it solely with interpersonal attraction, but despite an extremely detailed treatment, there is no definite indication of what alternative process is being suggested.

Interdependence and attraction also lie at the heart of social exchange, reinforcement, and equity approaches to the group. Social exchange approaches (Homans, 1961; Kelley and Thibaut, 1978; Secord and Backman, 1964; Thibaut and Kelley, 1959) emphasize the cost-benefit aspects of social relations. They reduce interaction to the transaction of rewards and costs, and simply state that interaction continues to the extent that rewards outweigh costs. Cohesiveness is considered to be the essential quality of groups, and its magnitude 'will be greater to the degree that rewards are experienced in belonging to the group' (Thibaut and Kelley, 1959, p. 114). However, since the unit of analysis is typically the dyad, cohesiveness in practice is interpersonal attraction based on interpersonal rewards. This link between cohesiveness and mutual interpersonal attraction is made quite explicit by Secord and Backman (1964).

Reinforcement approaches are even more explicit (B.E. Lott, 1961; Lott and Lott, 1961, 1965). Interaction that mediates goal achievement or is rewarding in some way is reinforcing, and hence results in interpersonal attraction. Cohesiveness is then defined as 'that group quality which is inferred from the number and strength of mutual positive attitudes among members of a group' (Lott, 1961, p. 279).

Equity theory (Berkowitz and Walster, 1976) defines the group in terms of 'equitable' (i.e. fair, just, etc.) interdependence between individuals: the perception of inequity creates pressures for its reinstatement or for the termination of interdependence, in which case the group has disbanded. It is assumed that equitable interdependence creates interpersonal attraction which functions to produce group cohesiveness.

In contrast to the treatments discussed so far, Festinger and Heider provide examples of theories that stress the role of preexisting similarities in attitudes and values between people in attraction and group formation.

Festinger's social comparison theory (Festinger, 1950, 1954; Suls and Miller, 1977) argues that people affiliate with others in order to validate their opinions, attitudes and beliefs. In the absence of physical, non-social means of validation, people rely on comparison with relatively similar others. The agreement of others — that is, their *similarity* to us in attitudes, and so on — gives us confidence in the correctness of our views, and so satisfies a basic need to evaluate ourselves and know that we are correct. Since similar others are rewarding in that they satisfy informational needs, we are attracted to them and affiliate with them. This idea has become a cornerstone of research on interpersonal attraction (e.g. Byrne's [1971] attraction paradigm). Festinger is explicit that we compare with other individuals, not groups, and that mutual interpersonal attraction reflecting shared attitudes is the basis of group formation. (The theory has been extended by Schachter, 1959, to include emotions.)

Heider's (1958) theory rests upon the principle of cognitive balance, which postulates a need within the organism for balance between different cognitions. He argues that positive sentiment relations (i.e. liking for others) and positive unit relations (a sense of togetherness, oneness, being linked, being the same) between individuals tend to go together. Interpersonal attraction and being in the same group are therefore inextricably interlinked. Heider's theory is somewhat different from the others in that attraction to similar others is seen to flow from a basic need for cognitive consistency, and there is an implication that group membership need not merely reflect interpersonal attraction but could also directly produce it. Newcomb (1968), however, in his application of cognitive balance concepts, argues that liking leads to positive unit relations rather than vice versa: that is, people we like are soon seen to be members of the same groups as ourselves.

Finally, social impact theory (Latané, 1981; Latané and Nida, 1980) specifies factors in a group that determine its impact on potential group members. Social impact is defined as 'changes in physiological states and subjective feelings, motives and emotions, cognitions and beliefs, values and behaviour that occur in an individual human or animal as a result of the real, implied or imagined presence or actions of other individuals' (Latané and Nida, 1980, p. 5). Social impact is the arithmetic product of three factors: (1) group size — the larger the number of physically present others, the greater the group's impact; (2) immediacy — the closer the others are in space and time, the greater the impact; and (3) strength of source — characteristics of the group and its members that are attractive to potential members (e.g. status, power, importance). For social impact theory, a group is simply a number of people. The cohesiveness of the group is a function of its degree of social impact, which in turn seems to be determined by its members' attractiveness for one another. Interpersonal attraction would seem to be the process, since number and proximity are important factors that magnify basically interpersonal effects.

Interpersonal attraction, therefore, lies not only at the heart of the concept of group cohesiveness, but also at the core of a wide array of superficially diverse conceptualizations of the social group. Current definitions of the social group (see Chapter 1) employ an admixture of components drawn from these theories. The group is essentially a numerically small face-to-face collection of individuals interacting to perform a task or fulfil shared goals. The members like each other and have role relations with respect to each other that emerge from intragroup structural divisions developed in the fulfilment of the group's purpose. A product of continued interaction is a sense of identity as a group member. However, the fundamental process responsible for the psychological formation of the group and the degree of solidarity and cohesiveness of the group in all these approaches is interpersonal attraction (see Figure 2.3).

Conclusion

This chapter has described the way in which group cohesiveness has been conceptualized and operationalized over the years. In practice, group cohesiveness as a psychological concept refers mainly to members' attraction to the group, which in turn is predominantly considered in terms of group members' liking for one another. The cohesiveness of the group as a whole is determined by summing or averaging across individual members' attraction to the group and/or each other. This conceptualization of cohesiveness does not only express itself in the formal concept of group cohesiveness, but also lurks beneath the surface of an array of other social psychological treatments of group solidarity and psychological group formation.

This perspective has framed a great deal of group cohesiveness research. Chapter 3 briefly summarizes this research and its findings, and describes the many scales that have been devised to measure the cohesiveness of groups.

Chapter 3

Research and measurement

This chapter provides a summary overview of what we know about the antecedents and consequences of group cohesiveness: what factors influence the cohesiveness of groups and what are the consequences of variation in group cohesiveness. Of course, in order to do this properly, a clear definition of group cohesiveness is required. In keeping with the conclusions drawn from the analysis provided in Chapter 2, I have selected attraction-to-group or interpersonal attraction as the most appropriate operational definition. I should stress that this is not because I necessarily endorse such a definition (see Chapters 4 and 6), but because attraction-to-group or interpersonal attraction is the most common operational definition, and therefore the most convenient for organizing a review of empirical findings.

It is important to note that this chapter is not intended to be a comprehensive empirical review. Rather, the intention is to summarize established empirical relationships, to give an indication of how robust the finding may be, and to sketch an overall idea of the sort of research that has been conducted: the general paradigms and the types of subjects and groups involved. Particular attention is given to anomalous, unusual and problematic findings.

A second aim is to summarize and review some of the scales that have been used to measure group cohesiveness. There are almost as many different ways to measure cohesiveness as there are studies of cohesiveness, but recently some attempts have been made to construct reliable and robust multidimensional multi-item group cohesiveness questionnaires. These questionnaires emerge almost exclusively from the sports psychology and group-therapy literature, rather than from what could be called mainstream social psychology of groups. Clearly, despite its conceptual problems, group cohesiveness is a phenomenon of great practical relevance and importance. My coverage of group cohesiveness scales is not intended to be comprehensive. I have tried to describe some of the major and recent scales and scale items in sufficient detail to bring them to life, and to allow researchers to select items or scales for their own use.

This chapter is intended to give a flavour of empirical research on group cohesiveness: the things that are looked at, the way in which they are looked at, the types of operationalizations and measures used, the subjects and groups that are investigated, and the things that are found.

Empirical antecedents and consequences of cohesiveness

There are a great number of empirical reviews of the cohesiveness literature, varying in detail, scope and specificity. Quite often, cohesiveness is reviewed as part of a more general review of group processes, or of a specific topic in group processes (e.g. productivity, leadership, sports teams). However, a reading of Lott and Lott (1965), Cartwright (1968), Shaw (1976), Zander (1979), McGrath and Kravitz (1982), and Levine and Moreland (1990) provides an overall and relatively comprehensive review of data published since the late 1940s on antecedents and consequences of group cohesiveness. Without a doubt, the most comprehensive and directly relevant empirical review is Lott and Lott (1965). For this reason the summary that follows is closely based on Lott and Lott, and updated, where necessary, in the light of more recent research.

Lott and Lott provide a comprehensive review of empirical antecedents and consequences of group cohesiveness, published between 1950 and 1962: the period during which basic group cohesiveness research was at its peak (see Chapter 4). They were concerned to document what had been found from 'investigations of real or simulated interaction among persons who are in association with one another on a relatively voluntary basis' (1965, p. 260), and self-confessedly did not examine problems of methodology and measurement.

For their review, Lott and Lott chose a definition of group cohesiveness as interpersonal attraction. This choice was based primarily not on their own theoretical preferences, but on recognition of the fact that most research operationalized cohesiveness in terms of interpersonal attraction: that is, 'the category of like and dislike "packages" most of the determinants of interaction' (Tagiuri, 1958, p. 317). Lott and Lott observe:

> When investigators have desired to manipulate the cohesiveness of groups . . .
> the operations performed have typically involved telling the members of some
> groups that they would probably like each other, be congenial, etc., while telling
> others just the opposite. Further, in measuring the cohesiveness of experimental
> or naturally existing groups, some sociometric device is generally utilized to

determine how much each member likes or is attracted to the other members. (1965, p. 259)

Table 3.1 summarizes Lott and Lott's findings. It lists all the variables they document as having an empirically established antecedent or consequent relationship with interpersonal attraction among members of a group (i.e. group cohesiveness). For each variable, the number of empirical studies cited that report a positive relationship (+), a negative relationship (−), or no relationship (0) is also displayed. The 'no relationship' category also includes studies producing internally inconsistent or contradictory findings, and studies employing contaminated or problematic independent or dependent variables. This information is tabulated in order to give an indication of the robustness of a particular empirical relationship. The text below simply summarizes the findings and the sort of research that produced them. Individual studies are cited only if they raise problematic or interesting issues, or represent important work published subsequent to Lott and Lott's review.

Antecedents of cohesiveness

Interaction/propinquity
In general, propinquity and verbal and physical interaction increase positive affect among group members in classrooms, organizations, sororities, housing projects, summer camps, and military groups. There are, however, some very important exceptions. Forced propinquity can produce negative intragroup attitudes (e.g. Festinger's [1953] study of residents who were forced, by circumstances, to live in a housing project), and interaction/propinquity among people of different ethnic or racial backgrounds is not guaranteed to transform negative attitudes into positive attitudes, or even merely to neutralize negative attitudes (e.g. Cook, 1978; Gundlach, 1956).

This latter finding is consistent with the more general view that interaction/propinquity enhances intragroup attitude only if deep schisms grounded in emotionally charged prior or external group memberships (including large-scale category memberships based on race, ethnicity, nationality, 'disability', etc.) are not present (cf. Sherif, 1966). Recent ongoing research into the effects of intergroup contact on prejudice adds further complexity to the picture (see Hewstone and Brown, 1986; Johnston and Hewstone, 1990; Miller and Brewer, 1984).

Special characteristics of the group situation/atmosphere
Intragroup attraction is enhanced by conditions embodying a cooperative, as opposed to competitive, reward structure among children and adults in classroom settings and in experimental game-playing exercises. One important exception seems to be when interpersonal competition is a normative property of the group. For example, Myers (1962) found that members of more com-petitive rifle teams expressed greater esteem for one another than did

Table 3.1   *Variables with empirically established antecedent and consequent relationships with group cohesiveness as interpersonal attraction*

Variables	Number of studies		
	+	−	0
Antecedents of cohesiveness as liking			
Interaction/propinquity	19	2	3
Special characteristics of group situation/atmosphere			
Cooperation	6	2	−
Democracy	2	−	1
Acceptance by others	15	−	−
Frustration/threat	10	−	−
Status			
Status similarity	7	−	−
Status dissimilarity	9	−	−
Status congruence	4	−	−
Behaviour or personality characteristics	20	−	5
Similarity			
Background (race, ethnicity, occupation, age)	6	1	1
Attitudes	23	1	−
Values	8	−	3
Compatible personality traits	17	−	4
Success/reward			
Shared success or failure	8	2	5
Attraction to source of reward	6	−	−
Individual reward in presence of others	5	1	−
Attraction to successful persons	4	−	
Reduction of cognitive dissonance	3	−	−
Consequences of cohesiveness as liking			
Expression of aggression	5	−	−
Self-evaluation	6	3	1
Evaluation of the situation	4	−	−
Evaluation of others			
Perception of similarity	14	1	−
Favourable judgements of behaviour of liked others	4	−	−
Perceptual sensitivity	4	−	−
Perceived reciprocal attraction	6	−	−
Communication	12	−	−
Uniformity/conformity	29	−	8
Task performance	20	9	5
Learning	4	2	5

Note: This table is compiled from Lott and Lott's (1965) empirical review. The column head '+' indicates a positive relationship, '−' a negative relationship, and '0' no relationship. This last category includes flawed studies and internally inconsistent or contradictory findings.

members of less competitive teams: competition among group members was, however, in the service of a superordinate competition with other rifle teams.

Although there is some evidence that democratic leadership is associated with positive mutual attitudes among group members, more detailed analysis indicates that leadership style *per se* may not be the causal agent. Rather, groups which achieve their goals, due to any effective leadership regime, are characterized by greater attraction.

Porter and Lawler (1965) have reviewed a large number of studies of work groups in large organizations, concluding that increasing group size is associated with decreasing satisfaction and cohesiveness. From a detailed study of organizational groups by Indik (1965) it becomes clear that it is not group size *per se*, but rather factors usually contingent on increasing size (e.g. poor communication, hierarchical command structures) that diminish cohesiveness.

Acceptance by others

People who feel accepted by the group and its members express more liking for the group and its members. Acceptance has been operationalized directly in terms of rejection/selection, or indirectly via liking, status, or favourable rating, in task-orientated or role-playing laboratory groups, and in dormitories and organizational groups.

Frustration/threat

Frustration and threat do not influence cohesiveness in a deterministic manner. Rather, their effect is dependent on the absence or presence of a number of qualifying conditions. Frustration or threat that is imposed from outside the group, is shared by the group members, is not attributable to deficient skill and ability on the part of group members, and for which there is no realistic individualistic way out, produces enhanced intragroup cohesion and liking (see review by Stein, 1976). These conditions seem to suggest that only frustration or threat that accentuates the perceived entitativity (cf. Campbell, 1958; see Chapter 2) of the group enhances cohesiveness (see Chapter 6).

Status

Studies of status have generally focused on occupational, professional and task status, 'demographic' status (e.g. age), and status as indicated by over-selection within the group. The sorts of groups studied include laboratory teams, discussion groups, housing projects, military groups, and organization and work groups. The general findings are that high-status individuals like one another, all group members like higher-status group members more than lower-status group members, and groups with a high degree of status congruence (irrespective of the status level) are cohesive.

There is an interesting qualification. Kelley (1951) and Cohen (1958) both found that in mixed-status laboratory groups, where status was defined in terms of desirability of job performed in the group, lower-status members who perceived no job/status mobility (i.e. they were non-mobile) showed high regard for fellow lower-status members but did not express liking for the higher-status members. The effects of intragroup (and possibly intergroup) status on cohesiveness may be mediated by perceptions of the mutability or otherwise of the status differential (see Chapter 6).

Behaviour or personality characteristics

People whose behaviour is likely to promote friendly, pleasant interaction in groups are liked more than those whose behaviour is unlikely to have this outcome. Such behaviour, which includes warmth, equalitarianism, good adjustment, sensitivity and helpfulness, can be perceived to reflect enduring personality styles (traits) or situational factors. It should be noted, however, that a significant proportion of the studies in this area leave unanswered the question of causality: does positive behaviour influence relative attractiveness, or is the opposite the case?

There are some interesting qualifications to the positive behaviour/ intragroup attraction relationship. For example, Theodorson (1957) found that there was a positive relationship between liking for a group member and the value of that group member's contribution to the group, but only in groups that had an overall high level of cohesiveness. There are also data (see Homans, 1961; Jennings, 1950; Riecken and Homans, 1954) that liking for group members can be independently influenced by different classes of behaviour in the group: for example, someone can be liked as a 'good fellow' but disliked as a 'taskmaster' (see Chapter 7).

Similarity

Many studies of similarity and compatibility do not resolve the question of whether similarity or compatibility creates attraction, or whether the opposite is the case. Also, the relationship between subjective and objective similarity or compatibility is often not specified.

Actual or perceived similarity in religion, occupation, race, and socioeconomic status has been found to enhance attraction among members of schools, sororities, training groups, work groups and laboratory groups. There are some interesting qualifications which suggest that whether such 'background' variables influence cohesiveness depends on the importance of the variable to the group or the individual group member. So, for example, Seashore (1954) found attraction to be uninfluenced by similarity in age or socioeconomic status in industrial work groups: length of service in the group, which was significantly more central to group functioning, was the most important influence on liking. Similarly, Lazarsfield and Merton (1954) found enormous variation in the influence of 'background' factors on liking among members of housing communities. Finally, Byrne and Wong (1962) found that race was an influence on liking only among prejudiced group members.

Actual and perceived attitudinal and value similarity among members of housing projects, military groups, organizational groups, laboratory groups, college populations, and industrial relations groups has been found to enhance cohesiveness (cf. Byrne, 1971). An interesting exception is a study by Gage and Exline (1953) in which attitudinal similarity on dimensions relating to group processes was not associated with attraction as reflected in sociometric choice for leisure-time activities. Perhaps group processes and leisure-time activities are independent dimensions (see Chapter 6). For critical discussion of the problematic relationship between attitudinal similarity and group cohesiveness, see Brown (1984).

Assumed or actual compatibility of personality tends to enhance group cohesiveness. 'Compatibility' seems to refer to a complex admixture of similarities and differences in personality, but the term is rather ambiguously and unclearly defined. Negative findings have been reported by Bowerman and Day (1956), and Hoffman (1958). An interesting finding is that liking for work partners is influenced by the degree to which they are instrumental in achieving group-mediated goals. Personality similarity or dissimilarity may promote such achievement. Lerner and Becker (1962) and Israel (1956) report data showing that for cooperative interaction, personality similarity enhanced liking; while for more competitive interaction, personality dissimilarity enhanced liking.

Success/reward

Studies of shared success or failure in laboratory groups reveal a range of outcomes. Although intragroup liking is sometimes enhanced by group success (the predicted outcome), it is sometimes enhanced by failure, and sometimes it remains unaffected. For example, Zander, Stotland and Wolfe (1960) and Burnstein and McRae (1962) found no difference in intragroup attraction between succeeding and failing groups, and Shaw and Gilchrist (1955), Thibaut (1950), and Berkowitz, Levy and Harvey (1957) found an increase in cohesiveness in failed groups, particularly among central group members. Pepitone and Kleiner (1957) report evidence that lower-status (losing) teams, faced with the prospect of losing or of winning against another low-status team, manifested increased cohesiveness. Even when they were faced with the prospect of losing against a higher-status (winning) team, cohesiveness increased.

Some of these positive relationships between failure and increased cohesion may be interpreted in terms of shared external threat. However, this is controlled for in a study by Turner, Hogg, Turner and Smith (1984), in which groups that had unequivocally failed manifested heightened cohesion (see Chapter 7 for details of this experiment).

Other data on the relationship between success/reward and cohesiveness reveal that (1) people are attracted to group members who are disproportionately responsible for group success or goal achievement; (2) people who are rewarded or succeed in the presence of other group members tend to like the group as a whole and to like other group members; and (3) people tend to like other group members who are successful in task/group terms or more general terms.

Reduction of cognitive dissonance

Intragroup liking tends to be enhanced by the experience of an unpleasant initiation rite attached to entry to the group. There is some evidence for a positive relationship between liking and the severity of the unpleasant initiation (e.g. Schopler and Bateson, 1962).

Consequences of cohesiveness

Expression of aggression

Cohesive groups that have experienced frustration, or been insulted by external sources, tend to express greater aggression or hostility towards fellow team members or external sources than do less cohesive groups. Where the target of the aggression or hostility is not the instigator of the frustration or insult, aggression is a positive function of dislike for the target.

Self-evaluation

People tend, over time, to develop an evaluation of self that is consistent with the way liked others evaluate them: provided that these liked others do not evaluate them negatively. Self-evaluation is not affected by the views of disliked others. People also tend, over time, to develop a conception of self that is consistent with their own positive or negative evaluation of liked others. In the domain of performance evaluation, self-evaluation is generally affected by cohesiveness such that those who believe they are performing better than the group as a whole experience an exaggerated sense of superior performance, while those who believe they are performing less well than the group as a whole experience an exaggerated sense of inferior performance.

Evaluation of the situation

Liking among members of decision-making groups, work groups, therapy groups, and simulated laboratory groups is associated with a positive evaluation of the ambient circumstances of the group interaction, and of the interaction itself.

Evaluation of others

Liking among members of sports teams, sororities, college groups, marital partnerships, summer camps, military groups, and laboratory groups has been shown to accentuate perceptions of attitudinal, personality, and value similarity (see Byrne, 1971). Other research involving discussion groups, summer camps, air crews, and simulated groups reveals that the behaviour of liked individuals is evaluated more favourably than the behaviour of less liked individuals. Liking among group members also appears to enhance interpersonal sensitivity to the needs, feelings and beliefs of fellow group members. There is also substantial evidence from a wide array of group settings that group members assume that those whom they like or dislike reciprocate their feelings.

Communication

There is more communication, less inhibited communication, and better-quality communication among people in naturally occurring and laboratory dyads and groups characterized by greater interpersonal attraction. Under conditions embodying strong pressures towards conformity, cohesive groups tend to direct their communication towards deviant members in order to bring them back into line with group standards.

Uniformity/conformity

Studies of the effects of cohesiveness on uniformity/conformity have employed a wide range of groups, including classroom groups, decision-making conferences, fraternity groups, college students, boy scouts, summer camps, industrial work groups, housing projects, and actual or simulated laboratory dyads and groups. Cohesiveness has been manipulated directly (often by telling subjects that they will probably like one another, or find one another congenial) or indirectly (e.g. via cooperation, similarity, or task outcome), or established groups that differ in terms of intragroup attraction have been used.

The general finding is that people in cohesive groups who like one another conform to group standards and thus produce intragroup uniformity of conduct. People in cohesive groups tend to reject and not conform to deviates, and are themselves resistant to changing opinions that they share with members of the group to whom they are attracted. In general it is the most liked members of groups who have the greatest influence on members' behaviour. There are, however, some negative or contradictory findings (e.g. Bovard, 1953; Downing, 1958; McKeachie, 1954). Interestingly, Seashore (1954) found that more and less cohesive industrial work groups did not differ in degree of consensus on production levels, but that members of the more cohesive groups conformed to their production standards more closely than members of the less cohesive groups. Another way to describe this is that both groups were clear about the appropriate production norms, but behavioural conformity was enhanced by cohesiveness.

High cohesiveness in decision-making groups can produce excessive concurrence-seeking, to the detriment of optimal decision-making procedures.

This is what Janis (1972) referred to as 'groupthink' (see Chapter 8 for a critical discussion of groupthink).

Task performance
Research into the effects of cohesiveness on group productivity (task performance) has employed laboratory groups, summer camps, industrial work groups, supermarkets, conferences, military groups, college and school groups, and recreational groups. Attraction has been manipulated directly or indirectly, or left to vary naturally, and productivity measured on both intellectual and mechanical tasks. Some studies find that attraction increases and improves productivity, some find no effect, and yet others find that attraction decreases productivity.

These contradictory findings probably arise because attraction increases conformity to group standards, and such standards do not necessarily specify good performance or high productivity. For a discussion of the cohesiveness/performance relationship in sports teams, see Carron (1980); and in therapy, encounter and analogue groups, see Drescher *et al.* (1985). The relationship between cohesiveness and productivity/performance is discussed in more detail in Chapter 8.

Learning
Research in this area concerns the effects of attraction or group climate (positive, permissive, restrictive, traditional, etc.) on learning, mainly in classroom settings. Unfortunately, most of the research focuses on the role of the teacher or experimenter rather than the group that is doing the learning, so it is difficult to be confident about the effect of intragroup attraction on learning. Findings are inconsistent. Positive atmosphere, positive relations with the teacher/experimenter, or positive relations among subjects sometimes produce an increment in learning, sometimes a decrement, and sometimes no effect.

Summary

Taken together, Lott and Lott's (1965) review and subsequent research reveal that group cohesiveness is enhanced by: (1) relatively voluntary interaction/propinquity among people who do not differ too dramatically in terms of emotionally charged intergroup differences (e.g. race); (2) cooperative interaction or normatively prescribed competitive interaction; (3) acceptance by others; (4) externally imposed frustration or threat that is shared, not attributable to deficient skill or ability, and for which no individualistic avoidance strategy exists; (5) homogeneity of status, high status, or the impossibility of upward status mobility; (6) behaviour and personality characteristics that appear to help the group to fulfil its specific functions; (7) attitudinal, value, and 'background' similarities, and personality compatibilities, that are relevant to the group's existence and purpose; and (8) unpleasant initiation rites. Note that group success does not reliably enhance cohesiveness.

The effects of elevated cohesiveness are: (1) aggression in response to external insult; (2) self-evaluation in line with positive evaluations by liked others, and positive or negative evaluations of liked others; (3) exaggerated evaluation of the superiority or inferiority (as the case may be) of one's own performance relative to the group; (4) positive evaluation of the group and its immediate circumstances; (5) perception of interpersonal attitudinal, behavioural and personality similarity, and reciprocal positive regard, as well as accentuated sensitivity to others' internal states; (6) better, less inhibited, and more communication; and (7) conformity to group standards concerning attitudes and performance.

The measurement of cohesiveness

Group cohesiveness has been with us for more than forty years, and so one might be forgiven for assuming that during that time there could have been triangulation on to one – or a handful of – standardized and well-validated measure[s] of cohesiveness. This has not happened. There are almost as many measures of cohesiveness as people who have researched cohesiveness, and there is not even consensus on the parameters defining an appropriate measure. While cohesiveness remains imprecisely defined, it continues to be open season for the measurement of cohesiveness (see Chapter 4).

There have been attempts to measure cohesiveness by monitoring overt behaviour (Anderson, 1975; Cialdini, Borden, Thorne, Walker, Freeman and Sloane, 1976). Mobley, Griffeth, Hand and Meglino (1979), for example, monitored membership turnover (cf. Marshall and Heslin, 1975); while Yalom and Rand (1966) monitored attendance at group-therapy sessions. There have also been attempts to monitor non-verbal indexes of cohesiveness, such as tendencies for group members to stand or sit close together, focus their attention on one another, show signs of mutual affection, and display coordinated patterns of behaviour (Piper, Marrache, LaCroix, Richardsen and Jones, 1983; Tickle-Degen and Rosenthal, 1987). For example, Cialdini *et al.* (1976) monitored the behavioural display of membership emblems associated with expressions of group belongingness and commitment; while Kirshner, Dies and Brown (1978) used the duration of group hug at the conclusion of therapy groups. Since cohesive group members tend to engage in self-disclosure or collaborative narration, develop a special argot, and generally communicate freely, measures of verbal behaviour have also been developed and used (e.g. Cialdini *et al.*, 1976; Eder, 1988; Owen, 1985). In this vein, Atthowe (1961) monitored the proportion of 'we' and 'I' remarks made by group members.

The overwhelming majority of measures of cohesiveness, however, involve some form of self-report (Drescher *et al.*, 1985). What is usually measured is interpersonal attraction among group members (e.g. Festinger *et al.*, 1950; Lott and Lott, 1965; Terborg, Castore and DeNinno, 1976). This has been done via sociometric choice (e.g. Dimock, 1941) or by the very popular method of simply having subjects rate how much they like one another (e.g. Bovard, 1951; Jackson, 1959). Cohesiveness has also been measured by asking subjects to evaluate their feelings about the group as a whole (e.g. Bovard, 1951).

Another method that has been used rests on the not unreasonable assumption that group members are able accurately to perceive and represent the cohesiveness of their group as a whole. So, for example, Mann and Baumgartel (1952) asked group members to report whether they felt that their group was 'better than others at sticking together', and Martens and Peterson (1971) monitored members' perceptions of the 'closeness' of the group.

A fourth method for measuring cohesiveness is via expressed desire to remain in the group (e.g. Anderson, 1975). Schachter (1951) simply asked subjects 'Do you want to remain a member of this group?', 'How often do you think this group should meet?', and 'If enough members decide not to stay so that it seems this group might discontinue, would you like the chance to persuade others to stay?'. Libo (1953) used a more subtle projective picture-description test that correlated very highly with subjects' subsequent free decision to remain in or leave the group.

A final method involves monitoring identification or closeness with the group, via self-reported expressions of belongingness and commitment (e.g. Converse and Campbell, 1968; Steers, 1977). For example, Indik (1965) asked: 'How strong a "sense of belonging" do you feel you have to the people you work with?'.

While some studies employ only a single measure of cohesiveness (e.g. Festinger *et al.*, 1950), and some employ multiple measures of the same aspect of cohesiveness (e.g. Schachter, 1951), the majority employ composite indexes calculated from members' evaluations of each other and the group as a whole (e.g. Keller, 1986; Manning and Fullerton, 1988). These composite indexes range from relatively simple and idiosyncratic scales with only a few items, to complex multi-item scales with subscales, which have been used over and over again.

Seashore (1954) asked employees at a large manufacturing firm the following five questions: (1) 'Do you feel that you are really a part of your work group?'; (2) 'If you had the chance to do the same kind of work for the same pay in another work group, how would you feel about moving?'; (3) 'How does your work group compare with other work groups at [name of company] on each of the following points? (i) The way the men get along together, (ii) The way the men stick together, (iii) The way the men help each other on the job?'. Intercorrelations among questions ranged from .15 to .70, and the scale as a whole related meaningfully to various consequences of cohesiveness.

Scott (1965) found, in a longitudinal study of college fraternities and sororities, a significant relationship between a 7-item index of devotion to group and various behavioural measures. However, the devotion scale was not significantly correlated with measures of average interpersonal attraction among group members. Hagstrom and Selvin (1965) administered a wide-ranging 19-item cohesiveness questionnaire to female college students living in various different group situations (sororities, dormitories, etc.). The questions correlated positively and relatively highly, but clustered into two relatively separate factors reflecting 'social satisfaction' (instrumental attractiveness of the group) and 'sociometric cohesion' (intrinsic attractiveness of the group, and particularly its members).

Gross and Martin (1952) found no significant correlation between three different measures of cohesiveness administered to female college students in residential units, and Eisman (1959) found no significant correlation between five measures of cohesiveness administered to student groups. Moreover, a replication of the Eisman study, but with Dutch college students, obtained similar results (Ramuz-Nienhuis and van Bergen, 1960).

Group cohesiveness questionnaires

Sports psychology
It is in the area of sport and exercise psychology that the measurement of cohesiveness has been addressed most systematically. In 1971 Martens and Peterson published their Sports Cohesiveness Questionnaire (also see Martens, Landers and Loy, 1972) which, by the mid 1980s, had already been used in various permutations in at least twelve published studies.

The original questionnaire (Martens and Peterson, 1971) had 8 items in 3 groupings. The first group (4 items) monitored evaluations of other team members in terms of (1) interpersonal attraction; (2) their contribution to the team based on ability; (3) their contribution to the team based on being enjoyable to play with; and (4) their influence or power. The second group (2 items) monitored the respondent's relationship to the team; in terms of (1) strength of sense of belonging to the team, and (2) value of membership. The third group (2 items) monitored evaluation of the team as a whole in terms of (1) level of teamwork; and (2) how 'closely knit' the team was. Martens *et al.*'s (1972) variant is only very slightly different (see Table 3.2). It had 7 items,

Table 3.2   *Cohesiveness items from Martens, Landers and Loy's (1972) Sports Cohesiveness Questionnaire*

I *Individual to individual relations*

Interpersonal attraction:	'On what type of friendship basis are you with each member of your team?' (1 'good friend', 9 'not good friend')
Personal power/influence:	'For many reasons some of the members of a team are more influential than others. How much influence do you believe each of the other members of your team have with the coach and other teammates?'

II *Individual to group relations*

Value of membership:	'Compared to other groups that you belong to, how much do you value your membership on this team?'
Sense of belonging:	'How strong a sense of belonging do you believe you have to this team?'
Enjoyment:	'How much do you like competing with this particular team?'

III *Group as a unit*

Teamwork:	'How good do you think the teamwork is on your team?'
Closeness:	'How closely knit do you think your team is?'

---

all answered on 9-point scales: for example, the interpersonal attraction item was responded to on a scale labelled 'good friend' (1) and 'not good friend' (9). The Sports Cohesiveness Questionnaire has been criticized (see Widmeyer, Brawley and Carron, 1985) for not being developed on the basis of a conceptual model of cohesiveness, and for inadequate tests of its psychometric properties.

Feeling that a better measure of cohesiveness was needed, Yukelson, Weinberg and Jackson (1984) developed a 22-item Multidimensional Group Cohesion Instrument to monitor the cohesiveness of intercollegiate basketball teams. On the basis of extensive literature review and informed opinion, a 41-item instrument, with an 11-point scale response format, was constructed and administered to 196 intercollegiate basketball players from 16 teams. Factor-analytic techniques were used to produce a final 22-item instrument with 4 subscales (see Table 3.3). The entire scale had a very high alpha reliability coefficient of .93: for the subscales the values ranged from .79 to .88.

Widmeyer, Brawley and Carron (1985) feel that although Yukelson *et al.*'s Multidimensional Group Cohesion Instrument has at least some psychometric validity, it suffers from two other problems. It is rather specific to the sport of basketball, and it is 'without a theory upon which to develop hypotheses' (Widmeyer *et al.*, 1985, p. 10). To address these and other limitations, the research team of Brawley, Carron and Widmeyer have developed an 18-item 4-scale Group Environment Questionnaire (Widmeyer

Table 3.3   *Cohesiveness variables from Yukelson, Weinberg and*
Jackson's (1984) Multidimensional Group Cohesion
Instrument

Quality of teamwork ($\alpha = .86$)
Teamwork
Role compatibility
Support and mutual respect
Degree of unselfishness
Conflict resolution
Well-defined roles
Closely knit
Team task discipline

Attraction to the group ($\alpha = .88$)
Feelings of enjoyment
Continue group membership
Feelings of acceptance
Pride in group membership
Value placed on membership
Significant and worthwhile
Satisfied with friendships

Unity of purpose ($\alpha = .86$)
Team preparation
Commitment to team operations
Team goal clarity
Method to reevaluate goals

Valued roles ($\alpha = .79$)
Role valued by teammates
Role valued by coaches
Sense of belongingness

Note: See Yukelson *et al.* (1984, pp. 107–8) for wording of
questions monitoring each of these 22 variables.

et al., 1985; see also Brawley, Carron and Widmeyer, 1987; Carron, Widmeyer and Brawley, 1985).

The research team was extremely rigorous and systematic in reducing an initial 354-item pool to a final 18-item instrument. The researchers were explicitly guided by a theoretical conviction that it was important to distinguish operationally between individual and group levels of cohesiveness, and between task and social concerns of the group and its members. The final version of the questionnaire (published in Widmeyer, *et al.*, 1985) had 18 items clustered into 4 subscales, and a 9-point ('strongly agree' to 'strongly disagree') response format (see Table 3.4). The reliability of the subscales is relatively high. For example, a study of 247 athletes from 26 different Canadian interactive sports teams (Carron *et al.*, 1985) yielded Cronbach alphas of .64 for attraction to the group–social, .75 for attraction to the group–task, .76 for group integration–social, and .70 for group integration–

Table 3.4   *Cohesiveness items from the Group Environment Questionnaire*

Individual attraction to the group–social
- 'I do not enjoy being part of the social activities of this team'
- 'I am not going to miss the members of this team when the season ends'
- 'Some of my best friends are on this team'
- 'I enjoy other parties more than team parties'
- 'For me this team is one of the most important social groups to which I belong'

Individual attraction to the group–task
- 'I am not happy with the amount of playing time I get'
- 'I am unhappy with my team's level of desire to win'
- 'This team does not give me enough opportunities to improve my personal performance'
- 'I do not like the style of play on this team'

Group integration–social
- 'Members of our team would rather go out on their own than get together as a team'
- 'Our team members rarely party together'
- 'Our team would like to spend time together in the off season'
- 'Members of our team do not stick together outside of practices and games'

Group integration–task
- 'Our team is united in trying to reach its goals for performance'
- 'We all take responsibility for any loss or poor performance by our team'
- 'Our team members have conflicting aspirations for the team's performance'
- 'If members of our team have problems in practice, everyone wants to help them so we can get back together again'
- 'Our team members do not communicate freely about each athlete's responsibilities during competition or practice'

Note: The Group Environment Questionnaire is published in Widmeyer, Brawley and Carron (1985).

task. In another study, using a slightly expanded 24-item version with 212 athletes from 20 similarly diverse teams, Cronbach alphas of .58, .74, .61, and .78 were obtained for the 4 subscales.

'Therapy' groups

Another area in which there is a proliferation of formal instruments to measure cohesiveness is therapy, psychotherapy, counselling, and personal growth groups. Table 3.5 lists 9 items which Stokes (1983), writing from a group-psychotherapy perspective, believes are the most frequently used group cohesiveness tests. The first 7 items are taken from an often-used cohesion scale published by Schutz (1966). Principal components and reliability analyses of responses to the 9-item scale from 177 members of a wide range of personal change groups produced a single factor accounting for 42.6 per cent of variance, and associated with a relatively high Cronbach's alpha value of .81 (Stokes, 1983).

Lieberman, Yalom and Miles (1973) have administered a 7-item questionnaire to 161 encounter-group participants. The instrument contains items 1, 2, 4, 6, 8, and 9 from Table 3.5, and one additional item which is basically a rewording of Item 6, in which the statement 'I like my group . . .'

Table 3.5   *Nine commonly used items to monitor group cohesiveness*

1. 'How many of your group members fit what you feel to be the ideal of a good group member?'
2. 'To what degree do you feel that you are included by the group in the group's activities?'
3. 'How attractive do you find the activities in which you participate as a member of your group?'
4. 'If most of the members of your group decided to dissolve the group by leaving, would you try to dissuade them?'
5. 'If you were asked to participate in another project like this one, would you like to be with the same people who are in your present group?'
6. 'How well do you like the group you are in?'
7. 'How often do you think your group should meet?'
8. 'I feel that working with the particular group will enable me to attain my personal goals for which I sought the group.'
9. 'Compared to other groups like yours, how well would you imagine your group works together?'

Note: Taken from Table 1 in Stokes (1983, p.452) by permission of the American Group Psychotherapy Association.

invites responses ranging from 'like very much' to 'dislike very much'. Stokes (1983) reports values of Cronbach's alpha associated with these data: .86 for the 7-item scale, and .82 with the redundant additional item excluded.

Perhaps the most widely used scale (see Stokes, Fuehrer and Childs, 1983; Wright and Duncan, 1986) is that developed specifically for therapy groups by Yalom, Houts, Zimerberg and Rand (1967). This is an 11-item scale containing all the items in Table 3.5, except 3 and 5, but with the addition of items monitoring participants' feelings about their contribution to the group work, their feelings about the length of group meetings, their feelings about the group therapist, and their feelings about being ashamed to be in therapy.

In an attempt to produce a cohesiveness scale that can be used with a broader range of different groups, Evans and Jarvis (1986) developed a general 20-item Group Attitude Scale to measure attraction-to-group. On the basis of a conceptualization of cohesiveness as attraction-to-group, and a definition of attraction-to-group as 'an individual's desire to identify with and be an accepted member of the group' (p. 204) they constructed a 40-item scale with a 9-point Likert response format. This was administered to 178 members of 26 growth and therapy groups in order to arrive at a final 20-item scale (see Table 3.6). The final scale has been administered to 56 members of 7 growth groups at the beginning, middle, and end of the life of the group (Cronbach alphas of .93, .92, and .90 were obtained), to 27 members of 6 task-orientated educational groups (alpha of .96), and to 47 members of 8 growth groups at 4 points in the life of the group (alphas of .94, .92, .96, and .97) – see Evans and Jarvis (1986).

Although this scale appears to have high internal consistency (it is also reported to have good external validity – in terms of correlations with other scales and indexes of cohesion), it is not clear why Evans and Jarvis (1986)

Table 3.6   *Cohesiveness items from Evans and Jarvis's (1986) Group Attitude Scale*

1.   'I want to remain a member of this group.'
2.   'I like my group.'
3.   'I look forward to coming to the group.'
4.   'I don't care what happens in this group.'
5.   'I feel involved in what is happening in my group.'
6.   'If I could drop out of the group now, I would.'
7.   'I dread coming to this group.'
8.   'I wish it were possible for the group to end now.'
9.   'I am dissatisfied with the group.'
10.   'If it were possible to move to another group at this time, I would.'
11.   'I feel included in the group.'
12.   'In spite of individual differences, a feeling of unity exists in my group.'
13.   'Compared to other groups I know of, I feel my group is better than most.'
14.   'I do not feel a part of the group's activities.'
15.   'I feel it would make a difference to the group if I were not here.'
16.   'If I were told my group would not meet today, I would feel badly.'
17.   'I feel distant from the group.'
18.   'It makes a difference to me how this group turns out.'
19.   'I feel my absence would not matter to the group.'
20.   'I would not feel badly if I had to miss a meeting of this group.'

Note: These items are taken from Table 1 in Evans and Jarvis (1986, p. 207). © 1986.
Reprinted by permission of Sage Publications Inc.

believe that a scale constructed and validated almost exclusively on the responses of personal growth groups should necessarily be generalizable to other group situations.

Conclusion

There are many other group cohesiveness scales in addition to those I have singled out in this chapter. For example, there is Rosenfield and Gilbert's (1989) 10-item questionnaire, Gruber and Gray's (1981) 13-item questionnaire, and a general Group Environment Scale devised by Moos, Insel and Humphrey (1974), which has a cohesion subscale. In general the major activity in scale construction and validation occurs in the sports team and therapy/growth group areas. Some of these scales are very specific to the particular types of group being investigated. Others however, may have a more general application.

In conclusion to this section on cohesiveness scales, it should be noted that investigations of correspondence among different operationalizations of group cohesiveness have often indicated only weak or non-significant correlations (Bovard, 1951; Carron and Ball, 1977; Eisman, 1959; Jackson, 1959; Ramuz-Nienhuis and van Bergen, 1960; Scott, 1965), or the existence of separate cohesiveness dimensions (Bednar and Kaul, 1978; Gruber and Gray, 1981; Hagstrom and Selvin, 1965; Widmeyer *et al.*, 1985; Yukelson *et al.*, 1984). This confronts us with the thorny problem of deciding whether a group that is 'cohesive' by one measure, but not by another, is or is not a 'cohesive' group. How should one decide? This state of affairs can make interpretation of multidimensional measures difficult, and preference of any one operationalization over others inadvisable (see Chapter 4).

Conclusion

Fundamental research has generally adopted, implicitly or explicitly, an attraction-to-group or interpersonal-attraction definition of group cohesiveness. Within this framework, we have learned a great deal about those variables that have antecedent and consequent relationships with cohesiveness. There are persistent anomalous and problematic findings, but in general by the mid 1960s we could be relatively confident about many of the antecedents and consequences of cohesiveness in small interactive social groups. Subsequent research has not really altered that picture – given acceptance of the social cohesion model.

There are an enormous number of different ways to measure group cohesiveness, and there is often weak or non-significant correlation between different measures. Nevertheless, particularly in more applied areas of social psychology, a number of multidimensional, multi-item formal cohesiveness scales have emerged. Some of these scales have been carefully constructed – this is reflected in good internal consistency and external reliability; many, however, are rather specific to the type of group under investigation.

Having given a thumbnail sketch of the empirical state of play, I would like now to return to the main focus of this book: consideration of the conceptualization of group cohesiveness.

Chapter 4

Limitations and critiques

impact attractiveness

Chapter 2 described the origins and development of the scientific concept of group cohesiveness, and how it very rapidly changed its form to become mainly an attraction-based theory of group formation and solidarity. Attraction is a very important aspect of small interactive groups: people in small groups tend on the whole to like one another, and when they do not, group functioning may suffer, or the group may disintegrate. This is one reason why much research on group cohesiveness appears now to be concerned with how to measure attraction in groups. In Chapter 3 this work was surveyed, in order to describe some of the scales and questionnaires that have been devised and used. Chapter 3 also summarized what we know about the empirical antecedents and consequences of cohesiveness as interpersonal attraction. It was essentially concerned with operational and empirical, not fundamental theoretical, issues: this is, I believe, a relatively accurate reflection of current research concerns in this area.

What if we are wrong? What if it is a mistake to equate group cohesiveness with attraction in this way? Many people share this concern, but in general, concerns about limitations of the concept do not carry through to deliver viable alternatives. In exploring the reasons for this, it is valuable to relate the history of the concept of group cohesiveness to salient features of the history of ideas in social psychology. The first section of this chapter describes the way in which the concept of group cohesiveness has – since perhaps the late 1960s – suffered diminished popularity, particularly in mainstream social psychology. The next section relates this to relevant aspects of the history of ideas in social psychology. The rest of the chapter deals with limitations of the concept of cohesiveness: it documents the range of criticisms that can be – and often have been – levelled at this concept, in preparation for Chapters 5 and 6, where alternative conceptualizations are introduced.

The demise of group cohesiveness

Group cohesiveness has suffered diminished popularity in mainstream social psychology. In the 1950s and early 1960s, it was a major focus of attention. Prominent journals of the time always carried numerous articles on cohesiveness, and there were frequent major reviews of progress (e.g. Cartwright and Zander, 1953, 1960, 1968; Hare, 1962; Kelley and Thibaut, 1954; Lindzey and Borgatta, 1954; Riecken and Homans, 1954; Roseborough, 1953; van Bergen and Koekebakker, 1959). If the vicissitudes of interest in group cohesiveness are seen to shadow those of interest in small groups as a whole, then it is relevant to note that according to Hare (1962) the approximate per annum rate of bibliographical reference to small groups rose from 21 in the 1930s to 43 in the 1940s and 152 in the 1950s. Hare (1962, p. 3) lists 36 major reviews, published between 1951 and 1960, of small-group research.

By the mid 1960s, however, interest had waned, so that the last extensive reviews of group cohesiveness are generally considered to be those published by Lott and Lott in 1965, and Cartwright in 1968. For almost a quarter of a century, very little of significance on group cohesiveness has been published in mainstream social psychology. This is well illustrated by the fact that Levine and Moreland's (1990) review of progress in small-group research during the 1980s dedicated only two of thirty-six pages to 'cohesion'. Although group cohesiveness is now little researched in mainstream social psychology, there is continuing interest in more applied areas. Levine and Moreland concluded that most research 'involves military units, sports teams, or therapy groups, and is aimed at making those groups more successful by strengthening their cohesion. The main issue for these researchers is how the cohesion of a group should be conceptualized and/or measured' (1990, p. 603).

There is also, unfortunately, a distressing absence of scientific rigour in some of this literature. For instance, social psychological studies of military units tend to prefer the term morale or 'unit climate' to cohesiveness, yet it is not at all clear how these concepts differ at the level of psychological processes – they seem, ultimately, to refer to identical notions (e.g. Gal, 1986; Gal and Manning, 1987; Manning and Fullerton, 1988; Motowidlo and Borman, 1978).

Group cohesiveness is a pragmatically useful concept for those who are interested in interactive small groups. However, such pragmatic considerations do not appear to have helped to resolve fundamental conceptual problems. For example, Mudrack concludes that 'uncertainty and inconsistency have plagued four decades of research on group cohesiveness' (1989a, p. 38), while Evans and Jarvis complain that 'lack of clarity surrounds both its definition and its measurement' (1980, p. 359). Piper et al. (1983) believe that cohesiveness has 'considerable importance as a theoretical construct that facilitates our understanding of group phenomena . . . [but that] . . . there is little cognitive substance to the concept of cohesion and little cohesion in the cohesion research' (p. 94; cf. Bednar and Kaul, 1978). Stein (1976) notes that this problem extends to the relevant sociological literature. Although cohesiveness is alive and residing elsewhere, it is clearly not well.

Levine and Moreland (1990) are optimistic about the future of group dynamics. They feel that social psychology has run as far as it can with group dynamics, and it is right and timely that the torch should now be passed on. They feel that new advances will be made by organizational and other applied areas of social psychology. It remains to be seen whether this optimistic prognosis is borne out. As regards group cohesiveness specifically, the prognosis may not be so rosy, although the concept is still much used. Recent critical commentaries (e.g. Carron, 1982; Evans and Jarvis, 1980; Mudrack, 1989a), although they contain many useful insights, tend generally to ignore developments in mainstream social psychology since the mid 1960s. They recycle old and well-worn criticisms of group cohesiveness from social psychology and conduct a debate that is largely internal to the world of sports teams, therapy groups and military units. The approach thus has few of the enviable qualities of interdisciplinary endeavours, and does not appear to benefit from conceptual and metatheoretical developments in mainstream social psychology.

Historical trends in social psychology

There are many interrelated reasons why group cohesiveness may find itself on the sidelines of social psychology. One reason – which is quite inescapable if one glances at the pages of major social psychology journals over the past ten years – is the ascendancy of social cognition (e.g. Fiske and Taylor, 1991; Landman and Manis, 1983; Markus and Zajonc, 1985). Social psychology has placed an increasing emphasis upon the study of individual cognitive processes and representations. This work draws heavily and intentionally on (its understanding of) cognitive psychology and thinks in terms of schemas, memory, knowledge structures, judgemental heuristics, categorization processes, perceptual salience of information, and so on. There is little about 'feelings' or groups. The questions posed by social cognition researchers in order to construct theories rarely require research methods involving face-to-face human interaction. Generally, individual subjects now react on their own to computer simulations of information.

Clearly, group cohesiveness, with its emphasis on feelings and interaction, does not fit well with the *Zeitgeist* of contemporary social psychology. It should, however, be noted that social psychology has always been cognitive (Markus and Zajonc; 1985). For instance, Lewin's field theory (see Chapter 2) is a cognitive theory, as were the cognitive consistency theories (see Abelson *et al.*, 1968) that dominated the 1950s and 1960s: for example, Festinger's (1957) cognitive dissonance theory, Heider's (1958) cognitive balance theory, and Osgood and Tannenbaum's (1955) cognitive congruence theory. Attribution theories that dominated the 1970s were also cognitive (Harvey and Smith, 1977; Heider, 1958; Hewstone, 1983, 1989; Jones and Davis, 1965; Kelley, 1967; Kelley and Michela, 1980). In the 1980s it was social cognition.

It is true that social cognition has focused attention away from interactive groups. However, it has advanced our understanding of cognitive processes and representations, so that we may now be in a position to retheorize cohesiveness. Remember that one reason why group cohesiveness became so quickly simplified and reduced to interpersonal attraction was the problem of conceptualizing and operationalizing complex cognitive representational concepts such as 'the total field of forces', or 'group mind' (see Chapter 2).

The advent of social cognition is not the only – and is quite probably not the major – reason why there has been a marked shift of emphasis from the study of groups to the study of individuals. Many commentators have documented and commented upon this shift in great detail (e.g. Cartwright, 1979; Festinger, 1980; Pepitone, 1981; Steiner, 1974, 1983, 1986; Triandis, 1977), and proffered explanations in terms of pragmatic and ideological factors.

For example, Steiner (1974) notes that an empirical focus on the individual produces results more easily, more quickly and with less risk than research on interactive groups. Take, for example, an experiment on interactive four-person groups. Four subjects are needed to run a session, and every four-person group represents only one case for analysis. If only three subjects manage to show up for the session, then the session has to be abandoned. If a non-interactive paradigm could be adopted, then all sessions could be run irrespective of number of subjects who appear, and every subject would represent one case for analysis. Clearly the 'non-interactive' researcher requires significantly fewer resources: fewer subjects and less time. In any given year, the 'non-interactive' researcher will be able to conduct many more separate experiments, and hence publish more work. It is a sad fact of academic life that throughout the world volume of publication has increasingly become the measure of performance.

Another factor contributing to a diversion of interest from groups is suggested by Schaffer (1978), who argues that the discipline of social psychology has succeeded in isolating itself from sociology, and has expanded so much that no social psychologist could realistically hope to keep abreast of all developments across the discipline. As a consequence, social psychologists have become narrow specialists in small, well-circumscribed areas of social psychology, and in all cases they are largely ignorant of sociology. Specialization may be unavoidable, perhaps even desirable, but Schaffer's warning about isolation from sociology is worth consideration by group researchers. It is instructive to note how some of the more influential insights about the social psychology of group processes are predicated on sociological concerns: e.g. McDougall's (1921) group psychology, Moscovici's (1976) ideas about social change, Sherif's (1936) analysis of social norms, and Tajfel's (1974) analysis of intergroup relations.

G.W. Allport (1968), Knowles (1982), and Wegner, Guiliano and Hertel (1984) all feel that the failure of McDougall's (1921) 'group mind' helped to nudge social psychology in the direction advocated by Floyd Allport's statement that 'there is no psychology of groups which is not essentially and entirely a psychology of individuals' (1924, p. 4). One reason why McDougall's group mind succumbed so easily to Allport's attack is quite possibly, as was suggested in Chapter 2, that it was an idea before its time: containing vague specifications of cognitive representational concepts which may be properly explicated only as a consequence of recent advances in social cognition and the social psychology of intergroup relations.

A final factor to consider is that in much traditional small-group research, the dyad has assumed the role of prototype group — a turn of events that has inevitably shifted the conceptual emphasis away from interaction among members of groups towards interpersonal interaction in dyads (e.g. Kelley and Thibaut, 1978; see Clark and Reis, 1988). This shift in emphasis can be explained in terms of some of the reasons just discussed. However, those who consider research on the dyad to represent *group* research might argue that the status of the dyad as a prototype group is legitimized by evidence that naturally occurring interactive groups typically have a membership of two to seven, with a mean of three (Bakeman and Beck, 1974; Hollingshead, 1949; James, 1951, 1953; Jorgensen and Dukes, 1976; Lyndsay, 1972, 1976), and that 73 per cent are dyads (James, 1953).

However, the overriding reason why group cohesiveness, as a distinct group-level concept, has made little headway in social psychology is perhaps a metatheoretical one. As social psychologists we tend to develop theories of human social behaviour that explain group phenomena in terms of interpersonal interaction or properties of individuals. Group-level theories tend to dissolve readily into theories of interpersonal processes, and thus have no distinct theoretical status. This is a major critique that is central to the fundamental point of this book. It is discussed later in this chapter.

The reductionism of social psychology can be traced to our sociopolitical milieu, which stresses the primacy of the individual. More precisely, contemporary social psychology is largely a North American product — painstakingly developed in the USA, by Americans, and in an epoch of American hegemony. The liberal democratic political system that has characterized America and most Western nations for almost the entire history of experimental social psychology provides the ideological parameters, Garfinkel's (1967) 'hidden agenda', of theorizing. This system places the individual human being above and before all else. It is the individual that counts – a fact well understood by Iraqi propagandists in their warnings to Allied forces during the Gulf War of early 1991: that while Iraq could tolerate untold casualties, the Allies could not. The primacy of the individual is further reflected in the Western democratic political system. The collective will of the nation is arrived at through a process of aggregation of the will of individuals, and a government is elected to administer this aggregate expression of individual wills. Despite advertising and media interests, it is nevertheless promulgated that individuals can make truly independent, objective – and essentially asocial – social decisions.

It is not surprising that an individualistic ideology such as this would facilitate the development of theories of social behaviour that consider groups to be aggregates of individuals. Perhaps the historical lack of success and/or the relatively low profile of group theories that are distinct from – or are not reduced to – theories of interpersonal processes can be attributed at least partly to the sort of deep-seated taken-for-granted assumptions we make, and preconceptions we have, about the nature of human beings.

Limitations and criticisms of group cohesiveness

Having documented the relaxation of interest in group cohesiveness, and suggested some reasons why this may have happened, I must now deal with the many criticisms that have been levelled specifically at the concept of group cohesiveness over the years. These criticisms fall roughly into two categories: those that can be called *traditional*, as they are grounded in general acceptance of the underlying model of the social group; and those that can be called *radical*, as they are predicated on dissatisfaction with – and sometimes rejection of – this model (see Table 4.1).

Table 4.1 *Limitations and criticisms of the group cohesiveness concept*

Traditional criticisms
- Operationalization and measurement
- Group cohesiveness operationalized as attraction
- Group cohesiveness as an inadequate theory

Radical criticisms
- Aggregate vs structural attributes
- Reductionism
- The molecule simile
- Sociometric choice
- Motivation
- Definition of 'small group'
- Groups, categories and roles

Traditional criticisms

Traditional criticisms focus on the way in which group cohesiveness has been operationalized and measured, and on limitations of the attraction-to-group or interpersonal-attraction formulation, but do not mount an assault on fundamental assumptions underlying the nature of the social group.

Operationalization and measurement
The history of group cohesiveness is a continuous and unresolved debate about how to define and operationalize the concept. Because of the lack of a clear and unambiguous conceptual definition, there are no obvious criteria for admissible and inadmissible operationalizations. Thus, 'the question of how to measure cohesiveness remains open, and in consequence different researchers have operationalized cohesiveness in different ways' (Forsyth, 1983, p. 349). Details of the measurement of group cohesiveness have been given in Chapter 3, but it is worthwhile summarizing here the array of measures that have been and are used.

Measures of group cohesiveness typically involve self-report (Drescher *et al.*, 1985), but there have been attempts to monitor overt behaviour (Anderson, 1975; Cialdini *et al.*, 1976), non-verbal behaviour (Piper *et al.*, 1983; Tickle-Degen and Rosenthal, 1987) and verbal behaviour (Eder, 1988; Owen, 1985). What is usually measured is (1) interpersonal attraction among group members (e.g. Festinger *et al.*, 1950; Lott and Lott, 1965; Terborg *et al.*, 1976); (2) expressed desire to remain in the group, via self-report (Anderson, 1975), behaviour (Marshall and Heslin, 1975), or membership turnover (Mobley *et al.*, 1979); or (3) identification or closeness with the group, via self-reported expressions of belongingness and commitment (Indik, 1965; Steers, 1977), or unobtrusive observation of verbal and behavioural display of membership emblems (Cialdini *et al.*, 1976).

Composite indexes calculated from members' evaluations of each other and the group also abound (e.g. Keller, 1986; Manning and Fullerton, 1988). In the group-psychotherapy context, for example, Rosenfield and Gilbert (1989) have a 10-item questionnaire, Lieberman *et al.* (1973) a 7-item questionnaire, and Yalom *et al.* (1967) an 11-item measure. The latter is the most widely used (Stokes *et al.*, 1983; Wright and Duncan, 1986). In sport and exercise psychology, the Sports Cohesiveness Questionnaire (Martens *et al.*, 1972) and the 18-item 4-scale Group Environment Questionnaire (Brawley *et al.*, 1987; Carron *et al.*, 1985; Widmeyer *et al.*, 1985) are widely used to monitor cohesiveness, but numerous other instruments also exist, such as Gruber and Gray's (1981) 13-item questionnaire, and Yukelson *et al.*'s (1984) 22-item Multidimensional Group Cohesion Instrument. Evans and Jarvis (1986) have developed a general 20-item Group Attitude Scale to measure attraction-to-group. There is also a general Group Environment Scale devised by Moos *et al.* (1974), which has a cohesion subscale.

Investigations of correspondence among different operationalizations of group cohesiveness have often indicated only weak or non-significant correlations (Bovard, 1951; Carron and Ball, 1977; Eisman, 1959; Jackson, 1959; Ramuz-Nienhuis and van Bergen, 1960) or the existence of separate cohesiveness dimensions (Bednar and Kaul, 1978; Gruber and Gray, 1981; Hagstrom and Selvin, 1965; Widmeyer *et al.*, 1985; Yukelson *et al.*, 1984). If a group is 'cohesive' by one measure but not by another, then is it or is it not a 'cohesive' group? How should one decide? This state of affairs makes interpretation of multidimensional measures difficult, and preference for any one operationalization over the others inadvisable. We have already seen how researchers were sensitive to this problem very early on: Gross and Martin (1952) objected to an operationalization purely in terms of interpersonal attraction as constituting at best an incomplete or partial index.

Group cohesiveness operationalized as attraction

Group cohesiveness is, nevertheless, generally operationalized in terms of attraction to the group. Carron agrees that 'operational measures of cohesion based upon attraction underrepresent the concept' (1980, p. 237; see also 1982), and that attraction is neither a unitary concept nor the only force binding members to the group. Carron also raises two other objections. First, attraction-to-group fails to account for cohesion under conditions where group members actually dislike each other: for example, Lenk (1969) found that although members of a rowing 'eight' disliked each other, they worked together as a cohesive team. Second, attraction may not be necessary for group formation: for example, Anderson (1975) found consensus on task procedures to be a stronger determinant than attraction, and Carron notes that in sports teams individuals 'may not know each other initially, they may never come to like one another, but they may stay together (cohere) in order to continue to compete in the league' (1982, p. 127).

Hogg and Turner and their colleagues have conducted a number of experiments that support these last two points (Hogg, 1987; see Chapter 7 for details of some of these experiments). They have found group solidarity in unattractive groups – groups that have failed (Turner *et al.*, 1984) or are unpopular (Turner, Sachdev and Hogg, 1983), and among individuals who dislike one another (Hogg and Turner, 1985a, b). In the first of these experiments, Turner *et al.* (1984) allowed individuals to choose to join an artificial laboratory group for a task in which they had to find synonyms. Their performance was evaluated, and they were subsequently informed that they had succeeded or failed (under conditions in which the failure could not be denied, attributed to the activities of an outgroup, or otherwise explained away). Members of groups that had failed expressed greater cohesiveness (attraction to the group, its members and activities; behavioural ingroup favouritism and preference; identification with the group; and other measures of group behaviour) than did those who had joined a group that succeeded.

In the second experiment, Turner *et al.* (1983) created artificial laboratory groups (employing a variant of the minimal group paradigm – e.g. Billig and Tajfel, 1973) that were allegedly popular (i.e. contained members who were liked by all subjects in the experiment) or unpopular (i.e. contained members who were disliked by all subjects in the experiment). Unpopular groups were found to be more cohesive (monitored similarly to above) than popular groups. The last two experiments again involved artificial laboratory groups, and similar measures of cohesiveness. Hogg and Turner (1985a) found that randomly categorized groups of individuals were more cohesive when members disliked rather than liked one another, and Hogg and Turner (1985b) found that group cohesiveness was unaffected by interpersonal relations among group members, but was influenced by the nature of the relations between in- and outgroup such that relatively more attractive ingroups were more cohesive than relatively less attractive ingroups.

Related to these findings is robust evidence that interpersonal attraction can be inversely related to group cohesiveness under conditions of team success. For example, among successful basketball teams (Fiedler, 1954, 1960), rifle teams (McGrath, 1962), soccer teams (Veit, 1970) and bowling teams (Landers and Luschen, 1974), more cohesive teams were characterized by less interpersonal attraction than less cohesive teams. Others have found no significant relationship between interpersonal attraction and cohesiveness: e.g. Martens and Peterson's (1971) study of basketball teams.

Group cohesiveness as an inadequate theory

A number of reasons have been proposed or implied to explain why the concept of group cohesiveness fails to meet scientific criteria for an adequate theory. These all argue for a reconceptualization, but tend to emphasize different strategies and approaches. Some critics believe that the problem is largely one of impoverished operational definition, which can be overcome by dealing mainly with the measurement problem (e.g. Carron, 1980, 1982; Mudrack, 1989b). Others feel that 'because cohesiveness is a high-order theoretical construct, [it] is not directly tied to any observable, measurable aspect of the group in a one-to-one fashion' (Forsyth, 1983, p. 349); in other words, the concept in its present form is simply too broad and complex to be captured operationally (Levine and Moreland, 1990). Bednar and Kaul (1978) conclude from their review of experiential group research that there is little cognitive substance to the concept of group cohesiveness, and that it should simply be 'dropped from the empirical vocabulary' (p. 802) in preference for more representative alternatives.

Radical criticisms

Radical criticisms call into question underlying assumptions concerning the social psychological nature of the social group. Specific criticisms concern aggregate versus structural attributes of groups, reductionism, the molecule simile, sociometric choice, motivation, definition of 'small' group, and the relationship between groups, categories and roles.

Aggregate versus structural attributes

Another account of the limitations of the group cohesiveness concept rests upon a suspicion that conceptualizing and measuring group-level phenomena in terms of individuals and interindividual interactions is somehow intrinsically problematic. Very early in the development of the concept, it was recognized that the many usages of the term cohesiveness seemed to reflect two broad categories of referent. For example, Schachter *et al.* felt able to 'categorize these assorted meanings into two classes. One class of definitions centers chiefly around particular aspects of group behavior or process and the word "cohesiveness" refers to such things as the morale, efficiency, or "spirit" of the group. . . . The second class of definitions is concerned exclusively with the attractiveness of the group for its members' (1951, p. 229). Festinger *et al.*'s original conceptualization falls into the latter category, and indeed subsequent treatments of cohesiveness tend to try to explain the former in terms of the latter. It is here that the crux of the problem may lie.

For example, Evans and Jarvis (1980) argue that 'cohesion is uniformly recognized as a group phenomenon, yet its measurement generally involves measuring the levels of attraction of individual members and averaging them. This technique assumes, with little justification, that the whole is no greater than the sum of its parts' (p. 359). In a similar vein, Mudrack (1989a) notes that 'researchers are forced to examine *individuals* in order to gain a glimpse of *the group*' (p. 38; original emphasis). Researchers collect data from individuals and then 'aggregate these data . . . in some way so as to draw conclusions about phenomena occurring at the *group* level' (*ibid.*, original emphasis). As we saw in Chapter 2, this is precisely the method adopted by Festinger *et al.* (1950), who determined the cohesiveness of the group by computing the number of ingroup relative to outgroup friendship choices.

Evans and Jarvis's (1980) and Mudrack's (1989a) concerns about individual and group levels of analysis clearly relate to the issue of reductionism in social psychology. They view as problematic how to describe accurately the cohesiveness of a group in terms of the individuals within it without resorting to some sort of mechanical arithmetical procedure. This version of a critique of reductionism may stem from a particular view of social psychology. As psychologists we analyze psychological entities (i.e. individuals) because the material arena of psychological phenomena is the individual human brain, while as analysts of group processes we are making summary statements about human aggregates. The latter are non-psychological entities because psychology cannot occur outside the human mind, or among separate psychological entities. Group and individual levels of analysis are thus independent.

This reasoning resonates with Scott and Scott's (1981) distinction between two types of attributes of collectivities: aggregate attributes (average characteristics of members) and structural attributes (relations among members). Cohesiveness, as traditionally defined, is a structural attribute to do with affective relationships among group members, and thus may not be simply transformable into aggregate terms.

Evans and Jarvis, and Mudrack, in their metatheoretical criticisms of group cohesiveness, may be identifying a tendency for group cohesiveness researchers to analyze aggregate properties of groups in terms of structural properties of groups. This kind of criticism of levels of analysis is very different to that mounted by, say, European social psychologists, and indeed Evans and Jarvis, and Mudrack, do not really *explore* the issue of reductionism. Nor do they document or cite the critical literature on reductionism, or the many concerted attempts to develop non-reductionist theories in social psychology.

Reductionism

I will discuss the reductionist critique in some detail, because it forms the critical framework of this book. It also lies at the heart of the alternative formulations of group cohesiveness proposed by the social identity and self-categorization theories described in Chapter 6.

There is a considerable critical literature in social psychology that traces the limitations of social psychological theorizing to reductionism: the tendency to explain phenomena in terms of the concepts and language of a 'lower' level of explanation. One possible hierarchy of levels of analysis is (from top to bottom) social history, sociology, small-group dynamics, individual psychology, physiology, biology, chemistry, physics. That is, social history can be explained by sociology, sociological phenomena by group dynamics, group dynamics by the properties of individuals, and so on. The implication is that finally it should be possible to use physics (social psychology's prototype of science) to explain *all* higher-level phenomena.

Although it would clearly be quite absurd to claim that knowledge about the workings of the atom can inform us (in any other way than simile) about the workings of society (but see Kellerman, 1981, and earlier discussion), a smaller reduction from, say, chemistry to physics could be theoretically useful. The point is that too great a reduction in level of analysis makes it impossible to answer many of the important questions posed at the original higher level. For example, an environmentalist enquiring into forest conservation would find little of use in an explanation articulated in terms of osmotic pressure, ion pumps, and so on, when the question requires (in this example) an analysis in terms of the interests of capital. Likewise, putting one's arm out of the car window to indicate an intention to turn can be explained in terms of muscle contraction, nerve impulses, understanding of and adherence to social conventions, and so on. If the level of explanation does not match the level of the question, then the question remains essentially unanswered.

Much social psychological theorizing is reductionist. Specifically, group-level phenomena such as conformity, prejudice, discrimination, intergroup conflict, stereotyping, group formation, collective behaviour and, of course, group cohesiveness, are all theorized in terms of interpersonal processes and/or properties of the individual. The critique of reductionism in social psychological theorizing has been mounted by social psychologists in both Europe (e.g. Billig, 1976; Doise, 1978, 1986; Israel and Tajfel, 1972; Moscovici, 1972; Tajfel, 1972a, 1981a, b; Taylor and Brown, 1979: Turner and Oakes, 1986; see also Hogg and Abrams's [1988, pp. 10–14], overview), and North America (e.g. Cartwright, 1979; Festinger, 1980; Gergen, 1973; Pepitone, 1981; Sampson, 1977, 1981; Steiner, 1974, 1983, 1986; Triandis, 1977; Zander, 1979). It is in Europe, however, that it has had the most widespread and visible impact, with the development – particularly since the mid 1960s – of a distinctive European tradition of social psychology (see Doise, 1982; Jaspars, 1980, 1986; Tajfel, 1972b, for historical background). This 'European' tradition is now, of course, no longer confined to Europe or to Europeans. The agenda has been to forge a non-reductionist social psychology which would be able to theorize the dynamic relationship between individual and society without sociologizing or individualizing it – that is, a truly social dimension to explanations of human behaviour (cf. Tajfel, 1984).

This critique can be – and has been – applied systematically to group cohesiveness (Hogg, 1983, 1985b, 1987; Hogg and Abrams, 1988, pp. 92–115; Turner, 1982, 1984). Chapter 2 documents how an explicit theorization of group cohesiveness in terms of interpersonal attraction is quite common. It also demonstrates that even where no such explicit statement is to be found, the underlying general model of the social group is nevertheless one in which people come together, spontaneously or deliberately, to the degree that they have individual needs capable of mutual satisfaction through interdependence. Such shared need satisfaction is reinforcing and produces mutual attraction as the basis of psychological group formation and group solidarity. At least some limitations of the group cohesiveness concept are common to a broad range of social psychological conceptualizations of the social group that represent a social cohesion or interpersonal interdependence model. Group cohesiveness, as attraction-to-group or as interpersonal attraction, is a reductionist formulation.

Doise has developed (1986; Lorenzi-Cioldi and Doise, 1990) a variant of the reductionist critique in social psychology. He proposes that four broad levels of explanation are employed in social psychology (see Table 4.2): (I)

Table 4.2   *Doise's four levels of analysis*

I   *Intrapersonal*
Analysis of psychological processes to do with individuals' organization of their experience of the social environment (e.g. research on cognitive balance).

II   *Interpersonal and situational*
Analysis of interindividual interaction within circumscribed situations. Social positional factors emanating from outside the situation are not considered. The object of study is the dynamics of relations established at a given moment by given individuals in a given situation (e.g. some attribution research, research using game matrices).

III   *Positional*
Analysis of interindividual interaction in specific situations, but with the role of social position (e.g. status, identity) outside the situation taken into consideration (e.g. some research into power and social identity).

IV   *Ideological*
Analysis of interindividual interaction that considers the role of general social beliefs, and of social relations between groups (e.g. some research into social identity, social representations, and minority influence; studies considering the role of cultural norms and values).

Note: This table is based on Lorenzi-Cioldi and Doise (1990, p. 73), and Doise (1986, pp. 10–16).

intrapersonal; (II) interpersonal and situational; (III) positional; and (IV) ideological. Doise recognizes that there is a reductionist tendency in social psychology, but feels that it is not reductionism *per se* that is the problem, but rather the lack of 'articulation' of different levels of analysis. Doise is using the French sense of 'articulation': 'organization of different elements which contribute to the functioning of a whole. . . . Interlinking of two processes' (*Dictionnaire le Robert*, 1979, p. 109). Doise feels that a complete and satisfactory explanation of most social behaviour requires the articulation of different levels of explanation, because explanations in terms of only one level represent an oversimplification, and thus a distortion, of the social behaviour under examination.

This analysis would identify group cohesiveness as a theory firmly located at Level II (the interpersonal and situational level of explanation). Limitations of the group cohesiveness concept exist not because – or not only because – it is a Level II explanation, but because this level of explanation is not articulated with explanations at Levels I, III and IV. The implication is that, in order properly to explain group solidarity and cohesiveness, conceptualizations of cognitive representations, cognitive processes, social interaction, social category dynamics, and widely shared cultural prescriptions and expectations need to be articulated.

No contemporary discussion of reductionism is complete without some mention of discourse analysis (e.g. Potter, Stringer and Wetherell, 1984; Potter and Wetherell, 1987; Potter, Wetherell, Gill and Edwards, 1990).

Discourse analysis does not refer only to the analysis of discourse – it is much more than that. It often lays claim to being the only true critique of – and solution to – reductionism, and to being the new – or rising – paradigm in British social psychology. Discourse anlaysis has its origins in a mêlée of post-structuralist thought (e.g. Foucault, 1972), ethnomethodology (Garfinkel, 1967), ethogenics (Harré, 1977, 1979), and Goffman's (1959) dramaturgical model. The central idea of discourse analysis is that social reality is constructed through discourse, and that nothing outside this constructed reality is of any significance for social behaviour. An implication of this analysis is that groups, individuals and cognition do not 'exist': they are all social constructs produced by discourse.

Although this analysis has not been applied specifically to group cohesiveness (discourse analysts do not study group cohesiveness), it is quite easy, and interesting, to see what some of its arguments might be. The concept of group cohesiveness reifies the notions of 'individual' and 'attraction', and fails to attend to the role of language and discourse (as opposed to communication) in constructing individuals and their affective relations to one another. From a discourse perspective group cohesiveness might be seen as a linguistic category or rhetorical device produced through discourse: something which constructs individuals in relation to one another as members of a 'group', and in contrast to other 'groups'.

It should be noted that discourse analysis has recently come under attack for being too extreme in its rejection of cognition as an explanation of human behaviour (Abrams and Hogg, 1990b; Hogg and McGarty, 1990). Indeed, discourse analysis may, paradoxically, be a reincarnation of radical be-haviourism: in denying cognition it seems also to be denying the existence of any intervening constructs in the production of social behaviour. If one considers the social group from the perspective of discourse analysis, it is merely a reification, perhaps for rhetorical purposes, of a linguistic category constructed through discourse. Is this idea not actually rather close to Floyd Allport's ultra-reductionist view that the group is merely a nominal fallacy (see Chapter 2)?

The molecule simile

In the context of the reductionist critique, I have elsewhere (Hogg, 1987) discussed a number of specific limitations of group cohesiveness, in addition to the operationalization problems stemming from conceptual imprecision. The implicit – and often explicit (e.g. Kellerman, 1981; Raven and Rubin, 1983, p. 405), 'molecule' simile for the social group, where the group is likened to a molecule in which individual atoms are people and interatomic forces are interpersonal attraction, has only very limited utility and may actually be conceptually misleading. Through hypostatization the simile entrenches an interpersonal attraction conceptualization of group cohesiveness and acts as a barrier to reconceptualization. Although simile can be a useful aid to communication and understanding, there is a very real danger of hypostatization. In the case of the molecule simile for group cohesiveness, when 'like' becomes 'is' the simile has outlived its usefulness. The simile ought, therefore, to be avoided (cf. Mudrack, 1989a, b).

Sociometric choice
The molecule simile introduces another problem: it encourages the use of sociometric choice measures of interindividual attraction as an index of group cohesiveness. The technique of sociometric choice was formalized by Moreno (1934) to chart who chose whom in a group for activities of varying intimacy. When it is employed simply to determine who likes whom in a group, this technique has a number of limitations (Golembiewski, 1962). The most relevant here is that it is largely unidimensional (A.I. Cohen, 1981; Hare, 1962; but see Jennings, 1947a, b) and thus fails to allow for the possibility of a qualitative difference between choice as an indicator of interpersonal friendship and choice as an indicator of attraction between group members (Hagstrom and Selvin, 1965; Scott, 1965). Friendship-based liking may be different to group-membership-based liking.

Indeed, recent research by Schwarzwald and colleagues (e.g. Schwarzwald, Laor and Hoffman, 1986; Schwarzwald, Moisseiev and Hoffman, 1986) indicates that differences in the way in which sociometric choices are obtained can have dramatic implications for what may actually be being measured. For example, Schwarzwald, Laor and Hoffman (1986) had high-school students either *nominate* three classmates with whom they would be willing to engage in activities of low, moderate or high intimacy, or *rate* their willingness to engage in these activities with each classmate. The nomination technique revealed strong ingroup preferences on the basis of sex and ethnicity, while the rating method did not. The two methods may have been accessing different bases of sociometric choice.

A similar sort of problem may exist in the use of Bales's (1950) 'interaction process analysis' method to study communication patterns in small groups. This method stresses the *quantity* of communication directed by one person to another in terms of categories based on task-management functions and the valence of socioemotional reactions, but makes no allowance for any qualitative distinction between intragroup and interpersonal relations.

Motivation
A third problem concerns the motive base for psychological group formation and elevated cohesiveness. The oft-encountered sentiment in social psychology that joining a group entails sacrifice of individual freedom (e.g. Gergen and Gergen, 1981) implies that groups suppress individuality and that individuality is superior, antithetical, and ontogenetically prior to group 'haviour (see Chapter 2, and the beginning of this chapter). So – why do

people join groups, and what is the motive for increased cohesiveness? The prevalent view (but see Moreland, 1987; also Chapter 5 below) is that similar or interdependent needs or goals drive people to affiliate, and that mutual satisfaction of such needs and goals generates interpersonal liking and thus elevated group cohesiveness (see Chapter 2). These needs and goals can range from very specific and elaborated goals to fundamental drives for affiliation (Watson and Johnson, 1972), reinforcement, identity (Knowles, 1982) and validation of beliefs.

This analysis invites a rather fundamental question concerning the origins of specific human needs and goals, and their relationship to group membership. Although some human needs (e.g. for food and air) may be relatively asocial, a large majority are constructed by group memberships. For example, Punks have a 'need' for outrageous hairstyles largely because they are Punks, not vice versa. In many cases common group membership produces specific common or interdependent goals. Another example: Christians hold similar beliefs at least as much because they are Christians, as they are Christians because they have similar beliefs.

The possibility exists, therefore, that there is an underlying psychological process responsible for group belongingness, and that – among other things – common or interdependent goals, affiliation (group members coming together in the same place at the same time), and group-based liking are all effects of this process. In so far as group memberships determine similarities between people, then, they also determine interindividual bonds and variations in cohesiveness, and are not merely an effect of purely individual motives and needs. Group cohesiveness may thus contain an element of mutual liking and attraction-to-group, but it is not caused by or isomorphic with interpersonal liking.

Definition of 'small group'
A fourth problem concerns the definition and theoretical status of the 'small group'. Group cohesiveness is a small-group concept, and as such it is important to understand its range of theoretical applicability. What constitutes a 'small' group, and what is the conceptual basis for separating 'small' groups from 'large' groups? The group-size criterion for group cohesiveness is problematic and should probably be rejected. In general, most researchers are not explicit about this parameter and simply assume that sports teams, therapy groups, tank crews, sororities, and the like are small and thus amenable to a group cohesiveness analysis. Attempts to specify a rigorous size criterion are generally unsuccessful. For example, although convinced that 10 people constitute a small group and 30 a large group, Shaw (1976, 1981) concedes that a cohesive 25-person group is 'small' while a non-cohesive 15-person group is 'large'. Group size, then, is not the real parameter of 'small' groups or group cohesiveness.

A slightly more accurate parameter might include the provision that individuals are in the same place at the same time and interacting with one another in a task-orientated manner . These conditions are, of course, likely to promote and/or lend high profile to interpersonal (affective) relations, thus suggesting one reason why group cohesiveness has generally been conceptualized ultimately in terms of interpersonal attraction. The cohesiveness of larger groups (e.g. large audience, crowd, army, nation) obviously cannot be properly analyzed in this manner because interpersonal interaction among all members is not possible. Yet large groups exhibit solidarity and cohesiveness, just as small groups do. This suggests the possibility that (1) there is no discontinuity between smaller and larger groups at the level of psychological processes responsible for group behaviour: the underlying psychological processes responsible for cohesiveness in large and small groups are identical; and (2) interpersonal attraction is not the mechanism responsible for cohesiveness. Cohesiveness as interpersonal attraction merely redescribes inter*personal* relations within groups that are small enough to permit mutual interindividual interaction, rather than addressing truly intra*group* phenomena. It would seem profitable to reconceptualize group cohesiveness in terms of processes equally applicable to groups of all sizes.

The point here is not that group size has no effect on the group, but that the definition of what constitutes a psychological group should not depend on group size: that is, whether an aggregate is 'small' or 'large'. Group size clearly will affect the group in so far as it affects, for example, members' social impact on one another (Latané, 1981), the type of intragroup communication structures that are possible (Bavelas, 1950), the perceived strength of group consensus (Moscovici, 1976; Turner, 1991), and the tendency to yield to or remain independent of majority influence (Allen, 1965, 1975; Wilder, 1977).

Groups, categories and roles

A final problem with the small–group perspective, also related to the group-size issue, is a distinction between groups, on the one hand, and categories and roles, on the other. 'Category' refers to large-scale affiliations such as nationality, sex, class or religion; and 'role' refers to an individual's position in a small interactive group, such as leader, gossip or comic. However, 'role' is often used also to refer to position within the small group, based on large-scale group membership. That is, category memberships based on sex, ethnicity, age, education, and so on can act as criteria for role assignment in small interactive groups. For example, the role of 'minute-taker' in many committees is often occupied by a female. Groups (e.g. committee) and categories (e.g. female) are thus treated as conceptually distinct psychological phenomena. The analysis of social groups is quite separate and distinct from that of social categories – the latter may impinge on the former only through the concept of role.

If membership size is largely all that distinguishes groups from categories, then (given the problems, discussed above, with the size criterion) groups and categories may actually be psychologically identical. In that case the term 'role' becomes problematic in discussing the effects of 'large-scale' group membership within a 'small-scale' group. A more appropriate analysis might be in terms of intergroup relations. An analysis of *group* processes that recognizes the unique features of face-to-face interaction among a small collection of individuals, but theorizes the social group in terms of underlying processes that are independent of group size, appears more parsimonious. The same mechanism may be responsible for cohesiveness in both small groups and large-scale social categories.

The concept of status stumbles upon similar difficulties. This has led Berger, Fisek, Norman and Zelditch (1977) to distinguish, in their expectation states theory, between two distinct types of social status: (1) *Specific status characteristics* are directly related to the focal activities and purpose of the group (e.g. athletic skill in sports groups). These are virtually membership-defining, or prototypical, characteristics. (2) *Diffuse status characteristics* are not directly related to the focal activities of the group. They are essentially social category membership characteristics (e.g. sex, age, ethnicity, socioeconomic status) that give rise to stereotypic expectations about how the person 'might' perform as a group member. Thus, the notion of diffuse status characteristics deals with the impact of wider social categories on small, interactive, task-orientated groups.

Conclusion

In this chapter the diminished popularity of group cohesiveness among mainstream social psychologists has been documented, and explained in terms of pragmatic and ideological factors in the history of social psychology. The main body of the chapter concerns limitations of the concept of group cohesiveness that have been suggested. There appear to be two general classes of objection. The first lies within the traditional small-groups perspective, because the social cohesion or interpersonal interdependence model of the social group is not questioned. The focus is on operational consequences of the definitional ambiguity of the concept – or, more specifically, on the inadequacy of an exclusively attraction-to-group formulation. The second class of objections is more radical because it questions, in various ways, the reductionist model of the social group on which group cohesiveness is based: specific problems include the molecule simile, the motive base of group belongingness, and the group-size criterion. Groups of all sizes can be cohesive, yet the concept of group cohesiveness only redescribes interpersonal relations among small numbers of physically present individuals. Group cohesiveness remains unexplained. These two classes of objection have spawned rather different remedies. The remainder of this book concerns reconceptualizations of group cohesiveness.

Chapter 5

Reconceptualizations and alternative perspectives

Chapter 4 covered limitations and criticisms of group cohesiveness. Although there has been an energetic clamour of dissatisfaction with the concept, this has generally produced few systematic alternative conceptualizations. Rather, there has been a lively debate over the dimensional structure of cohesiveness, and how best to measure it. Alternatives have tended to involve refinements of operationalization rather than reconceptualization. The plethora of different group cohesiveness scales, mainly in the sports psychology and group psychotherapy settings, has already been documented (see Chapter 3 for details).

There are, however, a number of attempts to reconceptualize cohesiveness. These are critically discussed in the first part of this chapter. The second part focuses on a group socialization perspective on group solidarity. The remainder of the chapter is dedicated to a discussion of alternative approaches to the conceptualization of facets of group solidarity. Although group cohesiveness has been experimental social psychology's principal attempt at theorizing group solidarity and psychological group formation, there are other group phenomena and other theories that are relevant. For example, other important dimensions of small-group solidarity include conformity, deindividuation, and loss of self-awareness. Research in these areas has spawned concepts and theories that all have relevance for an understanding of group solidarity, though cohesiveness itself may not be mentioned.

All these parallel or *re*-conceptualizations of group cohesiveness suffer, to varying degrees, from limitations that are discussed in this chapter. Many of these – and other – limitations may be overcome by adopting an intergroup perspective (social identity theory and self-categorization theory). Chapter 6 is dedicated to this new approach.

Reconceptualizations of group cohesiveness ═══════

Multidimensional conceptualizations

We have already seen that although group cohesiveness was originally intended to be a multidimensional concept, it very rapidly became unidimensional: attraction-to-group, or interpersonal attraction. There have, however, been many attempts to explore its bi- or multidimensional nature. (For details of some of the scales mentioned below, see the section in Chapter 3 on measurement of cohesiveness.)

A distinction is often made between, on the one hand, task-related processes and factors to do with the achievement of task-related objectives, and, on the other, social-related processes to do with the development and maintenance of harmonious social relations in groups (e.g. Anderson, 1975; Carron, 1982; Carron and Chelladurai, 1981; Enoch and McLemore, 1967; Hagstrom and Selvin, 1965; Homans, 1950; Lewin, 1948; Parsons and Shils, 1951; Sakurai, 1975; Schriesheim, 1980; Stogdill, 1972; Yukelson *et al.*, 1984; Zaccaro and McCoy, 1988). For example, Hagstrom and Selvin (1965) conducted a factor analysis of nineteen different measures of cohesiveness to produce two distinct factors: social satisfaction (satisfaction with the group and the group's influence upon behaviour) and sociometric cohesion (personal friendships with other group members). Carron and colleagues (e.g. Carron, 1982; Carron and Chelladurai, 1981), in a sports team context, distinguish between the development and maintenance of an effective task-orientated group, and the maintenance of positive interpersonal relations within a group.

Anderson (1975) argues that both task-related and socioemotional functions exist in all groups, but with varying relative emphases. Principally task-orientated groups 'exist to accomplish a task whose primary importance is to manipulate the environment' (p. 69), while people belong to principally socioemotional groups 'for the emotional satisfaction they derive from participation, that is, support of one's self-conception, consensual validation about the world etc.' (p. 69).

In addition to task and socioemotional dimensions, some researchers have suggested the existence of a third dimension. Donnelly, Carron and Chelladurai (1978) and Feldman (1968) believe that the normative force that restrains an individual within the group independent of the group's specific properties can produce cohesiveness. How this normative force operates psychologically is not explored. Stokes (1983) nominates risk-taking as a third factor in cohesiveness, in addition to instrumental value and intermember attraction. Stokes's analysis, however, is very specific to the unique conditions of personal change groups.

The picture becomes more complicated by research identifying four or more underlying dimensions. Yukelson *et al.* (1984) report four meaningful factors within a 41-item questionnaire administered to 196 college sports team members in the United States: attraction-to-group, unity of purpose, quality of teamwork, and valued roles. Gruber and Gray (1981) factor-analyzed a 13-item cohesiveness questionnaire administered to 515 university basketball players. They found six cohesiveness factors, but team performance satisfaction and task cohesion were the strongest.

There are, however, those who are sceptical about the empirical evidence for cohesiveness as a multidimensional construct (e.g. Stokes, 1983; Wright and Duncan, 1986), or believe that the dimensions are often correlated (e.g. Fisher, 1973; Wheeless *et al.*, 1982). Piper *et al.* (1983) have objections of a more metatheoretical nature. They feel that the treatment of group cohesiveness as a multidimensional construct 'seems to be another way of saying that quite different, at times independent, concepts have been involved despite the fact that at some time they have all been labeled cohesion' (p. 95). They feel that while the use of multiple measures 'is an improvement over relying on a single measure it leaves basic questions about the meaning of cohesion unanswered' (*ibid.*). The implication is that while solidarity may manifest itself in a variety of forms (and thus a range of indexes is needed), it would be both more parsimonious and more profitable to investigate the possibility of a single underlying process responsible for the range of group-solidarity-related behaviours.

Perhaps the pursuit of different dimensions of cohesiveness serves a taxonomic function. It helps to classify different types of groups on the basis of the relative preponderance of different dimensions of cohesiveness. While this is an important research activity in its own right, it may not actually contribute to a reconceptualization of the underlying *process* of cohesiveness. Whether groups are more or less task or socioemotionally orientated, the implicit psychological mechanism responsible for solidarity remains attraction based on interpersonal reward.

The distinction between task and socioemotional aspects of cohesiveness contains the implication that socioemotional aspects are to do with interpersonal relations among individuals in small interactive groups, while task-related aspects are more to do with the group. Sakurai (1975) goes even further by arguing that quite different social-influence processes operate in mainly 'attraction biased' socioemotional groups than in mostly 'interdependence biased' task-orientated (instrumental/rational) groups. He draws on Deutsch and Gerard's (1955) distinction between normative (social-approval-based) and informational (reality-confirmation-based) social influence. He argues that normative influence predominates in socioemotional groups, and informational influence in task-orientated groups. In other words, there are entirely different processes associated with solidarity and cohesiveness in task-orientated or socioemotional groups. It is worth noting that the validity of the two-process dependency model of social influence that Sakurai is invoking to account for cohesion in different types of group has been questioned (e.g.

Hogg and Turner, 1987a; Turner, 1985). This issue is discussed in detail later in this chapter.

Group cohesiveness as commitment-to-group

A different direction in reconceptualizing group cohesiveness is taken by those who feel that there are insurmountable problems in theorizing or describing cohesiveness as a group-level phenomenon on the basis of an attraction-to-group formulation. For example, Mudrack (1989a) recommends rejection of both the attraction-to-group formulation and the underlying 'atom metaphor', in preference for a commitment-to-group formulation. Goodman, Ravlin and Schminke (1987) are more specific: they recommend a focus on commitment to the group task.

Steers's (1977) correlational study of organizational commitment and employee turnover makes no reference to cohesiveness, yet it deals with issues identical to those dealt with by the social psychological concept of cohesiveness. Steers defines commitment in terms of a member's desire to maintain membership in the organization, willingness to exert effort on behalf of the organization, and acceptance of the organization's goals and values.

Piper *et al.* (1983) also advocate commitment-to-group. They provide evidence from a twenty-item questionnaire study of six-person learning groups that an independent commitment-to-group factor was the best predictor of cohesion. Members were bound to the group not through attraction but through commitment. This bond of commitment is considered to be of three types: member–member, member–leader, and – interestingly – between the member and 'his conception of the group as a whole' (1983, p. 95). The first two forms of commitment differ regarding status relations (equal versus unequal), but in other respects they reflect interindividual commitment. The consequences of such commitment presumably include trust, loyalty and attraction. The third form is quite different: it implies commitment to an abstract idea of what the group as a whole represents. The consequence of this form of commitment is, presumably, group-consistent behaviour (normative, stereotypical behaviour). This analysis is a step forward, mainly because it may allow us to ask the correct questions about group solidarity. As it is, however, it lacks detailed specification of how commitment operates: how it arises and how it produces its presumed effects. It also lacks an analysis of how the abstracted representation of the group is formed and, indeed, of precisely what form it takes..

Evans and Jarvis (1980) suggest a conceptual separation of cohesion from attraction-to-group. The former refers operationally to homogeneity of perceptions, attitudes and feelings. The latter refers to 'the individual's degree of identification with the group' (p. 368) and is reflected in feelings and attitudes about the group, feelings of acceptance, and a sense of involvement.

This suggestion is applauded by some (e.g. Stockton and Hulse, 1981). It was actually implemented by Wright and Duncan (1986), who found that a direct measure of attraction-to-group was a simple and viable alternative to a more complex cohesiveness measure.

Ingraham and Manning (1981) make a similar distinction: between cohesion (the group level of analysis) and individual morale (the individual level of analysis). Their research, however, leads to an analysis which is actually in terms of the latter: cohesiveness involves 'creating common experiences and facilitating face-to-face interactions' (p. 8).

A dialectical approach

A more radical alternative to traditional approaches is suggested by Budge (1981), who characterizes the concept of cohesiveness as one that emphasizes attraction-to-group and positive 'we-feelings'. The main objection, however, is that traditional analyses treat cohesiveness as a static property of the group which remains unchanged over time and invariant across members. In other words, cohesiveness is theorized synchronically: as if somehow cohesiveness-contingent outcomes do not themselves influence cohesiveness. Traditional analyses are concerned to establish the cohesiveness of the group as a whole at some particular time, and then to investigate the effects of this property on performance, self-disclosure, attitudes, and so forth.

In contrast, Budge urges a dialectical longitudinal approach that focuses on the impact of interindividual dynamics within the group on cohesiveness as a whole. The idea is that group members experience opposing forces for individuation (separateness, difference) and unity (oneness, similarity). In the life of the group there is a continual dialectical process: resolution of individual differences at one level spawns recognition of differences at a different level, which in turn is resolved, and so on. Perceptions of internal and external threat to the group feed into and out of this process. The underlying mechanism is an individual psychodynamic one. Very briefly, interpersonal conflicts, based on recognition of difference, are resolved by a process of identification, in the Freudian sense (see Chapter 2), and mutual reinforcement of 'we-ness'.

This perspective is valuable for its attention to dialectic. It is important to study cohesiveness as a dynamic property of groups that is both responsive to and influential of inter- and intragroup dynamics. However, there are a number of limitations to Budge's analysis:

1.   Budge does not actually offer a redefinition of cohesiveness. Sometimes it is equated with 'bonded' (e.g. 1981, p. 15), but at other times it is spoken of in terms of unity, similarity, uniformity, and so forth. Budge seems to be defining the group as an interactive goal-orientated

aggregate, and is concerned only with the way in which interpersonal conflicts arise and are resolved.

2.   The analysis is quite explicitly catered to the relatively specific and unique circumstances of psychotherapy groups, and may not be readily or appropriately generalized to diverse group contexts.

3.   In focusing exclusively on interpersonal dynamics, Budge does not readily permit theoretical consideration of the intergroup context of intragroup processes – ingroups exist, by definition, in contradistinction to relevant outgroups, and the perceived nature of this relationship is an important influence on intragroup dynamics (cf. Tajfel, 1972b).

4.   The adoption of a psychodynamic framework may be problematic for the development of a general analysis of group cohesiveness. Inter- and intragroup processes are often not satisfactorily explained in terms of intra-individual dynamics (see Billig's [1976] detailed critique of psychodynamic models of intergroup relations and group processes; see also Chapter 2).

A metaphor analysis

In a similar vein – but more promising, because it is not framed by a psychodynamic perspective – is Owen's (1985) intriguing 'metaphor analysis' of cohesiveness in small discussion groups. Owen believes that 'cohesive groups are those in which a sense of "we-ness" emerges to transcend individual differences and motives. Communication is the process by which members generate cohesiveness in the form of shared meaning structures, whether literal or metaphorical' (1985, p. 416). This formulation is contrasted with the traditional interpersonal attraction or attraction-to-group formulation.

The analysis proceeds from the fact that in order to concretize and simplify the nebulous and intangible, people represent and communicate complex concepts and experiences in the form of metaphor (i.e. 'A *is* B', where 'B' is a vivid and clearly expressed object or event, and 'A' is a less clearly understood object or event) (cf. Lakoff and Johnson, 1980). So, for example, we often tend to represent and communicate mood 'as if' happy is up ('That *boosted* my spirits') and sad is down ('I *fell* into a depression').

Owen (1985) believes that the social group is a highly complex and nebulous nexus of similarities, differences, agreements and disagreements that encourages members to construct a consensual reality through metaphorical communication and representation. To illustrate this process, he sampled the speech of a five-person classroom discussion group over four months. He discovered that idiosyncrasies in metaphor usage (i.e. use of kinaesthetic, visual and auditory metaphors) gradually disappeared, so that at the final meeting a single class of metaphors (in this case, visual ones) dominated. A consensual reality had emerged to replace awareness of individual differences with a sense of we-ness. For Owen, then, the group is cohesive because a shared metaphor (representing a shared meaning structure) is used.

This refreshingly novel analysis of cohesiveness is, as yet, sketchy and provisional, but it is promising, as it provides a social process (communication) motivated by an individual cognitive need (concrete and simplified representations) to explain the active construction of a group identity. However, it has a number of limitations:

1. It is restricted to small interactive discussion groups – though there seems to be little reason not to extend it to deal with more widely shared representations obtained through channels of mass communication;
2. It does not incorporate theoretically the intergroup context;
3. It does not explain the process through which construction of a consensual reality actually produces a sense of we-ness or other manifestations of cohesiveness, such as ethnocentrism, intergroup discrimination, or intragroup attraction; and
4. In practice, Owen may simply be reinventing, with different terminology, a phenomenon already very well documented in social psychology – that is, conformity to an emergent linguistic group norm, or group-stereotypical communication norm. (Conformity is discussed later in this chapter.)

Owen's analysis resonates with Moscovici's theory of social representations (e.g. Farr and Moscovici, 1984; Moscovici, 1961, 1981). Although Moscovici does not explicitly deal with group cohesiveness, it is worth briefly describing social representations here, as it is an account of how consensual representations emerge through conversation. Social representations are consensual understandings shared among group members. They emerge through everyday informal communication in order to transform the unfamiliar and complex into the familiar and straightforward. Moscovici's original analysis focused on psychoanalytic theory. Through informal lay conversation, this highly formalized theory has been simplified and distorted to become a shared 'common-sense' framework for much twentieth-century thought – in other words, a social representation (other examples might include Marxism, AIDS, relativity theory, evolutionary theory, and dietary and health fads).

For Moscovici, social representations function very much like ideologies in that they have a degree of inertia and tend to assimilate new information to fit in with and confirm the representation. Social representations, like stereotypes, define the parameters of social groups and facilitate simplified prejudgements of people and events. They change in response to social change. In these respects, Moscovici goes much further than Owen. However, the theory of social representations does not deal explicitly with cohesiveness.

76   *Reconceptualizations and alternative perspectives*

Also, it is a vague and imprecise theory (Augoustinos and Innes, 1990; Hogg and Abrams, 1988, pp. 81–2; Potter and Litton, 1985) which fails to define the group and does not identify a process that relates consensuality to the group.

The importance that Owen places on conversation and linguistic representation in the genesis of cohesiveness (defined in terms of shared linguistic representations) also resonates with some aspects of the recent discourse analysis approach in social psychology (Potter and Wetherell, 1987; see Chapter 4 for details). Discourse analysts do not deal with cohesiveness, but rather with the way in which situated discourse among people may construct shared social realities. However, since they consider groups, individuals and cognition largely not to 'exist' but rather to be linguistic constructs produced through discourse, it is difficult to envisage what direct relevance this work has for an analysis of group solidarity.

Finally, in shifting the emphasis from attraction to shared representations and we-ness, Owen's approach to cohesiveness has some similar terms of reference to those framing the social identity analysis of group processes – discussed in Chapter 6 (e.g. Hogg and Abrams, 1988).

Sense of community

Another interesting alternative to cohesiveness as interpersonal attraction or attraction-to-group comes from community psychologists, who adopt a more sociological framework. They tend to speak of communities rather than groups, and in so doing are often dealing with groups that are neither numerically 'small' nor quite as large and dispersed as large-scale social categories. The term 'community' has two major uses: territorial and geographical communities (e.g. neighbourhood, town, city) and 'relational' communities to do with the character of human relationships (e.g. professional, spiritual) (Gusfield, 1975). 'Sense of community' is considered to be equally applicable to both.

Riger and Lavrakas (1981) have proposed two distinct but correlated dimensions of sense of community: *social bonding*, which relates to feelings of being part of and belonging to a neighbourhood, and *behavioural rootedness*, which relates to material investment in a community in terms of numbers of years' residence, ownership of property, and so forth. Riger and Lavrakas's analysis is tied to territorial communities, and lacks analysis of underlying psychological processes. However, it is revealing that 'bonding' rather than, say, 'belonging' is the term used to refer to the more immediately social psychological dimension.

In contrast, McMillan and Chavis (1986) have proposed a general theory of sense of community. They define sense of community as 'a feeling that members have of belonging, a feeling that members matter to one another and to the group, and a shared faith that members' needs will be met through their commitment to be together' (p. 9). There are four dynamically interrelated elements here: (1) membership, (2) influence, (3) integration and fulfilment of needs, and (4) shared emotional connection. McMillan and Chavis treat membership as a 'sense of belonging and identification' (p. 10) with a normatively defined and clearly bounded social entity. Influence refers not only to the normative consequences of majority influence on individual community members, but also to members' sense of having influence on the community. Effective mutual influence renders the group more rewarding (thus attractive, close and cohesive) through consensual validation of reality and recognition of self-efficacy. Integration and fulfilment of needs enhances sense of community through the usual processes of mutual need satisfaction and interdependent interaction. Finally, shared emotional connection appears to refer principally to rewarding interpersonal interaction which produces positive feelings and closeness (cf. Lofland's [1981] suggestion that any emotional connection may produce cohesion).

McMillan and Chavis's model is too complex to be described in detail here. The important point, however, is that although group solidarity and cohesiveness are still conceptualized largely in terms of interpersonal processes that produce attraction through mutual reinforcement, this is not the entire story. An important role is given to identification or belonging to a normatively bounded social entity. However, the social psychology of this idea is not pursued.

Group socialization

Although it is not intended to be a treatment of group cohesiveness in the strict sense, Moreland and Levine's (1982, 1984; Levine and Moreland, 1985) model of group socialization is relevant to a discussion of cohesiveness for at least two reasons: (1) It applies 'primarily (but not exclusively) to small, autonomous, voluntary groups whose members interact on a regular basis, have affective ties with one another, share a common frame of reference, and are behaviorally interdependent' (Moreland and Levine, 1982, p. 139). These are precisely the sorts of groups that traditional group cohesiveness research usually deals with; and (2) It necessarily contains a perspective on the psychological formation of small groups (Moreland, 1987).

Moreland and Levine characterize their model of group socialization as an attempt 'to describe and explain the passage of individuals through groups' (1982, p. 139). They feel that much social psychology of groups suffers from a tendency to adopt a synchronic or narrow temporal perspective, and a unidirectional social perspective which focuses on the group's effect on the individual. To redress this imbalance, Moreland and Levine adopt a dynamic reciprocal perspective: focusing on the dynamic interrelationship of group and individual members across the lifespan of the group.

The adoption of a group socialization perspective at least partially reflects Moreland's (1987) view that group formation is not a binary event in which one is suddenly transformed from non-member to member. Rather, it is a continuous process of "'social integration", or strengthening of the bonds among persons' (p. 81). There are four distinct aspects of social integration:

1. *Environmental integration* refers to the way certain physical, social or cultural environments provide resources (e.g. proximity, communication networks) that strengthen bonds between people;
2. *Behavioural integration* refers to mutual interdependence in order to satisfy individual needs;
3. *Affective integration* refers to the strengthening of bonds on the basis of shared feelings; and
4. *Cognitive integration* refers to the role of recognition of shared personal characteristics in the strengthening of bonds.

Group solidarity and cohesiveness are a function of social integration, and thus the strength of bonds among people.

Three basic psychological processes are involved in group socialization: evaluation, commitment, and role transition. *Evaluation* refers to an ongoing process whereby individuals assess the past, present and future rewardingness of the group against the rewardingness of potential alternative relationships (cf. Thibaut and Kelley, 1959). Simultaneously the group evaluates individuals in terms of their contribution to the life of the group. Behind this idea lies an assumption that people, individually or as a group, have goals and needs that create expectations − normative expectations in the case of groups. To the extent that expectations are − or are likely to be − met, social approval is expressed. Actual or anticipated failure to fulfil expectations invites social disapproval and actions to modify behaviour, or actions to reject individuals or the group.

Evaluation affects *commitment* of the individual to the group, and vice versa, in a relatively straightforward manner:

$$C = (PR_c - PR_a) + (R_c - R_a) + (FR_c - FR_a)$$

Commitment (C) is the weighted sum of the difference between rewardingness of the current relationship (subscript 'c') and alternative relationships (subscript 'a') in the past ($PR_c - PR_a$), the present ($R_c - R_a$), and the future ($FR_c - FR_a$). All things being equal, these three temporal components are unequally weighted so that present relationships (R_c, R_a) are most important and future relationships (FR_c, FR_a) are least important. At any given time, commitment disequilibrium may exist such that the individual is more committed to the group or the group to the individual. This state of affairs endows the least committed party with relatively greater power, and so is unstable. There is general pressure towards commitment equilibrium.

Moreland and Levine consider commitment to be a unitary construct that embodies 'acceptance of the group's goals and values; positive affective ties to group members; willingness to exert effort on behalf of the group and to fulfill group expectations; and desire to gain or maintain membership in the group' (1982, p. 148). These can be labelled: consensus, cohesion, control and continuance (cf. Kanter, 1968, 1972).

Role transition refers to discontinuities in the role relationship between individual and group. These discontinuities overlay a continuum of diachronic variation in commitment, and are governed by groups' and individuals' decision criteria for the occurrence of a transition. There are three general role regions: (1) non-member: including prospective members who have not joined the group and ex-members who have left it; (2) quasi-member: including new members who have not yet attained full member status and marginal members who have lost that status; and (3) full member. Full members are those who are 'most closely identified with the group and who have all of the privileges and responsibilities associated with group membership' (Moreland and Levine, 1982, p. 149). Role transitions can be smooth and easy where individual and group are equally committed, and share the same decision criteria. However, commitment disequilibrium and unshared decision criteria can introduce conflict over whether a role transition should or did occur. For this reason, transition criteria often become formalized and public, and rites of passage become a central part of the life of the group.

Equipped with these conceptual building blocks, Moreland and Levine (e.g. 1982, 1984) provide a detailed account of the passage, marked by role transitions, of individual members through the group. Very briefly, they identify five distinct phases of group socialization, each involving reciprocal evaluation and influence by group and individual: (1) *investigation* by and of prospective members; (2) *socialization* of new members; (3) *maintenance* of full membership; (4) *resocialization* of marginal members; and (5) *remembrance* by and of ex-members.

Moreland and colleagues have conducted research on specific transitions, particularly those associated with becoming a member (e.g. Brinthaupt, Moreland and Levine, 1991; Moreland, 1985; Moreland and Levine, 1989; Pavelchak, Moreland, and Levine, 1986). Although they do not talk directly about group cohesiveness or solidarity (this is explicitly *not* a 'group-level' theory), it can easily be inferred that commitment may relate to – or possibly even be responsible for – solidarity, as full members are most committed to the group, and commitment entails consensus, cohesion, control and continuance. Commitment may be the individual-psychological-level process reponsible for 'group-level' phenomena such as cohesion.

Although Moreland and Levine do not conceptualize commitment in a narrow interpersonal-attraction sense, they are quite explicit that commitment produces its effects through perceptions of rewardingness: 'Our analysis is . . . based on the concept of rewardingness' (1982, p. 145). However, the idea of role discontinuity introduces the notion that group solidarity may be underpinned, at least to some extent, by cognitive shifts in self-perception. So, for example, for the high levels of solidarity associated with full membership to emerge, there must be a social redefinition of self that is internalized by self (cf. Moreland, 1985).

It should be noted that while some role transitions (e.g. new member to full member) can readily be understood to occur within the context of an already formed group, others (e.g. prospective member to new member) would seem more likely to mark a qualitative shift from non-member to member. In other words, the 'special *event*' (Moreland, 1987, p. 81) in the formation of groups that Moreland seeks to avoid in his 1987 social integration model may be resurrected in a different form.

Other aspects of group solidarity

Group solidarity has many facets. These might include ingroup loyalty, trust and attraction, ethnocentrism, normative and stereotypical perception and conduct, conformity and homogeneity of attitudes and behaviours, group identity, and intergroup competitiveness and discrimination. The group cohesiveness concept does not necessarily deal directly with all these phenomena but assumes, more or less explicitly, that the behaviour of cohesive groups is mediated by attraction-to-group, or interpersonal attraction. In contrast, social psychology has also dealt with many of these phenomena quite independently, without explicit reference to the group cohesiveness concept. The remainder of this chapter covers two of the most important of these areas of social psychology (i.e. conformity, and deindividuation/self-awareness), with the aim of uncovering processes that may help to reconceptualize group cohesiveness.

Conformity phenomena

A characteristic feature of cohesive groups is relative similarity of attitude and conduct. People in cohesive groups tend to agree with one another and behave in similar ways, and are thus relatively undifferentiated and homogeneous. Group behaviour is characterized by conformity to group standards or norms. This aspect of solidarity comes to the fore in the reconceptualizations of group cohesiveness discussed above: it is reflected in notions such as normative forces, unity of purpose, homogeneity of perceptions, attitudes and feelings, shared meaning structures, consensual representations, normatively bounded entities, and shared emotional connections.

Group cohesiveness theory generally tends to treat similarity as an unproblematic antecedent of attraction-to-group or interpersonal attraction: individuals with similar goals congregate to form groups. There is, however, an enormous body of social psychological literature on the causes of increased similarity as a consequence of group pressure: conformity.

Traditional theoretical treatments of conformity contain a number of conceptual distinctions. However, recent critical discussions (e.g. Abrams and Hogg, 1990c; Hogg and Abrams, 1988, pp. 165–7; Hogg and Turner, 1987a; Turner, 1991) argue that these distinctions can be simplified to a relatively straightforward distinction between two social-influence processes which together share the burden of explanation: *normative* and *informational influence* (following Deutsch and Gerard's [1955] terminology). Both processes revolve around one individual's dependence on another – dependence for social approval in the case of normative influence, and dependence for information about reality in the case of informational influence. Conformity is thus explained in terms of a two-process dependence model. Table 5.1 lists some of the different terminologies that have been employed to refer to these two distinct processes of social influence.

Normative influence (Deutsch and Gerard, 1955; Kelley, 1952) is based on *pressure to comply* (Abrams and Hogg, 1990c): it results from the

Table 5.1 *Different terminologies to refer to two distinct processes of social influence*

Researchers	Two distinct terminologies	
Deutsch and Gerard (1955) Kelley (1952)	Normative influence	Informational influence
Kiesler and Kiesler (1969)	Public compliance	Private acceptance
Kelman (1958, 1961)	Compliance, identification	Internalization
Festinger (1950, 1954)	Group locomotion	Social reality testing, social comparisons
French and Raven (1959) Raven and Kruglanski (1970)	Coercive power, reward power, referent power	Expert power, informational power
Jellison and Arkin (1977) Sanders and Baron (1977)	Cultural values	——
Burnstein and Vinokur (1977) Vinokur and Burnstein (1974)	——	Persuasive arguments
Moscovici (1976) Mugny (1982)	Majority influence	Minority influence
Abrams and Hogg (1990c).	Pressures to comply	Reasons to agree

Note: This table is based, by permission of Routledge, on Table 8.1 in Hogg and Abrams (1988, p. 165).

individual's need for social approval and acceptance. It creates merely *public compliance* with – rather than *private acceptance* (Kiesler and Kiesler, 1969) or *internalization* (Kelman, 1958, 1961) of – the group's attitudes, opinions, beliefs or behaviours. The individual merely 'goes along with' the group for instrumental reasons such as attainment of group goals (called *group locomotion* by Festinger, 1950) or avoidance of punishment, censure or rejection for deviation, or in order to attract social approval and acceptance. There is no internal change. Normative influence arises under conditions in which the group (or individual) is perceived to have *coercive power* (i.e. the power to criticize, derogate, threaten, punish, or enforce laws and regulations for which there are penalties attached for non-compliance), or *reward power* (the power to reinforce compliance or administer affection, praise and material rewards) (French and Raven, 1959; Raven and Kruglanski, 1970).

According to Hogg and Turner (1987a) normative influence may also underpin the *referent power* (Raven and Kruglanski, 1970) of a group: that is, its power to exact conformity on the basis of being a relevant reference group for the individual. Since reference groups are implicitly defined in terms of emotional attachment on the basis of liking and admiration (see Kelley, 1952) it is likely that pressures for uniformity in such groups are based on a desire for approval, acceptance, and so forth. This analysis probably still holds, despite Kelman's (1958, 1961) use of the term *identification* to classify the conformity process underlying referent power. Kelman considers that reference groups comprise significant reference others who are people to whom one is attracted, and with whom one therefore wishes to maintain a relationship. Thus conformity via referent power is actually a relationship-maintenance process.

Informational influence (Asch, 1952; Deutsch and Gerard 1955; Kelley, 1952), in contrast, is based on subjectively valid *reasons to agree* (Abrams and Hogg, 1990c). It is 'true influence' in that it produces *private acceptance* or *internalization* of beliefs, attitudes and behaviours resulting from the individual's need to be correct. The power of informational influence resides in the perceived expertise or *expert power* (i.e. possession of knowledge that others repeatedly need to draw upon), or the *informational power* (possession of a specific piece of information that is needed) of others (French and Raven, 1959; Raven and Kruglanski, 1970). The precondition for effective informational influence is subjective uncertainty, or lack of confidence in the objective validity of one's own beliefs, opinions, and so forth, which cannot be directly resolved by objective tests against physical reality. Under these conditions, social comparisons (Festinger, 1954) or social reality tests (Festinger, 1950) are conducted.

A very similar two-process model underlies explanations of other group-influence phenomena, specifically group polarization and minority influence. Group polarization is the tendency for group discussion to produce group decisions that are more extreme than the average of members' pre-discussion opinions, in the direction initially favoured by the group (Isenberg, 1986;

Moscovici and Zavalloni, 1969; Myers and Lamm, 1976; Wetherell, 1987). Traditional explanations invoke *cultural values* (Jellison and Arkin, 1977; Sanders and Baron, 1977) and *persuasive arguments* (Burnstein and Vinokur, 1977; Vinokur and Burnstein, 1974) as the two major classes of explanatory process (see critical discussions by Hogg and Abrams, 1988, pp. 177–80; Hogg and McGarty, 1990; Turner, 1985). Cultural values relates to normative influence, and persuasive arguments to informational influence (see Table 5.1).

Much conformity research tends to focus on how numerical majorities exact conformity from minorities or individual group members. To redress the balance, Moscovici and Mugny and their associates have conducted a great deal of research into how active minorities can change the views of the majority: i.e. minority influence (e.g. Moscovici, 1976; Mugny, 1982; Paicheler, 1988; Pérez and Mugny, 1990). A close reading (see Abrams and Hogg, 1990c; Hogg and Abrams, 1988, pp. 180–2) of this very complicated literature reveals that the two-process model has been resurrected, albeit in a slightly different guise. Majorities exact conformity through normative channels (they have power to administer rewards and punishments, impose sanctions, mobilize surveillance, etc.), while minorities do so by informational influence (they provide an alternative and more 'truthful' version of reality, one which appears more convincing and better able to resolve contradictions, etc.).

There are a number of limitations of the two-process dependence model (summarized in Hogg and Abrams, 1988, pp. 167–71; see also Turner, 1991). Perhaps the most important to highlight here are:

1. Conformity can occur under conditions where neither influence process is operative: that is, when there is no subjective uncertainty to be resolved, and when behaviour is anonymous and not under surveillance by the group (e.g. Deutsch and Gerard, 1955; Hogg and Turner, 1987a).
2. Given surveillance and subjective uncertainty some people simply do not conform.
3. By emphasizing interpersonal dependence for reward or reality validation, the role of norms is not theoretically elaborated. Norms are quintessentially products of group processes, and they have powerful prescriptive properties. The questions of how norms arise and how they influence behaviour are left unanswered. The analysis of conformity as adherence to norms, or as normative behaviour, cannot simply be conjured out of a collection of separate interpersonal processes.

Traditional theories, then, appear to leave conformity incompletely explained. Although homogeneity of opinion and behaviour is a major aspect of group solidarity, we still do not have a completely satisfactory explanation of how it arises.

Deindividuation and loss of self-awareness

The analysis of conformity and normative behaviour focuses on the relative uniformity of attitudes and action in groups. A similar concern with the explanation of uniformity of action was shared by LeBon (1908, 1913) and McDougall (1921) in their early explanations of the crowd (see Chapter 2 for details). These early researchers, however, placed a much greater emphasis than have conformity researchers on the role of 'self' in group behaviour. They thus draw attention to the fact that a cohesive group is very much one in which the unique idiosyncratic individual self is relatively subservient to the group: there is an apparent reduction in self-awareness, a reduction in individuality. These can be subsumed by the term deindividuation.

Deindividuation generally refers to a loss of personal identity, and is believed to be associated with antisocial aggressive behaviour and lack of self-consciousness. A range of factors including anonymity, coaction, diffusion of responsibility, and large group size have all been proposed as preconditions for deindividuation. Until the mid 1970s deindividuation research seemed to lack precision and clarity: it produced contradictory findings and incompatible theoretical statements (e.g. Dipboye, 1977; Zimbardo, 1970; see Hogg and Abrams, 1988, pp. 140–7).

In 1980 Diener published a clarification of the area by equating deindividuation with loss of self-awareness. He argued that 'people who are deindividuated have lost their self-awareness and their personal identity in a group situation. . . . Thus prevented from self-attention . . . they become more reactive to immediate stimuli and emotions and are unresponsive to norms and to the long term consequences of their behaviour' (Diener, 1980, p. 210). This is consistent with the view of self-awareness theories (e.g. Carver and Scheier, 1981; Wicklund, 1982) that societal standards are embodied by the ideal self-image, and that self-focused attention highlights the discrepancy between ideal and actual self. This discrepancy is aversive and motivates behaviour aimed at bringing the actual self into line with the ideal self: i.e. conformity to societal norms (see discussion by Abrams, 1990). For example, Wicklund writes:

> To the extent that individuals collect in deindividuated units, thus transforming the unit of analysis from 'I' to 'we', the potential of each individual member for the discomfort of self-focus is thereby reduced . . . [thus] lowered control via values and personal standards . . . a condition just opposite to self-awareness will arise – that of deindividuation – which entails the relaxing of standards and morals. (Wicklund, 1982, p. 226)

Situational factors present in a group are considered responsible for the degree of self-awareness, and thus group members (and the group as a whole) can vary in the degree of loss of self-awareness. In this respect, deindividuation/

self-awareness theory is a theory of group solidarity and psychological group formation.

In response to evidence that behaviour in groups conforms to group norms and is not by any means anormative, and to evidence that some forms of self-attention promote rather than inhibit group normative behaviour, the simple equation of deindividuation with lack of self-awareness became problematic. In its place a distinction was made between private and public self-attention (Carver and Scheier, 1981; Greenwald, 1982; Prentice-Dunn and Rogers, 1982; Scheier and Carver, 1981). Private self refers to aspects of self such as personal attitudes, values, feelings and motives, while public self is what one presents because it is socially appropriate and desirable. Attention to private self produces independence and self-consistent behaviour, while attention to public self produces conformity to the group and socially desirable behaviour. Deindividuation is based on lack of private self-attention, while the amount of public self-attention simply determines the course of action taken by a group member.

The private/public distinction quite clearly reflects the informational/ normative influence distinction discussed previously. Presumably the private self is associated with informational social influence processes (reasons to agree), while the public self is associated with normative social influence processes (pressures to comply) (Abrams and Hogg, 1990c).

The deindividuation/self-awareness model of group solidarity/uniformity remains complicated and contradictory – perhaps this is reason enough to be cautious (but see Figure 5.1 for some clarification). For example, deindividuation as lack of self-awareness produces uniformity presumably

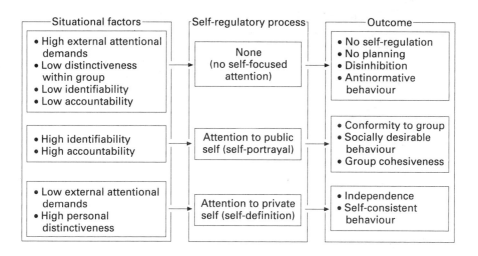

Figure 5.1 *The self-awareness/deindividuation model of self-regulation in groups. (This figure is based on Figure 6.1 in Abrams and Hogg (1990a, p. 91).)*

because all group members react relatively automatically and 'thoughtlessly' (self is not involved) to the same transitory cues that are present in the group. Lack of private self-awareness produces a similar effect, because internalized standards are not employed to guide action. On the other hand, deindividuation as loss of public self-awareness is associated with idiosyncratic non-uniform behaviour, because self-presentational demands are unimportant. In other words, public self-awareness produces conformity to group norms because of self-presentational demands, while private self-awareness produces independent self-consistent behaviour. Group uniformity and solidarity is thus produced by a social-influence process predicated on a need for social approval. So, although the language of self-awareness theories is very different to that of the group cohesiveness approach, the psychological mechanism responsible for group solidarity is the same: some form of attraction based on positive reinforcement for socially/group desirable behaviours. (See Abrams [1990] and Hogg and Abrams [1988] for summaries of more specific limitations of the deindividuation/self-awareness model of group behaviour.)

Conclusion

In this chapter, a number of remedies for limitations of cohesiveness have been presented. The major effort appears to be invested in clarification and refinement of the dimensional structure and measurement of cohesiveness: ultimately, this has been largely a methodological exercise. An additional feature of this sort of approach is that at the theoretical level there is an implication that different processes may be responsible for cohesiveness in different types of 'cohesive' group (e.g. work versus recreational groups).

Attempts to reconceptualize the underlying mechanism of cohesiveness, although promising, are rather few, tend to point in a direction rather than present a properly elaborated coherent theory, are largely not related to any specific body of theory of group processes, and tend not to be grounded in contemporary social psychology. These attempts focus on commitment-to-group, dialectical processes, metaphor and shared representations, and sense of community. They include an emphasis on norms, commitment-to-group, identification with the group, group boundaries, construction of a consensual reality through communication, and dynamic longitudinal analyses.

Moreland and Levine's work on group socialization does not offer a reconceptualization of group cohesiveness, but a diachronic and dialectical model of socialization in small groups. Group solidarity is contingent on commitment, which in turn is influenced by assessments of rewardingness, and by role transitions. Although this is a dynamic and wide-ranging model of the social group, it still retains some key elements of the social cohesion model discussed in Chapter 4: specifically, a lack of discontinuity between individual and group (although, as discussed above, there are conflicting statements here) and an underlying process relating to interpersonal rewards based on the perceived satisfaction of individual goals/needs.

A critical discussion was also presented of theories of conformity, group polarization and minority influence, and of deindividuation and self-awareness. These are areas of social psychological research that deal with important aspects of group solidarity, yet in general they simply parallel group cohesiveness research. Remarkably, there is virtually no explicit cross-fertilization of ideas. In the case of conformity, existing theories embody a two-process model where neither one process alone, nor both processes operating in conjunction, can satisfactorily account for uniformity of behaviour in groups. In the case of deindividuation and self-awareness, the same two-process model surfaces, with attendant problems.

In Chapter 6 an entirely different model of group cohesiveness, solidarity, and indeed the social group, is presented. This approach is generally more systematic and cumulative than alternatives that we have considered, and is grounded in contemporary social psychology, specifically the social psychology of intergroup relations and group processes. I intend to be somewhat partisan in proposing that it overcomes most of the limitations of other approaches, and thus represents a significant advance in our understanding of group cohesiveness. The remainder of this book is dedicated to the presentation, discussion and assessment of this new social identity and self-categorization perspective on group cohesiveness.

Chapter 6

Social identity, self-categorization, and group cohesiveness

The theory of group cohesiveness, formalized in the 1950s, rapidly became simplified to a theory of interpersonal relations among people interacting together. Ultimately the theory is one in which interpersonal attraction arising from mutual satisfaction of interdependent goals binds people together as a group. The concept of cohesiveness is replaced by the concept of attraction, and thus a group process is replaced by an interpersonal process. Chapter 2 documents this reduction in level of analysis, and Chapter 4 relates it to historical trends in social psychology.

Although group cohesiveness theory has been criticized from many directions and for many reasons, these can be roughly classified as 'traditional' or 'radical' criticisms. In Chapter 4 we saw that traditional criticisms operate within the reductionist social cohesion model, while radical criticisms contest the model itself. Reconceptualizations also vary along this dimension. In Chapter 5 we discovered that both traditional and radical reconceptualizations suffer from limitations that are at least partly due to a failure properly to overcome the reductionism of the original cohesiveness concept. Another problem with contemporary approaches to group solidarity is the relative conceptual isolation of attempts to reconceptualize cohesiveness from related topic areas in social psychology dealing with, for example, conformity, and with deindividuation and self-awareness.

A crucially important topic area not discussed in Chapter 5 is intergroup behaviour. Prejudice, discrimination and ethnocentrism are significant aspects of intergroup relations that are clearly related to the solidarity of large-scale social categories. A complete theory of group solidarity must be able to explain cohesiveness at this macrosocial level as well as the level of small, task-orientated, interactive groups. Although there are, of course, differences between groups that differ in size, longevity, dispersion, structure, function, purpose, and so forth, it is very probable that these differences may be mainly 'surface' or 'content' differences, and that there are one or more fundamental psychological processes that are uniquely associated with groups: processes that have as little to do with interpersonal relations as interpersonal processes have to do with intra- and intergroup relations.

What is called for is a non-reductionist theory of group solidarity – or, more generally, the social group – that accounts parsimoniously for the entire range of group behaviours and is able to articulate (cf. Doise, 1986; see also Chapter 4) sociohistorical dimensions and the behaviour of the individual psychological entity. A theory such as group cohesiveness, which is crafted to deal with interpersonal relations among members of small interactive aggregates, cannot accomplish this. Attempts to modify the group cohesiveness concept to deal with social categories, but within the confines of the social cohesion model, are also likely to be problematic. A metatheoretical change in direction is needed.

The remainder of this book presents just such a change in direction. Out of – and in association with – a sustained critique of reductionism in social psychology (see Chapter 4) has arisen *social identity theory* and its more recent development *self-categorization theory*. These theories are presented in detail elsewhere (e.g. Hogg and Abrams, 1988; Tajfel and Turner, 1979; Turner, 1982, 1985; Turner *et al.*, 1987), so they will only be surveyed in this chapter. They are often considered together as representing an intergroup or social categorization approach. This is really rather appropriate here, as it identifies an important difference from the group cohesiveness perspective: the former originates in an analysis of large-scale intergroup relations, pivots on a cognitive definition of the social group, and theorizes in terms of categorization, while the latter originates in an analysis of small interactive aggregates, pivots on a largely affective definition of the group, and theorizes in terms of interpersonal attraction.

This chapter presents a self-categorization theory of group cohesion. In Chapter 7 this theory is examined in terms of related concepts and themes in the group cohesiveness literature as well as other areas of social psychology. Some data are presented, and problematic areas are discussed in the context of general criticisms of the social identity/self-categorization approach. Finally, Chapter 8 identifies prospects for the future and shows how this reconceptualization of group solidarity may be able to clarify some problematic group cohesiveness phenomena, and address phenomena beyond the scope of traditional formulations.

Social identity theory

Social identity theory grew out of Henri Tajfel's early work on perceptual accentuation effects (e.g. Tajfel, 1957, 1959), his lifelong interest in the social psychology of prejudice, discrimination, intergroup conflict and social change (e.g. Tajfel, 1963, 1969a, b, 1972c, 1973), and his desire to develop a non-reductionist, distinctly European, social psychology (e.g. Tajfel, 1972b, 1984). Although the theory was originally conceived by Tajfel, it was through collaboration with students and colleagues at the University of Bristol in the 1970s and early 1980s that it became formalized. The two major integrative statements of the theory come out of this period: Tajfel and Turner's (1979) discussion of intergroup relations, and Turner's (1982) cognitive redefinition of group membership. It was Turner and his colleagues who were then responsible for developing the approach and producing the more recent self-categorization theory (Turner, 1985; Turner *et al.*, 1987).

Groups versus individuals

Social identity theory is based upon a fundamental distinction between interpersonal and group processes, in which the latter cannot be explained in terms of the former. Social behaviour and relations among people vary along a continuum, with unique and idiosyncratic personal friendships at one extreme, and stereotypic and ethnocentric group behaviour at the other. This behavioural dimension is underpinned by a shift in self-conception from *personal identity* (one's conception of self as unique and distinct from all other humans, and/or in terms of unique interpersonal relationships) to *social identity* (one's conception of self in terms of the defining features of a self-inclusive social category that renders self stereotypically 'interchangeable' with other ingroup members and stereotypically distinct from outgroup members).

Group behaviour has characteristic features that distinguish it from interpersonal behaviour. These features include ethnocentrism, ingroup bias, intergroup competition and discrimination, stereotyping, prejudice, uniformity, ingroup cohesion, conformity, and so forth (cf. Brewer and Campbell, 1976). Social identity theory argues that a self-inclusive social category (e.g. nationality, religion, political affiliation, sports team, work group) provides a category-congruent self-definition that constitutes an element of the self-concept. The many groups to which we belong together furnish us with a repertoire of discrete category memberships, or social identities, that vary in relative overall or contextual importance in the self-concept. These social identities provide a relatively consensually recognized sense of who we are. They locate us in the complex network of social relationships existing in a community.

Category memberships are represented in the individual member's mind as a social identity that both describes and prescribes one's attributes as a group member. That is, when a specific social identity is the salient basis for self-conception, self-perception and conduct become ingroup stereotypical and normative, perceptions of relevant outgroup members become outgroup stereotypical, and intergroup behaviour acquires – to varying degrees, depending on the history of relations between the groups – competitive and discriminatory properties. Social identities have important self-evaluative consequences that motivate groups and their members to adopt strategies for achieving or maintaining intergroup comparisons that favour the ingroup, and thus the self.

Categorization and social comparison

The processes underlying and responsible for group behaviour are categorization and social comparison. The cognitive process of categorization has been shown to accentuate similarities among stimuli falling within the same category and differences between stimuli falling in different categories, on dimensions subjectively perceived to be correlated with the categorization (e.g. Doise, 1978; Eiser, 1980; Eiser and Stroebe, 1972; Tajfel and Wilkes, 1963). Where the categorization is of people, this accentuation effect accounts for the perceptual distancing and homogenization of outgroup members on stereotypic dimensions which characterize stereotyping. Social-categorization-contingent accentuation effects also arise in the perception of ingroupers and self, and occur on behavioural and affective dimensions as well as the more familiar attitudinal ones. In other words, contexts that make salient a specific social categorization produce stereotypic ingroup, outgroup and self-perception, ingroup normative behaviour (i.e. behavioural uniformity), and intergroup differentiation and discrimination.

Social comparison refers to comparisons between one's own attitudes, beliefs and behaviours, and those of others. Festinger (1954; Suls and Miller, 1977) originally maintained that we resort to social comparisons only when we cannot refer directly to reality to confirm the veracity of our beliefs. Social identity theory claims that no truth is self-evident, and that all knowledge is derived through social comparisons (cf. Turner, 1991). It is the establishment of consensus that provides us with confidence in the veracity or appropriateness of our attitudes and behaviours. Different visions of the world are offered by different groups precisely because the contours of groups are defined by discontinuity between one consensus and another.

When we make intergroup social comparisons – that is, between self as ingroup member and other as outgroup member (or between ingroup and outgroup as a whole) – we not only strive to maximize intergroup differences, but also – very importantly – try to secure an evaluative advantage for the ingroup. Because social categories contribute to the self-concept and thus serve to define and *evaluate* self, we continually try to make intergroup comparisons on dimensions that already favour the ingroup. We strive for evaluatively positive social identity through positive ingroup distinctiveness. Social identity theory argues that this reflects a basic human motivation for positive self-esteem through self-enhancement (see Hogg and Abrams, 1990, for detailed discussion).

Macrosocial dimensions

The self-enhancement motive is an important component of social identity theory that was introduced to help explain social change. In the competition for positive distinctiveness, the strategies available to groups are constrained by the perceived nature of intergroup relations: that is, by social belief structures concerning the stability and legitimacy of the status quo, and the permeability of intergroup boundaries (and thus the possibility of 'passing').

There are two major classes of social belief: (1) *social mobility*, in which intergroup boundaries are believed to be permeable and open, and thus allow one to 'pass' easily from subordinate to dominant group; and (2) *social change*, in which intergroup boundaries are believed to be impermeable and closed, and thus do not allow one to 'pass' easily. Social mobility is associated with individualistic strategies whereby members of subordinate groups (groups with relatively lower status and usually at a material and evaluative disadvantage) attempt to dissociate themselves from their group and become self-defined and accepted members of the dominant group.

Social change is associated with different strategies, depending on whether or not it is associated with *cognitive alternatives*. 'Cognitive alternatives' refers to a belief that there is a viable and achievable alternative to the status quo — that is, that the subordinate position of the group is neither legitimate nor stable, and real change is possible. Where a social change belief structure is *not* accompanied by cognitive alternatives, subordinate group members resort to strategies of social creativity — they may seek to change the dimensions of intergroup comparison, reverse the evaluative implication of their position on a dimension, or opt out of upward intergroup comparison in favour of lateral or downward intergroup comparison. Where a social change belief structure *is* accompanied by cognitive alternatives, subordinate group members engage in direct intergroup competition aimed at stripping the dominant group of its power over the subordinate group.

This macrosocial aspect of social identity theory has proved extremely profitable in explaining a range of large-scale group behaviours, for example ethnolinguistic intergroup relations (e.g. Giles and Johnson, 1981; Giles and St Clair, 1979; Sachdev and Bourhis, 1990; see Chapter 8) and other macrosocial phenomena (e.g. Hinkle and Brown, 1990; Van Knippenberg, 1984).

Self-categorization theory ===

Self-categorization theory (Turner, 1985; Turner *et al.*, 1987; see also Hogg and McGarty, 1990; Turner and Oakes, 1989) is a development of the social identity concept which differs from social identity theory more in emphasis than in content. It elaborates in much greater detail the operation of the categorization process as the cognitive basis of group behaviour, and focuses more on intragroup processes than on macrosocial intergroup relations. In so doing it makes little reference to self-esteem as a motivational concept, or to macrosocial strategies for social change. One significant difference is that the rather binary discussion of personal identity versus social identity is replaced by the idea that self-conception varies in level of abstraction: from the unique self that is differentiated from all other (in)group members to the entirely depersonalized self that is identical to all other ingroup members and different to all outgroup members. There is a dynamic tension between individuation and depersonalization (cf. Brewer's 1991 notion of optimal distinctiveness – see Chapter 7).

Self-categorization theory formalizes and systematizes many of the more imprecise aspects of social identity theory, to provide a more complete and rigorous theorization of the social group. As such it can provide an explanation of group cohesiveness that is theoretically related to the entire array of other group phenomena that occur in groups of all types.

For self-categorization theory, the basic mechanism of group phenomena is the cognitive process of categorization, which perceptually accentuates both similarities among stimuli (physical, social, or aspects of the self) belonging to the same category, and differences among stimuli belonging to different categories on dimensions believed to be correlated with the categorization (e.g. Tajfel, 1959; Tajfel and Wilkes, 1963). This process ultimately serves the function of rendering experience of the world subjectively meaningful, and identifies those aspects relevant to action in a particular context. Categorization clarifies intergroup boundaries by producing stereotypical and normative perceptions and actions, and assigns people to the contextually relevant category.

People can categorize themselves and others at a number of different levels of abstraction (e.g. Rosch, 1978). The most relevant one here is the level of ingroup–outgroup (defining one's social identity). Categorization of self and others at this level accentuates the group prototypicality, stereotypicality or normativeness of people. The individual is perceptually and behaviourally depersonalized in terms of the relevant ingroup prototype. For self-categorization theory, 'the depersonalization of self-perception is the basic process underlying group phenomena (social stereotyping, group cohesion and ethnocentrism, cooperation and altruism, emotional contagion and empathy, collective behaviour, shared norms and mutual influence process, etc.)'

(Turner, 1985, pp. 99–100). Nothing negative is implied by the term 'depersonalization'. It contains none of the implications of 'dehumanization' or 'deindividuation', but refers simply to a contextual *change* in the level of identity, not to a loss of identity.

For self-categorization theory, a prototype is a cognitive representation of the defining features of a social category. It is a relatively nebulous or fuzzy set of properties that the individual group member believes defines the category. Prototypes tend not to be abstract checklists of isolated features, but are embodied as a reified image of a 'most prototypical' group member – an ideal or representative category member. Prototypes encompass the whole range of interrelated properties that define the group and differentiate it from relevant outgroups, or from people who are not in the group. The prototype is the cognitive representation of the group norm or the group stereotype.

Categorization, therefore, accentuates perceived similarities between self or fellow group members and the prototype. This is what is meant by depersonalization: self and others are perceived not as unique persons but as embodiments of the prototype. Since prototypes are, by definition, shared among group members, one consequence of the depersonalization process is relative intragroup uniformity of perceptions, attitudes and behaviour. In this way the self-categorization process accounts for conformity to group norms (see below).

The social self-concept is context-dependent in so far as specific social self-categorizations are brought into play (i.e. become the basis of perception and conduct) by the social field. The cognitive system, in seeking to maximize meaning in a specific context, engages whatever categorization best accounts for the similarities and differences among stimuli. This process is guided by the accessibility to the individual of particular categorizations, and the degree to which stimulus properties fit that categorization. Accessibility is influenced by the individual's current intentions and past experiences. This 'accessibility x fit' formulation, which is based on the work of Bruner (1957), helps explain the contextual salience of different self-conceptualizations that govern perception, cognition and conduct.

Another way in which to approach salience is in terms of the principle of metacontrast. The contextually salient categorization is that which simultaneously minimizes perceived *intra*category differences and maximizes perceived *inter*category differences within the social frame of reference (Campbell, 1958; Turner, Wetherell and Hogg, 1989). Once they are formed on the basis of perceived similarities and differences among stimuli, categories are consequently used as a basis for the perceptual accentuation of these similarities and differences (Tajfel and Wilkes, 1963; see also Eiser and Stroebe, 1972; McGarty and Penny, 1988), thereby maximizing separateness and clarity. The terms 'social frame of reference', 'social field', and 'social comparative dimension' all refer to roughly the same idea: the range of positions on one or more comparative dimensions (e.g. attitudes, behaviour, dress, appearance, etc.) that are subjectively believed or perceived, in that context, to be occupied or occupyable by human beings.

Social influence in groups: conformity and normative behaviour

Traditional perspectives

A highly characteristic and central feature of group behaviour and group solidarity is attitudinal and behavioural uniformity. Traditionally, social psychologists have analyzed this phenomenon from a number of different and often compartmentalized directions. Stereotyping research (e.g. Ashmore and Del Boca, 1981) has investigated why people derogate outgroup members and perceive them as 'all the same'. This research also discusses, to some extent, auto-stereotyping and ingroup stereotyping. Behavioural uniformity tends to be approached under the headings of, for example, collective behaviour (e.g. R.H. Turner, 1964), conformity (e.g. Allen, 1975), deindividuation (e.g. Zimbardo, 1970) and polarization (e.g. Isenberg, 1986). An important feature of social identity and self-categorization theories is that this diversity of group uniformity phenomena is theorized in terms of a single process of social influence within groups. Let us explore this in the context of conformity and group polarization.

Traditionally, conformity and group polarization have been researched and theorized largely as separate phenomena. Conformity has been approached as an averaging process represented by behavioural or attitudinal convergence among members of a group on the group mean (e.g. Allen, 1965, 1975; Sherif, 1936). The underlying process is either subjective reality testing or self-presentation: called informational influence and normative influence by Deutsch and Gerard (1955; cf. Kelley, 1952). However, conformity occurs under conditions – and in ways – which are not well explained by either of these processes (e.g. see reviews by Abrams and Hogg, 1990c; Hogg and Turner, 1987a). (See Chapter 5 for critical discussion of traditional research into conformity.)

Group polarization, in contrast, has been characterized as a group decision-making bias in which groups make judgements that are more extreme than the average initial position of the group members in the direction initially favoured by the group mean. This is clearly not an averaging process (which would imply convergence rather than polarization), so it was not considered a conformity phenomenon. There are two broad classes of explanation – one focuses on the persuasiveness of the information carried by arguments produced in discussion (e.g. persuasive arguments theory: Burnstein and Vinokur, 1977; Vinokur and Burnstein, 1974); the other on self-presentational considerations (e.g. cultural values theories: Jellison and Arkin, 1977, Sanders and Baron, 1977). Although these processes can account for many instances of group polarization, there are a number of anomalous findings (see Wetherell, 1987), and neither process has unequivocal empirical support.

Social identity and self-categorization

In contrast to these traditional approaches, social identity and self-categorization theories consider the apparent discontinuity between conformity and group polarization to be a historical accident. The different 'phenomena' actually reflect different emphases (averaging versus shift) placed on the outcome of effective social influence within a psychologically salient group. The same two-process interdependence model of social influence quite clearly underlies the explanation of both conformity and group polarization (see critical discussion by Turner, 1985; also Abrams and Hogg, 1990c; Hogg and Abrams, 1988, pp. 165–71; Hogg and Turner, 1987a; Turner, 1991; and Chapter 5).

Social identity theory originally focused mainly upon conformity, and proposed a single process of social identification which produced conformity to group norms (see Figure 6.1). Turner (1981, 1982) called the social process referent informational influence (see also Hogg and Turner, 1987a, Hogg and

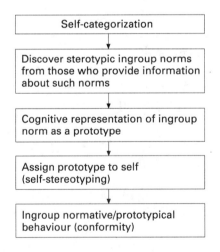

Figure 6.1 *Conformity through referent informational influence. (This figure is modified, by permission of Routledge, from Figure 8.1 in Hogg and Abrams (1988, p. 172).)*

Abrams, 1988, pp. 172–5). First, people categorize and define themselves as members of a distinct social category or assign themselves a social identity; second, they form or learn the stereotypic norms of that category; and third, they assign these norms to themselves; thus their behaviour becomes more normative as their category membership becomes more salient. Direct evidence for the operation of this process comes from a number of studies in which conformity to group norms is enhanced under conditions, such as explicit intergroup categorization, which would be expected to render social identity more salient (e.g. Abrams, Wetherell, Cochrane, Hogg and Turner, 1990; Hogg and Turner, 1987a; Reicher, 1982, 1984, 1987; Turner *et al.*, 1989; see also Hogg, 1985a; Hogg and Turner, 1987b).

Self-categorization theory takes referent informational influence theory one stage further by explicitly theorizing social identification as a process of self-categorization. As a consequence, it is now possible to specify more precisely the salient group norm upon which group members converge. Consider a salient social comparative dimension (attitude scale, behaviour dimension, etc.) which represents ingroup, including self, and outgroup or non-ingroup members. The relevant ingroup norm is that position on the dimension which simultaneously maximizes intergroup differences and minimizes intragroup differences. The ingroup member occupying this position, the most prototypical group member, is the person who is simultaneously most different to the outgroup and least different to the ingroup. This position can be identified by calculating a metacontrast ratio (see Hogg and McGarty, 1990, p. 16) for each member, such that the metacontrast ratio (MCR_k) for a specific ingroup position (I_k) in a frame of reference comprising m ingroup members (I_i) and n outgroup (i.e. non-ingroup) positions (O_i) is:

$$MCR_k = \left(\left(\sum_{i=1}^{n} \left| I_k - O_i \right| \right) / n \right) \bigg/ \left(\left(\sum_{i=1}^{m} \left| I_k - I_i \right| \right) / (m-1) \right)$$

The ingroup member with the highest MCR occupies the most prototypical or normative ingroup position.

It has been shown, from computer modelling of a very large number of ingroup and non-ingroup distributions, that as the mean ingroup position moves away from the midpoint of a comparative context, the prototype becomes even more extreme than the ingroup mean (McGarty, Turner, Hogg, David and Wetherell, 1992). In other words, allowing for ceiling effects, extreme ingroups have polarized norms.

Effective social influence within a group, mediated by self-categorization, produces conformity to the group norm (convergence on the prototypical position). Whether this norm (prototype) is extremitized or not depends upon the relative distribution of ingroup and non-ingroup positions on the social comparative dimension. Where the norm is more extreme than the mean but in the same direction, polarization occurs. The important points are: (1)

norms (which are likely to be extremitized) for specific groups can be derived from the social comparative context, and (2) polarization can be predicted owing to a process of conformity to these norms. Further details of this theory can be found in Hogg, Turner and Davidson (1990), Turner (1985, 1991), Turner *et al.* (1987, 1989), Turner and Oakes (1989), and Wetherell (1987).

Measuring social identity

Before moving on to discuss the self-categorization analysis of group cohesiveness, a few words regarding the measurement of social identity are in order. Social identity cannot be measured directly. However, the underlying process of self-categorization produces systematic general effects that can be measured: depersonalized group-prototypical perception of self and others, normative behaviour (thus conformity), ethnocentrism, ingroup favouritism, intergroup differentiation, ingroup liking. Although these are general effects, the way in which they manifest themselves is strongly influenced by a number of factors to do with general social beliefs, intergroup status relations, self-presentational goals, intergroup strategies, contextual norms, wider cultural prescriptions, and so forth. In other words, in order to measure social identity one has to understand the social content and context of the specific group being studied (cf. Tajfel's [1972a] warning against doing experimental research in a social vacuum).

So, for example, social identification in truly minimal groups (e.g. Billig and Tajfel, 1973) is measured via subjects' use of strategies of intergroup differentiation. These groups are designed to have no prior history, so they do not have specific group stereotypes of one another. On the other hand, social identification in ethnic groups will be expressed in vastly different ways, depending on the particular sociohistorical circumstances of the group (e.g. French-speaking Canadians in the 1990s in contrast to, say, thirty years ago) – Sachdev and Bourhis (1990; see also Chapter 8). Another similar example is social identification as male or female (see Hogg, 1985a; Smith, 1985).

General social identification scales are, therefore, likely to have only very restricted usage. For example, the distribution matrices used to measure social identification in minimal groups are only really designed for such groups. As soon as groups become less minimal (e.g. have some history of association, and status relations with other groups), then other measures must also be included (e.g. stereotypical evaluation – Hogg and Turner, 1987b). The measurement of social identification should be approached in a constructive manner that is mindful, on the one hand, of general effects of self-categorization, and, on the other, of the specific nature of the group and its social history of relations with other groups, and the immediate social context in which the group finds itself.

Social identity and self-categorization theories are theories of the dynamic social construction, representation, and expression of group membership/belongingness. So the measurement of group membership (i.e. its expression) rests on theoretical principles but is influenced by contextual considerations: that is, although different measures may be used for different groups, different types of group, different contexts of measurement, and so forth, all are derived theoretically from clear principles about the nature of group membership. It is in this respect that the measurement of group solidarity based on self-categorization theory differs starkly from that based on traditional treatments of group cohesiveness. In the latter, the underlying theory is unclear, so the construction of appropriate measures and scales is problematic (see Chapters 3 and 4).

Social attraction and cohesiveness

The social identity and self-categorization theories of group processes have a number of important features: (1) they are general theories of the social group, not constrained by the size, dispersion, longevity, and so forth of the membership; (2) they incorporate the role of the intergroup context in group behaviour; (3) they account for the range of group behaviours (e.g. conformity, stereotyping, discrimination, ethnocentrism, etc.) in terms of a limited number of theoretically integrated generative principles; (4) they are basically cognitive; and (5) they do not construct group processes from interpersonal processes. All this allows a reconceptualization of group cohesiveness. Earlier formulations are published elsewhere: see Hogg (1983, 1985b, 1987, in press), Hogg and Abrams (1988, pp. 105–12), Hogg and Hardie (1991, 1992a); Hogg and McGarty (1990); Hogg and Turner (1985a, b), Turner (1982, 1984, 1985).

As we have just seen, group solidarity – or simply group behaviour – has a number of components, including ethnocentrism, stereotypic perception, normative conduct, ingroup trust, respect and liking, and intergroup differentiation. All these 'symptoms' are produced by self-categorization, but local situational factors and the wider context of intergroup relations may influence the specific mix of behaviours that are manifested.

Interindividual attraction among ingroup members is, nevertheless, an important aspect of group solidarity. We tend to have a complex of positive feelings, a positive attitude, towards fellow group members, which is accentuated under circumstances that enhance one's sense of belonging to the group. For example, we tend to experience contextually enhanced liking for fellow supporters of a team during a match, or fellow members of a group or faction engaged in tricky negotiations. This sort of attraction, or interindividual attitude, is a group, not an interpersonal, phenomenon. More precisely, it is the product of a group process, not an interpersonal process. As such, it must be distinguished from interpersonal attraction.

Social versus personal attraction

In order to do this, a clear distinction can be drawn between two forms of attraction or interindividual attitude: *social attraction* and *personal attraction* (see Figure 6.2). The phenomenology of both is a positive feeling that one person has about another. However, the generative process underlying each is quite different. *Social attraction*, attraction among members of a salient social group, is quite different to genuine inter*personal* attraction, in that it is depersonalized liking based upon prototypicality and generated by self-categorization. It is actually attraction to the group as that group is embodied by specific group members, so that the object of positive attitude and feelings is not actually the unique individual person, but the prototype that he/she embodies. Targets are relatively interchangeable – they are depersonalized. John is not liked for being John, but for being a more or less exemplary embodiment of the prototypical properties of the group. How much individual group members are liked is thus a function of their perceived prototypicality and the degree to which the perceiver has a positive attitude towards the group as it is prototypically represented.

In contrast, *personal attraction* is idiosyncratic and grounded in specific interpersonal relationships. It is an interpersonal feeling or attitude based on assessment and perception of the whole person as a unique self-contained biographical entity. Personal attraction is tied to specific non-interchangeable targets. It is governed by personal preferences and the course of interpersonal relationships. How much someone is liked is a function of perceptions of the whole unique person and the history of his/her relationship to self. Attraction is highly personalized.

Social attraction is associated with group processes, and personal attraction with interpersonal processes. The two are therefore quite distinct at the level of generative process. Although both represent a positive feeling or attitude towards another person, social attraction is intricately linked to other group phenomena (e.g. conformity, stereotyping, intergroup differentiation), whereas personal attraction is not. To the extent that interactive contexts vary in the relative extent to which social or personal categorizations are salient, so will the degree to which interindividual attitude (e.g. liking) is more or less depersonalized. Where an interaction is almost entirely based upon common category membership, depersonalized social attraction will prevail. Where an interaction is almost entirely based upon an interpersonal relationship, personalized personal attraction will prevail.

An interesting special case is that of small groups, where the category is defined in terms of a small number of physically present individuals who

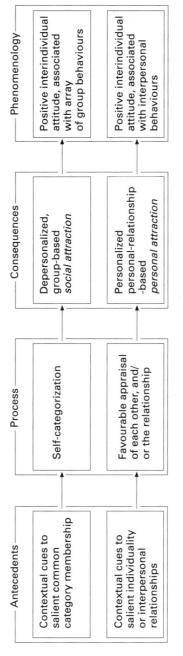

Figure 6.2 *Social attraction, personal attraction, and interindividual conduct*

usually all interact together repeatedly (e.g. a committee, work group, sports team). The circumstances of such groups (e.g. propinquity, repeated face-to-face interaction with the same people, high degree of shared beliefs) generally encourage the development of interpersonal relationships, so social and personal attraction may often coexist. It is very important, however, to keep clearly in mind that the two types of attraction are conceptually separate: people may like one another as group members as well as interpersonal friends, but the bases of these two feelings are quite distinct. You will recall that a major limitation of the traditional cohesiveness concept is that no such distinction is made. Instead, the analysis is solely in terms of interpersonal relationships. From a self-categorization perspective, the intragroup attraction aspect of group cohesiveness is depersonalized liking, and does not involve personal attraction.

Thus far we have spoken of social attraction as a positive attitude among members of a group. What about negative attitudes (e.g. dislike) and attitudes among members of different groups (intergroup attitudes)? Social and personal attraction are dimensions that can range from highly positive interindividual attitudes to highly negative interindividual attitudes. Interpersonal relationships, and concomitant personal attraction, encompass the entire range of feelings from warm and close friendships to violent and highly personalized dislikes and animosities. The personal nature of such relationships is clearly revealed by the way in which one person's close friend is another's despised fiend.

Dimensions of depersonalized social attraction

Social attraction is more complicated. As an interindividual attitude it can be more or less favourable: ranging from highly positive to highly negative. However, as a *group-based* interindividual attitude, social attraction can have as its target an *ingroup* member or an *outgroup* member. A proper understanding of social attraction must, therefore, be grounded in a discussion of intergroup relations.

Intergroup relations define groups, or rather the consensual relative value of groups; and the groups to which one belongs define self, including the valence of self. So there is continual innovation and competition to secure and maintain a relatively favourable evaluation of one's own group. One consequence of this is that ingroup prototypes are generally evaluatively positive. Social attraction for an ingroup member is associated with depersonalized perception of the target in terms of this prototype, and thus is unlikely to be negative. In other words, intragroup attraction (social attraction for a fellow ingroup member, or attraction that is depersonalized in terms of the ingroup prototype) may vary in terms of its positiveness, but is not usually negative.

The only instances that come immediately to mind where intragroup attraction may be negative are: (1) where a specific ingroup member is highly non-prototypical: this is relatively rare, since categorization of individuals as ingroup members accentuates their prototypicality, and highly non-prototypical 'members' are likely to be categorized as outgroupers or non-ingroupers; and (2) where the ingroup prototype is perceived to be highly negative: this is also rare, because of the creativity of group members in defining their groups in positive terms. In general, where such a state of affairs exists, the member is quite probably psychologically dissociated from the group, and so is not categorizing him/herself as a group member at all.

Social attraction for an outgroup member is attraction that is depersonalized in terms of an outgroup prototype. Since outgroup prototypes are generally evaluated relatively less favourably than ingroup prototypes, social attraction for outgroup members is generally negative, or at least not very positive. The more outgroup-prototypical outgroup members are, the less we like them. A possible exception to this pattern is the case where the outgroup prototype is highly desirable, but this would arise only where individuals were relatively dissatisfied with their group membership and striving to become accepted as members of the outgroup. Here, people may actually be categorizing themselves as outgroup members, even though such a self-categorization may not actually be recognized as legitimate by others (ingroupers or outgroupers).

Social attraction, then, is generally a positive attitude towards ingroupers and a negative, or less positive, attitude towards outgroupers. This arises from the way in which attitude is depersonalized in terms of a relatively positive ingroup prototype in the former case, and a relatively negative, or less positive, prototype in the latter case. This relatively symmetrical outcome of self-categorization may, however, be influenced by another factor.

Prototypes, as representations of groups, not only mediate *evaluation* of self and others, but also serve an important *structural* purpose. They pattern the social world into discrete, well-defined and meaningful social units. People strive to construct and maintain such meaningful structures and try to avoid the aversive consequences of uncertainty and chaos. People are, therefore, more comfortable when their prototypical expectations are confirmed than when they are disconfirmed (cf. Kuhn's [1962] analysis of the structure of scientific revolutions). One consequence of this is that people should have a more positive attitude towards those others who are relatively more than less prototypical, and therefore should like both ingroupers who are ingroup-prototypical and outgroupers who are outgroup-prototypical. Of course, highly non-prototypical in- or outgroup members will be disliked, particularly if, by being non-prototypical, they are actually being prototypical of the other group. This may explain the strong negative attitudes that exist towards traitors and 'black sheep' (cf. Marques, 1990).

Both ingroupers and outgroupers are liked for being prototypical of their respective groups because this confirms the clarity and meaningfulness of the existing categorization, and thus ultimately the way in which self is defined. This process interacts with the self-evaluative process described above to accentuate depersonalized liking for ingroupers, and moderate depersonalized dislike for outgroupers.

Depersonalized attraction is also affected by intergroup relations in a number of ways. Since depersonalized attraction is prototype-dependent, any factor that influences the nature of the prototype will influence who is considered more or less prototypical and hence prototypically attractive. Group norms, stereotypes and prototypes are not context-independent. Local or context-dependent frames of reference can produce polarized norms, and thus influence patterns of intragroup and intergroup social attraction. An ingroup member who is highly prototypical in one context may be marginally prototypical in another. This may be a transient effect, but it may also be an enduring effect if the context or frame of reference change is a lasting one. In general, any changes in the social comparative context influence the nature of ingroup and outgroup prototypes, and thus patterns of ingroup and outgroup social attraction.

Another way in which intergroup relations may influence social attraction is via people's subjective beliefs about the nature of the relations between groups and about what is considered legitimate or appropriate behaviour. Intergroup relations at the macrosocial level tend to be characterized by status and power differentials that cast groups into subordinate and dominant roles. The way in which these groups behave towards one another and the way in which members behave towards fellow members will be influenced by what is believed to be the nature of the relations between the groups (e.g. Sachdev and Bourhis, 1991). Of particular relevance are beliefs concerning (1) the permeability of intergroup boundaries and the possibility of 'passing' from one group to the other; (2) the stability of the existing status differential; and (3) the legitimacy of the status differential.

If a subordinate group believes that boundaries are impermeable, and therefore that it is impossible to 'pass', and that the status differential is both illegitimate and unstable (i.e. there are cognitive alternatives to the status quo), then direct intergroup competition to change the status quo would no doubt polarize prototypes, accentuate identification, and legitimize overt expression of outgroup hatred and ingroup liking. It is important to recognize that social attraction is not only a relatively automatic consequence of group processes, but also serves a communicative or rhetorical function in delineating loyalties and punctuating solidarity.

In contrast, a subordinate group which believes that boundaries are impermeable, but that the existing status differential is legitimate and stable (i.e. there are no cognitive alternatives to the status quo) is likely to behave very differently. Prototypical polarization is unlikely to be very pronounced, and overt expression of outgroup dislike is very unlikely to be considered a legitimate – or, indeed, wise – course of action. The relationship between intergroup relations, social belief structures and social attraction is undoubtedly a very complex one, but it is important to consider theoretically the effect of wider intergroup relations on the affective life of the group.

In summary, the valence and magnitude of social attraction is a function of at least: (1) the social relationship between individuals – intra- or intergroup; (2) the degree to which specific others are perceived to be prototypical of their respective categories (this will be influenced by immediate or more enduring contextual factors that affect the relative prototypicality of specific ingroup or outgroup individuals); and (3) whether a social change subjective belief structure is or is not accompanied by cognitive alternatives. This relationship could perhaps be expressed as a quasi-mathematical formula, of the type:

$$a \approx (o + Ip + Kos + X),$$

where 'a' is social attraction, 'o' is social orientation, 'p' is prototypicality, 's' is subjective belief structure, 'I' and 'K' are constants, and 'X' acknowledges that other factors will also be influential. Note that this 'formula' is purely illustrative, and is not intended to be predictive in any quantitative sense.

If however, we assign arbitrary values of $+1$ to intragroup relations (o), high prototypicality (p), and social change with cognitive alternatives (s), -1 to the obverse conditions, and 0.5 to the two constants (I and K), and if we exclude the variable 'X', we can roughly infer what sorts of conditions might produce more or less positive or negative social attraction. Clearly, the most social liking will be for a highly prototypical ingrouper where cognitive alternatives are present ($A = (1 + 0.5(1) + 0.5(1 \times 1)) = 2$), and most social dislike for a less highly prototypical outgrouper where cognitive alternatives are present ($A = (-1 + 0.5(-1) + 0.5(-1 \times 1)) = -2$).

Some intervening mechanisms

The social attraction hypothesis, then, explains attraction phenomena within and between groups in terms of attitudinal consequences of self-categorization-contingent depersonalization. The process whereby self-categorization depersonalizes ingroupers in terms of the ingroup prototype and outgroupers in terms of the outgroup prototype may influence social attraction in a number of ways – some of which work in conjunction with one another to amplify liking/disliking, and others in opposition to one another to moderate liking/disliking (see Figure 6.3):

1. The favourability of ingroup relative to outgroup prototypes produces a relatively more positive attitude towards ingroupers than outgroupers: ingroupers are liked more to the extent that they embody the (relatively

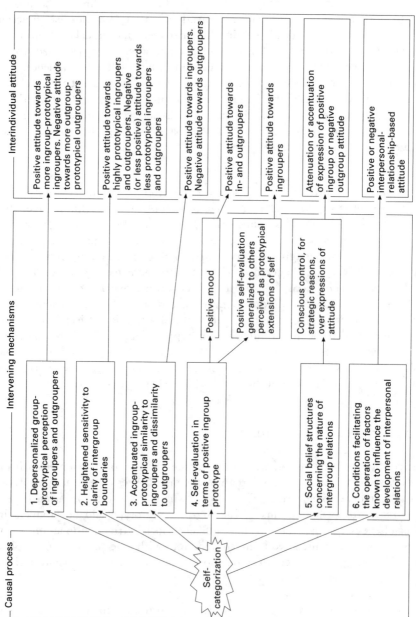

Figure 6.3   *Some mechanisms through which self-categorization may have its effects on interindividual attitude*

attractive) ingroup prototype; outgroupers are liked less to the extent that they embody the (relatively unattractive) outgroup prototype.

2. Irrespective of the content and relative valence of specific ingroup and outgroup prototypes, ingroupers and outgroupers who are highly prototypical of their respective groups are attractive because they confirm prototypical expectations and maintain intergroup distinctiveness. Marginally prototypical members of both in- and outgroup are less attractive because they muddy group boundaries and call into question group prototypes. People tend to seek confirmation for who they are, so they feel threatened by the insecurity and unpredictability communicated by marginally prototypical members, but comfortable and happy with the security and predictability communicated by highly prototypical members. This mechanism will tend to accentuate effects due to (1) above regarding ingroup liking (both mechanisms will accentuate liking for more prototypical ingroupers), and moderate effects due to (1) above regarding outgroup liking (increasing outgroup prototypicality will decrease liking via Mechanism 1, but increase it via Mechanism 2).

3. Self-categorization accentuates perceived similarities between self and fellow ingroupers on ingroup-prototypical dimensions, and accentuates perceived differences between self and outgroupers on both ingroup- and outgroup-prototypical dimensions. A straightforward similarity–attraction hypothesis (e.g. Byrne, 1971) would predict a more positive attitude towards ingroupers than towards outgroupers. It should be stressed, however, that from a social attraction perspective the relevant similarities and differences are prototypical ones based on depersonalized perception. They are not general similarities and differences based on relatively integrated and idiosyncratic personal perceptions of 'whole' persons.

4. Self-categorization depersonalizes self-perception in terms of the (evaluatively relatively positive) ingroup prototype, so it should generate a degree of positive self-evaluation or self-liking, and/or simply improve mood. One consequence of this might be an extension of favourable self-evaluation, manifested as other-liking, to fellow group members who are perceived as categorially relatively interchangeable with self. Fellow group members are treated as an extension of self. A similar logic is used by LeVine and Campbell (1972) to explain the intragroup attraction aspect of ethnocentrism: narcissism (self-love) is generalized to the group as a whole (see Chapter 7). McDougall (1921) has proposed a similar idea to explain the origin of positive ingroup sentiment (see Chapter 2). Another possibility is that if self-categorization has an elevating effect on mood, both ingroupers and outgroupers may be enveloped by a 'warm, rosy glow' that renders them relatively attractive.

5. Social belief structures to do with the nature of intergroup relations, and group norms to do with acceptable behaviour, may together influence the form and extent of expression of social attraction. Not only is social

attraction a relatively automatic expression of attitude produced by depersonalization, but since its expression also serves communicative and rhetorical functions within and between groups, groups have a degree of control over its expression.

6. Social attraction is quite distinct from personal attraction in that it is associated with uniquely group processes. Group life can, however, produce conditions that are conducive to the establishment of positive interpersonal relationships and hence interpersonal liking: for example propinquity, mutually enjoyable interaction, cooperation, general attitudinal similarity. Within groups, then, positive interpersonal relations may arise. This is particularly true of small interactive groups. It is, however, extremely important to remember that this personal attraction is not produced by a group process – it is simply that group processes can produce conditions that are incidentally favourable for personal relationships. It is just as true, of course, that group life can produce negative interpersonal relationships – relationships that are associated with personal dislike. The logic and dynamic of personal attraction within and between groups is theoretically unrelated to social attraction.

Although the cumulative or interactive effect of all these processes on attraction phenomena within and between groups is highly complex, it is possible to make distinct predictions that differentiate between social and personal attraction. The fundamental generative principle underlying social attraction remains straightforward: self-categorization depersonalizes attitude towards ingroupers in terms of the ingroup prototype and outgroupers in terms of the outgroup prototype.

Conclusion

This chapter has presented a self-categorization model of group cohesiveness that is grounded in the social identity and self-categorization theories of the social group. Two different forms of interindividual attitude, or attraction, are identified. *Social attraction* is an interindividual attitude that is depersonalized in terms of group prototypes and generated, along with other distinctive intra- and intergroup behaviours, by self-categorization. *Personal attraction* is an interindividual attitude that is personalized in terms of unique properties of individuals and close interpersonal relationships. Only social attraction relates to group solidarity and cohesiveness – it is a group phenomenon. Personal attraction has nothing to do with groups – it is an interpersonal phenomenon. The valence and magnitude of social attraction is influenced by a host of factors, including the nature of the social relationship between individuals, the perceived group prototypicality of people, and the perceived nature of intergroup relations.

In Chapter 7 this model is evaluated with reference to other conceptualizations of group cohesiveness, and with reference to related notions in other areas of social psychology. I also review and decribe some relevant studies and critical literature.

Chapter 7

Social attraction research

Chapter 6 described a self-categorization model of group cohesiveness, in which the process of categorization responsible for group behaviour generates intragroup attraction among individual members of a social group, whether the group is a small, face-to-face, task-orientated group or a large, transhistorical social category. Group cohesiveness can arise when two or more representatives of a social group of any size appraise each other under conditions which accentuate the salience of their shared group membership. This is not to deny – particularly in small face-to-face groups – that prolonged interaction may furnish conditions that also have effects on inter*personal* relations. However, these are conceptually separate from *group* cohesiveness. You can like someone as a fellow group member, and simultaneously dislike that person as a potential friend.

This model of group cohesiveness has a number of advantages over the traditional formulation. It is a general theory of group cohesiveness that is not limited by group size or dispersion; it deals theoretically with all aspects of group solidarity (e.g. ethnocentrism, conformity, discrimination, stereotyping, intragroup liking), not attraction alone; it is a clearly specified theory without the conceptual ambiguities of the traditional concept; it circumvents the problem of trying to construct the group level of cohesiveness from the individual level, by conceptualizing the group as represented within the individual rather than comprising a set of individuals. A cohesive group is one in which members identify strongly, via a process of self-categorization, and thus exhibit to varying degrees social attraction, ethnocentrism, normative conduct, and intergroup differentiation. Statements about the group as a whole are useful descriptive summaries about how 'most' or 'many' or 'some' members behave. They have no explanatory social psychological status.

In this chapter I discuss the relationship between the social attraction hypothesis and some other relevant concepts in social psychology. The empirical and metatheoretical status of the idea is also examined.

110

Related ideas in social psychology

Other reconceptualizations of cohesiveness

First of all, it is worth noting that the self-categorization model of group cohesiveness may provide a theoretical social psychological explication of aspects of cohesiveness that others have suggested pursuing in a reformulation of the concept (cf. Chapter 5). For example, Donnelly *et al.* (1978) suggest the existence of a normative force that restrains an individual within the group and thus produces cohesiveness. A number of people have advocated an analysis in terms of commitment-to-group (e.g. Mudrack, 1989a), and Piper *et al.* (1983) actually suggest that members can establish a bond of commitment between themselves and their 'conception of the group as a whole' (p. 95). Closely related to this idea is Evans and Jarvis's (1980) use of the term 'identification' to describe the underpinning of attraction-to-group. Owen (1985) emphasizes the way in which groups construct consensual realities and a sense of we-ness for their members through the communication and representation of metaphors. McMillan and Chavis (1986) discuss the cohesiveness of communities in terms of a concept called sense of community. This concept captures the way in which people identify with or belong to a normatively bounded social entity. Moreland and Levine's (1982) diachronic model of group socialization describes the way 'the individual moves through different phases of group membership' (p. 152). This process involves role transitions, and variations in type and magnitude of commitment to the group.

The self-categorization analysis of cohesiveness does not conflict with any of these ideas. Rather, it provides a comprehensive metatheoretical framework and a restricted set of explicit and interrelated theoretical social psychological constructs to account for commitment, identification, normative force, consensual realities, sense of community, role transition, and so forth.

Interpersonal attraction and personal relationships

At the core of the self-categorization analysis of group cohesiveness lies the crucial distinction between group-membership-based, depersonalized social attraction, and interpersonal-relationship-based, idiosyncratic personal attraction.

This distinction is similar to that made by Jennings (1947a) between 'sociogroups, . . . where sociometric structure is based on a criterion which is *collective*' (p. 71) and 'psychegroups, . . . where sociometric structure is based on [a] strictly *private* criterion which is totally *personal*' (p. 71). Jennings (1947b) proposes that 'the psychegroup . . . is an interpersonal structure where the uniqueness of the individual as a personality is appreciated. . . . [W]here one counts "altogether" as a person, not merely as an individual or as a group member', while in a sociogroup 'only certain aspects of personality are appreciated by other members, as only certain aspects are appropriate to the tasks important in the specific sociogroup life' (p. 33). Jennings observes that 'within the sociogroup, there may be many members chosen by others as sociogroup members who *at the same time* are rejected or unchosen by these same individuals in the latter's several psychegroups' (pp. 33–4).

Anderson's (1975) distinction between socioemotional and task-related functions of groups also has a passing resemblance to a distinction between personal and social attraction. On closer examination, however, it becomes clear that Anderson is distinguishing not between interpersonal and group levels of processing, but simply between different types of groups on the basis of their goals and purposes. Cohesiveness expresses itself differently depending upon the principal or primary function of the group – as interpersonal attraction in socioemotional groups, and as willingness to stay in the group (*inter alia*) in task-orientated groups.

Although much of the interpersonal attraction and relationships literature assumes that 'the phenomena of attraction are undifferentiated (except in degree)' (Newcomb, 1960, p. 104) – that is, 'may be described in terms of sign (plus or minus) and intensity' (Newcomb, 1961, p. 6), there are those who feel that profound qualitative differences exist. Marlowe and Gergen, for example, write: 'The differences among such phenomena as the comradeship felt by members of a team, the respect held for a powerful leader, sexual attraction for a person of the opposite sex, a mother's devotion for a child, and the gratitude of a person relieved of distress far outweigh the similarities' (Marlowe and Gergen, 1969, p. 622; see also Berscheid, 1985; Huston, 1974; McCarthy, 1981).

For example, Newcomb (1960) has discovered that interindividual attraction in highly cohesive groups tends to be based primarily on admiration and value support, while in less cohesive groups it is based on perceived reciprocation. Similarly, Segal argues for a theoretical separation of 'interpersonal affect based on pair relationships from feelings of respect based on individual behaviour seen as benefiting the group' (Segal, 1979, p. 260), and furnishes evidence that friendship is mutually reciprocated affect, while respect and liking are more unidirectional and group based. Along similar lines are Roger Brown's (1965, pp. 71–93) distinction between symmetrical solidarity relationships (characterized by use of the French familiar pronoun 'tu') and asymmetrical status relationships ('vous'), Rubin's (1973) distinction between affection and respect, and Triandis's (1977) distinction between – *inter alia* – liking and admiration. Finally, Hare (1962) urges caution in sociometric studies to distinguish between liking based on interpersonal factors and liking based on group membership.

Recent trends in research on personal relationships (see Mikula, 1984) include an emphasis on the way true personal relationships (and concomitant attraction) develop out of attraction phenomena based in more general and less idiosyncratic or personal relationships between individuals (see Huston and Levinger, 1978). Duck, for example, writes: 'One clear difference between liking relations is that some are long term (with a past history of complex interdependency, shared experience and so forth) and some are short term (spontaneously evoked liking towards a perfect stranger)' (Duck, 1977a, p. 15). He believes that 'at the most early points of an encounter the two people in an interaction are stimulus *objects* for each other rather than stimulus *persons*. It is not until later that their personalities emerge for one another and they become people rather than things or role occupants or stereotypes' (*ibid.*, p. 96). This diachronic model is not inconsistent with Fiske's (1982; Fiske and Neuberg, 1990) continuum model of impression formation, which I discuss below.

In contrast to the familiar view that belief and attitude similarity lead to attraction (Byrne, 1971; Griffitt, 1974), Duck believes that beliefs and attitudes are reliable cues to deeper construct similarities, where constructs are people's theories about the world (Kelly, 1955, 1970). Construct similarity facilitates interaction and thus generates attraction (Duck, 1973a, b, 1977b, c). Duck believes that close personal relationships 'provide opportunities to test the most subjective (and otherwise untestable) constructs: namely, those about other people's personality' (1977c, p. 386). Running through Duck's account is a clear distinction between short-term attraction based on widely shared constructs, and long-term friendship based on deep and idiosyncratic personal constructs. Although this maps fairly well on to the social versus personal attraction distinction I have proposed, Duck does not ground the former in a conceptualization of group membership – his concern is explicitly to theorize interpersonal relationships.

Along similar lines, Lea (1991; Lea and Duck, 1982) distinguishes between common and uncommon value similarity. General liking relationships among relative strangers are influenced by perceived similarity of common values (i.e. widely shared in the relevant population). Over time, as the relationship endures, friendship becomes less influenced by common value similarity, but dependent on uncommon value similarity (i.e. similarity regarding values that are not widely shared by others in the relevant population). From a self-categorization perspective, we could replace the terms common and uncommon value similarity with the terms group-prototypical similarity and idiosyncratic interpersonal similarity, and then relate these different levels of similarity to social and personal attraction respectively.

This brief and intentionally selective section on interpersonal attraction and relationships reveals that distinctions are made between different forms of attraction that resonate to varying degrees with a distinction between group-based and interpersonal attraction.

Interpersonal and group-level cognitive processing

Social identity theory considers that social behaviour varies along a continuum from entirely interpersonal to entirely inter- and intragroup. This behavioural continuum is underpinned by a continuum of self-conceptualization: from entirely in terms of personal identity to entirely in terms of social identity. Associated with these continua is a discontinuity between personal-identity-based interpersonal behaviour (including personal attraction) and social-identity-based group behaviour (including social attraction). The latter is theorized in terms of social categorization processes.

Self-categorization theory attributes the qualitative discontinuity between interpersonal and group processes to the level of abstraction of categorization. Intermediate-level categorization of people in terms of groups depersonalizes perception in terms of group prototypes – producing social attraction. Categorization of people as unique idiosyncratic individuals individuates or personalizes perception – producing personal attraction.

Related ideas exist. For example, Brewer (1988) has suggested a dual-process model of impression formation in which top–down, category-based information processing is distinguished from bottom–up, data-driven, person-based (personalized) information processing. Automatic stimulus appraisal (called 'identification') determines whether the threshold for further information processing is reached. If it is, a combination of stimulus and situational properties influences degree of 'self-involvement', which in turn determines whether subsequent conscious processing is category- or person-based. High self-involvement (i.e. feeling closely related to or interdependent with the stimulus person, or being ego involved in the task) selects the data-driven, person-based mode. This mode is bottom–up in that impression construction proceeds from the most concrete until a 'satisfactory' representation is reached.

The preferred mode of processing, however, is category-based, as it is cognitively more parsimonious. It is top–down in that impression construction proceeds from the most abstract until a 'satisfactory' representation is reached. For category-based processing, 'satisfactory' refers to an optimal level of distinctiveness (Brewer, 1991), in which a fundamental human tension between a need for similarity and a need for difference is resolved within the context of an overarching categorization.

Brewer does not, however, deal directly with the relationship between these cognitive processes and attraction. In contrast, the depersonalized attraction hypothesis explains how self-categorization produces group-based liking. In this way it deals with the important relationship between cognition and affect, or valenced judgement. Fiske (1982) argues that although a distinction must be drawn between affect, which relates to arousal and activation, and evaluation or preference, which relates to attitude or valenced judgement, the two are generally highly correlated and so tend to come together as a package. She goes on to describe what she calls a continuum model of the cognitive production of affective reaction (Fiske, 1982, 1988; Fiske and Neuberg, 1990; Neuberg and Fiske, 1987). (See Fiske and Taylor [1991, pp. 409–61] for a detailed overview of other perspectives on the relationship between cognition and affect.)

A distinction is made between piecemeal and schema-based information processing. The latter involves holistic, category-based processing of people which can occur at different levels of consensuality ranging from highly consensual cultural schemas, through intermediate subcultural schemas, to idiosyncratic individuating schemas. Schema-based processing takes priority, as it satisfies the dictates of cognitive parsimony. It is only on the rare occasions when a person does not fit into any preexistent schema that piecemeal processing is resorted to. Piecemeal processing involves elemental, data-driven information processing, in which affect is constructed from isolated elements of valenced information. Schema-based affect comes automatically attached to the relevant schema.

There are striking similarities between this model and the self-categorization notion of levels of abstraction. The former distinguishes between degrees of consensuality of a schema, while the latter distinguishes between levels of abstraction of a category and attendant prototype. The principal difference is that although Fiske talks of 'stereotypic or schema based evaluation' (1982, p. 61), hers is not a theory of group behaviour – rather, it is an explanation of individual social information processing. Fiske's linkage of cognition and affect resonates quite nicely with the depersonalized attraction idea. Specifically, where Fiske talks of affect based on relatively consensual schemas at the subcultural level, self-categorization theory would talk of social-identity-based attitude, or social attraction; and where she believes that once activated, 'schematic match determines affective response' (Fiske, 1982, p. 61), self-categorization theory talks about group prototypicality determining interindividual attitude.

Together, Brewer's dual-process model and optimal distinctiveness theory, and Fiske's continuum model, add convergent validity to the notion of depersonalized attraction.

The intergroup dimension

Perhaps the metatheoretically and theoretically most important and novel aspect of the self-categorization/social identity perspective on group cohesiveness is that it treats inter- and intragroup relations as inextricable. One cannot be theorized social psychologically in isolation from the other, since they are both psychologically produced by the same processes.

Ethnocentrism

The first point about an intergroup dimension is that it relates to Sumner's notion of ethnocentrism, in which he argues that 'The insiders in a we-group are in a relation of peace, order, law, government, and industry to each other. Their relation to all outsiders, or others-groups, is one of war and plunder, except in so far as agreements have modified it' (Sumner, 1906, p. 12). In other words, all things being equal, intragroup attraction is positive (liking) and intergroup attraction negative (disliking). LeVine and Campbell (1972) suggest that the intragroup liking aspect of ethnocentrism may arise as an expression of self-love (i.e. narcissism) at the group level (i.e. group narcissism). That is to say: in groups, love of self is generalized to the group as a whole.

The notion of ethnocentric attraction also surfaces in, for example, Andreyeva and Gozman's (1981) discussion of interpersonal attraction in an intergroup context. They distinguish between intragroup and intergroup attraction, and argue that such group-level attraction is determined by stereotypic perceptions such that whether one likes an ingroup member or an outgroup member depends on the valence of the relevant stereotype. Although Andreyeva and Gozman do not explore the implications of this idea in terms of theories of intergroup relations, group processes, social identity, self-categorization, prototypicality, and so forth, they are clearly thinking along similar lines to that embodied by the notion of depersonalized attraction.

The depersonalized attraction idea provides a theory to explain not only intragroup attraction, but also intergroup attraction, and therefore accounts for ethnocentrism. Sumner originally believed that ethnocentrism would occur on all dimensions of group difference; however, subsequent research has shown that this is not the case. The dimensions on which ethnocentrism is expressed depend on specifics of the intergroup context (Brewer and Campbell, 1976). However, Brewer (1981; Brewer and Campbell, 1976) identifies a limited number of universal dimensions of ethnocentrism, which embrace affective components such as trust, honesty and loyalty. Presumably we could include attraction here.

Intergroup conflict

Literature on intergroup aspects of cohesiveness tends to focus mainly on the relationship between intergroup conflict and intragroup cohesion. We are all familiar with this phenomenon, ranging from enhanced national solidarity in times of international conflict (e.g. the 1991 Gulf conflict) to accentuated team cohesion during competitive team games. Sumner believed that there was a direct and functional relationship between intergroup conflict and intragroup cohesion: 'The exigencies of war with outsiders are what make peace inside, lest internal discord should weaken the we-group for war' (Sumner, 1906, p. 12).

Indeed, research tends to support this view, both at the macrosocial level of international and interethnic relations (see Brewer and Campbell, 1976; LeVine and Campbell, 1972) and at the microsocial level of small interactive groups (see Dion, 1979). For example, intergroup conflict has been found to increase ingroup cohesion among boys at a summer camp (Sherif, 1966), soldiers at a training camp (Julian, Bishop and Fiedler, 1966), workers at an American car plant (Stagner and Eflal, 1982), members of a rifle team (A. Myers, 1962) and subjects in a prisoners' dilemma experiment (Deutsch, 1949b).

However, intergroup conflict/threat does not inevitably enhance cohesion. If individualistic responses are available or are preferred, then intergroup conflict/threat can cause group disintegration (see Fisher, 1990; Stein, 1976). For example, from a study of international conflict and intranational cohesion in seventy-one countries over a six-year period, Wang (1977) found that while moderate international conflict always enhanced intranational cohesion, extreme conflict did so only in politically integrated and economically developed countries. In other countries, extreme international conflict produced internal conflict (see Fisher, 1990, pp. 64–8). Other research, employing the minimal group paradigm (e.g. Billig and Tajfel, 1973; see below), has repeatedly shown that ethnocentrism (ingroup favouritism, intergroup discrimination, ingroup liking) can readily be produced by social categorization *per se*, in the complete absence of conflictual intergroup relations (also see Sachdev and Bourhis, 1984, 1985, 1987, 1991). Intergroup conflict may not, therefore, be necessary for ingroup cohesion, but it quite definitely can be instrumental in its accentuation.

Sumner (1906) believed in a reciprocal relationship between intergroup conflict and intragroup cohesion. We have noted that intergroup conflict may not be necessary for intragroup cohesion, but that in general it does enhance it. However, there is little evidence for the reverse relationship: that enhanced cohesion produces intergroup conflict. For example, in one of the very few experiments to address this question, Dion (1973) experimentally manipulated the cohesiveness of *ad hoc* groups (via false feedback of attitude and value similarity) and assessed subsequent behaviour and attitude towards ingroupers and outgroupers. He found that increased cohesiveness was associated with more cooperative behaviour towards the ingroup but no significant decrement in cooperative behaviour towards the outgroup (see Figure 7.1). This effect was also obtained on measures of attitude towards ingroupers and outgroupers.

There is an important lesson here. Intragroup relations are affected by the nature of the relevant intergroup context, while the nature of intergroup relations cannot be inferred so easily from an analysis of intragroup relations in isolation from the intergroup context. This, of course, is a pivotal argument in the critique of individualism that frames the social identity perspective (see Chapter 4).

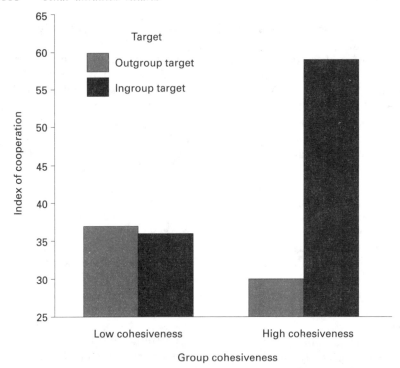

Figure 7.1 *Cooperative behaviour towards ingroup and outgroup targets as a function of ingroup cohesiveness. (This figure is based on data from Dion (1973).)*

Patterns of attraction within groups

Intergroup conflict appears to produce a more differentiated intragroup structure (e.g. Stagner and Eflal, 1982). This can be associated with differential intragroup attraction in which fringe members are made scapegoats for the group and are consequently disliked. For example, Lauderdale, Smith-Cunnien, Parker and Inverarity (1984) found that a legal discussion group whose continued existence was called into question by a high-status 'expert' (who was disapproving and critical of the quality of their discussion) distinguished sharply between the least popular member in the group and the rest. Those groups not so threatened were much less rejecting of the unpopular member. The critical 'expert' can be considered to represent a conflictual relationship with an outgroup. Intergroup conflict, then, produced enhanced cohesion among the group – perhaps at the cost of an evaluative downgrading of fringe members.

A similar finding emerges from recent research into what has been called the 'black-sheep effect' (Marques, 1990; Marques and Yzerbyt, 1988;

Marques, Yzerbyt and Leyens, 1988). In a series of experiments, these authors were able to show that in an intergroup comparative context an equivalent relatively poor performance (on a relevant dimension of intergroup comparison) by an ingroup member and an outgroup member was evaluated differently. The ingrouper was significantly downgraded relative to the outgrouper on attitudinal dimensions: this is dubbed the black-sheep effect. For example, Marques and Yzerbyt (1988) had Law students compare their feelings towards a fellow Law student (ingrouper) and a Philosophy student (outgrouper), where both had given a bad speech, or both had given a good speech. As predicted, the fellow Law student who had given a bad speech was downgraded relative to the Philosophy student who had given an equally bad speech (see Figure 7.2).

These studies suggest that intragroup attitude is more sensitive to variations in members' behaviour on protoypical (e.g. important, group-defining) dimensions than is intergroup attitude. This intragroup sensitivity may even manifest itself in the development of differentiated prototypes of the

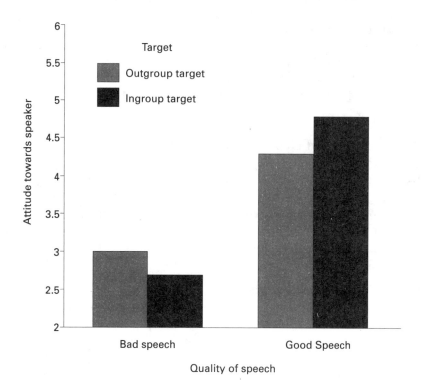

Figure 7.2 *Attitude towards good and bad speakers as a function of speakers' group membership. (Data from Marques and Yzerbyt (1988). This figure is adapted from Figure 8.4 in Marques (1990, p. 146). © 1988 John Wiley & Sons. Reprinted by permission of John Wiley & Sons.)*

'best' and 'worst' group members. For example, Charles (1982) found that forest rangers in Yellowstone National Park had clear prototypes of the 'naturalist' ranger (understands and appreciates the scenic wonder of the park, welcomes visitors as guests, and deals with rule violations educationally) and the 'policeman' ranger (cares little about the scenic wonders of the park, views visitors with suspicion and alarm, and deals with rule violations punitively). There was wide agreement that it was better to be a 'naturalist' than a 'policeman'.

Direct empirical issues

There is potentially an enormous empirical literature that could be reviewed to assess the depersonalized attraction perspective on group cohesiveness. It is not my intention to do this here, as comprehensive and detailed reviews of much of this literature already exist (e.g. Lott and Lott, 1965) and I have summarized empirical findings from this literature in Chapter 3. The emphasis of this book is conceptual, so I will restrict myself here to a summary of some examples of findings that are *problematic* for a traditional attraction formulation of cohesiveness. I shall dwell in more detail on a small number of recent direct tests of social attraction predictions.

Necessary and sufficient conditions for group solidarity

Research shows that group cohesiveness, traditionally defined, generally enhances group productivity (e.g. Schachter *et al.*, 1951) and performance (Goodacre, 1951), increases conformity to group norms (Festinger *et al.*, 1950), improves morale and job satisfaction (Exline, 1957; Gross, 1954), facilitates intragroup communication (Knowles and Brickner, 1981), reduces intragroup hostility and directs it towards an outgroup (Pepitone and Reichling, 1955), and increases feelings of self-worth. However, there are many exceptions (see Hogg, 1987; Lott and Lott, 1965). For example, factors that usually create liking (e.g. proximity, attitude similarity, cooperation) do not elevate cohesiveness if there is an emotionally charged or salient category boundary (e.g. class, ethnicity) between interactants, and succeed in elevating cohesiveness only within the confines of an already well-established common category membership (e.g. Brewer and Silver, 1978; Brown and Turner, 1981; Byrne and Wong, 1962; Doise, Csepeli, Dann, Gouge, Larsen and Ostell, 1972; Gundlach, 1956; Kandel, 1978; Sole, Marton and Hornstein, 1975).

Groups which suffer failure presumably do not mediate rewards for their members and consequently should experience reduced cohesiveness. However, everyday experience tells us that such groups (e.g. sports teams) can often bounce back with enhanced solidarity. This tallies well with historical documentation of national, ethnic or military groups through the ages which emerge from defeat or deprivation with heightened solidarity (see Herodotus's account of classical Greek history). There is also experimental evidence for this (e.g. Turner *et al.*, 1984).

Social anthropology furnishes rich examples of social groups that do not appear to depend on interpersonal attraction for their existence, maintenance or solidarity. For example, Ruth Benedict's ethnography of the Dobu of North West Melanesia describes them as a social unit that abides by shared norms and engages in collective rituals, yet is not characterized by interpersonal attraction (Benedict, 1935, pp. 94–119). Instead, liking is used as a strategic weapon to inflict revenge on adversaries in a cutthroat world of dog-eat-dog. In Chapter 8 I discuss in detail two further problematic areas: groupthink and group productivity.

The thesis that interpersonal attraction, or attraction-to-group, is the defining feature of group cohesiveness is perhaps most difficult to accept in the light of findings from studies adopting the minimal group paradigm: a paradigm in which experimental subjects are explicitly categorized as, for example, X or Y group members on a minimal (e.g. alleged preference for painters) or completely random (e.g. toss of a coin) basis. In addition to the absence of all the usual preconditions for interpersonal attraction, group membership is also anonymous. These experiments repeatedly and consistently find that group behaviour (e.g. intergroup discrimination, ingroup favour-itism, homogeneous group perceptions, ingroup liking) can occur in the absence of all the traditional determinants of interpersonal attraction (see Tajfel, 1982b, p. 24). The necessary and sufficient condition seems to be the explicit categorization of a person as a group member (e.g. Billig and Tajfel, 1973; Sachdev and Bourhis, 1991).

Friendship, liking, categorization, and cohesiveness

A crucial experimental focus is the comparison of categorization and interpersonal attraction *per se* in the production of group behaviour. Turner *et al.* (1983; see Hogg, 1987) conducted a minimal group study in which subjects were randomly (toss of a coin) aggregated (simply had similar code numbers) or categorized (into group A or B). Other subjects were aggregated or categorized by the explicit criterion that they were with 'the people that on the whole you like', or that they were with 'the rest' (on the basis of a pre-test questionnaire). So there were aggregates or groups of people whom everyone in the session allegedly liked (popular individuals), or did not like (unpopular individuals), or about whom there was no liking information. The results can be interpreted as showing that in the absence of explicit social categorization, people discriminated more in favour of those whom they and others liked (see Figure 7.3). Categorization strongly enhanced ingroup favouritism and transformed the subjective meaning of the attraction information: the absence or presence of a criterion of group membership now acquired greater importance than the valence of the attraction information constituting the criterion. Subjects discriminated more in favour of a criterial category (popular or unpopular) than a random category.

Hogg and Turner (1985a; see Hogg, 1987) modified this experiment to investigate the role of interpersonal attraction *per se*, unconfounded with the consensual and intergroup dimensions contained in the manipulation of popularity. Subjects in a minimal group study were aggregated with individuals whom they believed (on the basis of a pre-test questionnaire) they would like or dislike. They believed that attraction was the criterion of aggregation. Other subjects were explicitly categorized on this basis, while a third group of subjects were randomly categorized and led to believe that 'by

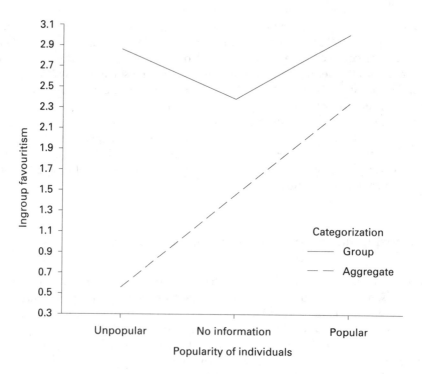

Figure 7.3 *Ingroup favouritism as a function of categorization and popularity. (This figure is compiled from Factor 1 cell means in Table 2 in Turner, Sachdev and Hogg (1983, p. 233).)*

chance' it had 'turned out' that they would like, or dislike, their fellow group members. There was greater solidarity among members of an uncategorized aggregate of people who liked one another than disliked one another (see Figure 7.4). Criterial categorization accentuated this effect, while – most interestingly – random categorization abolished it, and on some variables reversed it. These findings illustrate how interpersonal effects can be transformed by categorization. In this case, random categorization dissociated interpersonal liking from the group such that incidental information about liking became irrelevant to group solidarity. Criterial categorization explicitly linked interpersonal attraction to the group, thus making member valence relevant to the life of the group. Hence, positive (liked) members were liked more than negative (disliked) members. The fact that this effect is stronger in a group than in an aggregate suggests that different processes may be operating.

In another minimal group study (Hogg and Turner, 1985b; see Hogg,

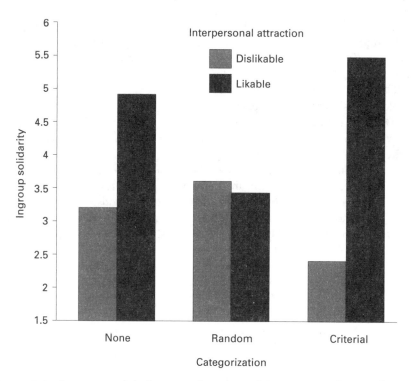

Figure 7.4 *Ingroup solidarity as a function of interpersonal attraction and categorization. (This figure is compiled from cell means in Table 3 in Hogg and Turner (1985a, p. 59). 'Ingroup solidarity' is a composite index from the principal variables of liking, group favourableness, and ingroup favouritism, in a group identification factor.)*

1987) we conducted a further investigation of the difference between interpersonal attraction and group-based social attraction. Subjects were explicitly categorized or merely aggregated, ostensibly as five-person groups, and formed impressions of three-item personality profiles of ingroup and outgroup members. The profiles were carefully constructed so that both ingroup and outgroup members were idiosyncratically likable or dislikable (the personal attractiveness variable), and ingroup members had a common likable trait while the outgroup members had a common dislikable trait, or vice versa (the social attractiveness variable). To try to distinguish between interpersonal and group effects, subjects were asked to evaluate their impressions of individual ingroup and outgroup members, and their impressions of the groups as a whole. The reasoning behind this – admittedly relatively crude – attempt to distinguish between interpersonal and group perceptions is that while depersonalized prototypical perceptions and feelings would underpin equally reactions to the group as a whole and specific group members, a focus on specific individuals, as opposed to the group as a whole, would elevate the relative salience of interpersonal relations against a background of depersonalized perception. We found that subjects explicitly categorized as a socially attractive ingroup expressed differential intergroup behaviour favouring the ingroup, but were unaffected by the personal attractiveness of group members. In contrast, interpersonal perceptions were unaffected by categorization or social attractiveness: subjects simply preferred likable to dislikable individuals.

There is further evidence for a distinction between social and personal attraction. For example, in his well-known boys' camp studies, Sherif (1966) allowed close interpersonal friendships to form during the first few days of the camp. In constituting the groups, he then made sure that each boy's nominated best friend was in an opposing group. Group cohesion was not reduced or undermined by the absence of close friends. Furthermore, the initial existence of intergroup interpersonal friendships had little effect in reducing ingroup loyalty and intergroup hostility. In fact, by the end of the study 90 per cent of boys nominated ingroup members as best friends.

There is other evidence that contexts which make shared reference groups salient increase mutual intermember attraction (e.g. Boyanowsky and Allen, 1973; Burnstein and McRae, 1962; Feshbach and Singer, 1957; Minard, 1952). Relatedly, Gaertner, Mann, Dovidio and Murrell (1989) had subjects conceive of themselves as six unique individuals, two three-person groups, or one six-person group. The usual preferential liking for ingroup over outgroup was obtained in the two-groups condition. Liking for erstwhile outgroup members increased in the one-group condition, where they were now considered fellow ingroup member. This demonstrates how the valence of social attraction for the same person depends on whether that person is considered an in- or outgroup member. Liking for erstwhile ingroup members actually *decreased* in the six-individuals condition. This illustrates two important points: (1) interpersonal attraction among aggregated individuals is not the same thing as social attraction among group members, and (2) group membership can accentuate positive attitude towards people.

Another interesting datum comes from Bakeman and Helmreich's (1975) study of four-person groups living in a deepsea chamber. These groups were continually monitored by television for one week, and it was discovered that cohesiveness (operationalized as how often groupmates helped one another) was significantly related to time spent on task activities but not significantly related to time spent in friendly gregarious interaction. Once again, friendly interpersonal relations (interpersonal attraction) are unrelated to group behaviour.

Finally, Bonacich (1972) found that friendliness and solidarity increased among members of a mutually cooperative five-person group playing a prisoners' dilemma game (PDG), but that the friendliness did not generalize beyond the PDG context. This effect can be interpreted in social attraction terms − the contextually discontinuous friendliness and liking may be group-based social attraction contingent on self-categorization in terms of the PDG group, rather than true interpersonal attraction. Another PDG study by Dion (1973) pitted dyads against each other to investigate the relationship between group cohesiveness and intergroup discrimination. The hypothesized positive relationship did not emerge. This is not surprising. Group cohesiveness was operationalized as interpersonal compatibility and congeniality regarding general interests, personality, etc. − all of which are more likely to create personal than social attraction, and to be unrelated to group processes.

Depersonalized attraction and group solidarity

The depersonalized attraction hypothesis produces a range of testable predictions, of which only a few have so far been addressed. However, the core idea that self-categorization depersonalizes the basis of interindividual attraction, such that ingroup individuals (and self) are liked in proportion to their perceived group prototypicality, does have some support. It is perhaps important to reiterate here that social and personal attraction differ regarding their generative base, but are both subjectively experienced as a positive or negative sentiment by one individual for another.

Lott and Lott (1965) document studies showing that people are attracted more to ingroup members who are perceived as 'better' than their fellows in ways relevant to or important for the group (e.g. more successful, correct, competent, normative). Codol (1975) has provided more recent evidence for this effect from a long series of experiments investigating the *'primus inter pares'*, or PIP, effect. From a review of sociometric choice studies, Hare (1962) concludes that despite some evidence for generically attractive personality traits (e.g. Hunt and Solomon, 1942), 'popularity appears to be related to the extent to which a person exemplifies the group ideal' (1962, p. 141), and 'the "popular" person may represent the "ideal" or "norm" of the group' (*ibid.*, p. 142). Hare's observation that 'friendliness involves two-way or reciprocated choices, whereas popularity involves only one-way choices' (*ibid.*, pp. 141–2) is reflected in Segal's (1979) distinction between mutually reciprocated affect (friendship) and unidirectional group-based affect (respect and liking).

Some direct evidence for the prototypical nature of depersonalized ingroup liking is provided by an experiment in which four-person single-sex groups made estimates of autokinetic movement under conditions accentuating individuality or sex-category membership (Hogg and Hardie, 1992a). The degree of convergence of estimates within the group across trials (i.e. conformity) was an index of group behaviour and identification with the group. Dependent measures monitored liking and perceptions of proto-typicality within the group, so that it was possible to compute the amount of intermember agreement on who was liked most and who was most prototypical. As predicted, female groups in the high salience condition converged more sharply and had a more consensual pattern of liking and perceived prototypicality. The results for males were less consistent. However, across all subjects we found that groups that converged most sharply had the most consensual patterns of liking and perceived prototypicality. This suggests that in psychologically salient groups, liking is related to prototypicality.

This same idea was tested under more controlled experimental conditions allowing for accurate location of the ingroup prototype. We conducted two very similar studies (Hogg and Hardie, 1992b) employing a conformity/group polarization paradigm (see Chapter 6), in which subjects were exposed to ingroup and outgroup positions on a choice dilemma in anticipation of group discussion and intergroup debate. It was possible to measure the relationship between how much, on the one hand, subjects liked fellow group members, and, on the other, how prototypical of the group they felt fellow members were, and how similar to self they felt they were. There were also measures of self-prototypicality and feelings about the group as a whole. In both experiments, the relationship between liking and interpersonal similarity was unrelated to the relationship between liking and perceived group proto-typicality of fellow members – in other words, as predicted, interpersonal similarity and group prototypicality were separate and unrelated bases of interindividual attitude. Furthermore, the positive prototypicality/liking relationship was strengthened for those subjects who categorized themselves more strongly as group members (i.e. rated themselves highly group-prototypical, expressed stronger ingroup preference, and conformed more strongly to group norms). The positive similarity/liking relationship was unaffected or weakened by self-categorization.

In another study (Hogg, Hardie and Bailey, 1991), university students

($N=334$) enrolled in either the Arts or the Science faculty formed an impression of a five-trait profile which was highly Arts- or highly Science-faculty prototypical. The two profiles were carefully constructed to be equally likable. For half the subjects, faculty membership was made salient through verbal and written instructions; for the others it was not. The focal dependent variables, for the purpose of the brief description given here, were: (1) attitude towards the profiled student (a composite of liking, trust, respect, similarity, and desire to meet the student); (2) correlation between attitude and perceived faculty-prototypicality of the profiled student; and (3) correlation between this relationship and perceived faculty prototypicality of self.

The results for Science students were complicated, but Arts students behaved as predicted (see Table 7.1). Faculty salience produced an ethnocentric preference for ingroup over outgroup by reversing a low salience preference for the outgroup profile. In the high salience condition, attitude towards and perceived faculty prototypicality of the ingroup target were more highly correlated than in the other conditions. This relationship was positively related to perceived self-prototypicality. Together, these suggest that category salience transforms the basis of interindividual appraisal to one based on prototypicality, and that the magnitude of such a transformation is a function of prototypical self-perception.

A further test of the role of prototypical perception in liking in groups focused on the prediction that while overall interpersonal similarity would influence liking where group membership was not salient (cf. Byrne's [1971] similarity–attraction hypothesis), only similarity on prototypical dimensions would have any effect under conditions of group salience. In a rather complicated experiment (Hogg, Hardie and Reynolds, 1992) we manipulated information about interindividual similarity on two dimensions, under conditions accentuating group membership or accentuating interpersonal relationships and individuality. One dimension was potentially prototypical of the group. We found that subjects' attitude (a composite of liking, wanting to meet, and wanting to work with the target person) towards the target was

Table 7.1 *Attitude, and attitude × prototypicality relationships, as a function of faculty salience and group membership of target: Arts faculty students*

Dependent variables	Cell means			
	Low salience		High salience	
	Ingroup	Outgroup	Ingroup	Outgroup
Attitude	4.72	5.22	5.15	4.95
Attitude × target prototypicality	−.01	.11	.18	.03
Self-prototypicality × (attitude × target prototypicality)	.13	.18	.30	.00

Note: Adapted from Tables 1 and 2 in Hogg, Hardie and Bailey (1991). Means are Pearson's correlation coefficients, except attitude, which can take values between 1 and 9.

affected as predicted (see Figure 7.5). In the interpersonal condition attitude was not significantly affected by whether the target was similar or different on the prototypical dimension, but in the group condition a significantly more favourable attitude was expressed towards the prototypically similar target than the prototypically dissimilar target. The prototypically dissimilar and prototypically similar targets were rated by subjects not to differ significantly regarding overall interpersonal similarity to self. The obtained effect on attitude thus appears to reflect perceptions of depersonalized prototypical similarity under conditions of salient self-categorization.

An additional finding was that group subjects who identified more strongly with the group (in terms of perceiving themselves fitting into the group, and enjoying working with the group) had a more favourable attitude towards the target. The correlation between attitude and identification was stronger for the prototypically similar target (see Figure 7.6). A final correlational analysis revealed that group subjects' attitude towards the target

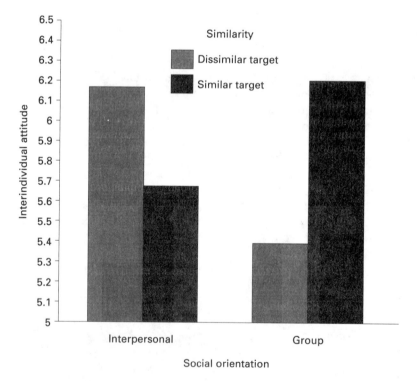

Figure 7.5 *Interindividual attitude as a function of social orientation and prototypical similarity. (This figure is compiled from cell means in Table 3 in Hogg et al. (1992). Interindividual attitude can take values from 1 to 9. F(1,211) = 15.71, p<0.001. The difference between dissimilar and similar targets in the interpersonal condition was not significant.)*

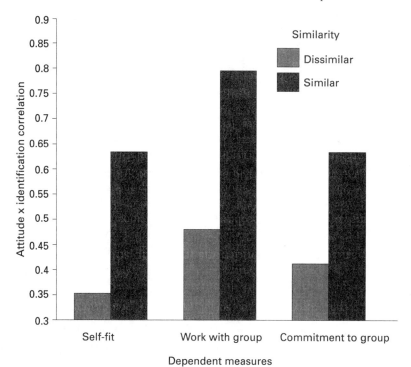

Figure 7.6 *Correlation between attitude and group identification, and attitude and target commitment, as a function of prototypical similarity. (This figure is compiled from means in Table 5 in Hogg* et al. *(1992).)*

was positively correlate with the perceived commitment to the group of the target, and that this was stronger for prototypically similar than for dissimilar targets (see Figure 7.6).

To complement these laboratory experiments, we conducted a field study of an Australian football team (Hogg and Hardie, 1991). A questionnaire was administered at a team practice session to elicit subjective perceptions of prototypical features of the team, and a rating of self-prototypicality. Respondents then rank-ordered fellow members in terms of prototypicality, social attraction, and personal attraction. These last two were elicited by special instructions making the team or interpersonal friendships, respectively, salient. As predicted, we found a significantly stronger relationship between social attraction and target prototypicality than between personal attraction and prototypicality. We also found that this effect was strongest for those subjects who identified most strongly with the team, and saw themselves as highly prototypical. In addition, there was a stronger relationship between being socially popular (i.e. consensually liked as a team member) and prototypically popular (i.e. consensually rated as highly prototypical) than personally popular (i.e. consensually liked as a personal friend) and prototypically popular. Members who were most socially and prototypically popular were also those who themselves identified most strongly with the team, and defined themselves as most prototypical (cf. Hogg, Cooper-Shaw and Holzworth, in press).

One implication of the depersonalized attraction idea is that lay explanations for social attraction will tend to rely less on stable internal idiosyncrasies of the target (i.e. personality – cf. Weiner, 1986) than will lay explanations for personal attraction. Another way to put this is that lay explanations for social attraction will be less prone to what Ross (1977) has called the fundamental attribution error (the tendency to make internal attributions for others' behaviour) than will lay explanations of personal attraction. The attribution literature has not addressed the sorts of explanations people give for group- or interpersonal-based liking (see Harvey and Weary, 1984; Hewstone, 1989; Kelley and Michela, 1980; Ross and Fletcher, 1985). As a preliminary investigation of this idea (Hogg and Hardie, 1990) we content-analyzed 477 students' lay explanations for their feelings about likable and dislikable friends of theirs, and people they knew who were members of the same – or different – groups as themselves. A number of dimensions, including personality, emerged. We then constructed profiles to convey information relevant to all the dimensions obtained, and had subjects rate the importance of each dimension in influencing their feelings about the profiled hypothetical person. The profiles were presented as being of ingroup members, outgroup members, or personal acquaintances. As predicted, personality was considered a significantly less important reason for liking an ingroup or outgroup member than a personal acquaintance (see Figure 7.7).

Metatheoretical issues

A central theme of this book is that traditional conceptualizations of group cohesiveness are, to varying degrees, reductionist. They approach the group from the perspective of interpersonal relationships among interactive individuals in small groups, and because of this they produce explanations that are conceptually dissociated from other group phenomena. In this and the previous chapter I have described and promoted an alternative non-reductionist approach that employs concepts dealing with the entire range of group behaviours.

To what extent does this new perspective satisfy claims (1) that it is non-reductionist, and (2) that it explains phenomena that are problematic for the traditional social cohesion model? The latter claim is addressed by the studies described in this chapter, and by issues dealt with in Chapter 8. The former – metatheoretical – claim is worth dealing with here.

This book is about group cohesiveness, so the emphasis has been upon

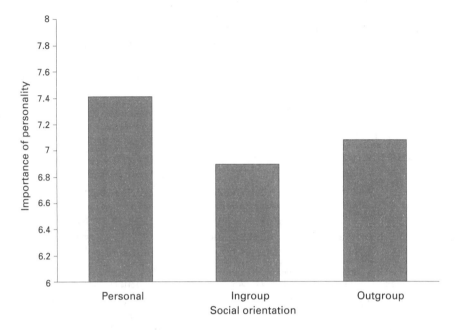

Figure 7.7 *Importance of personality as an explanation for liking, as a function of social orientation. (This figure is compiled from means in Table 2 in Hogg and Hardie (1990). 'Importance of personality' can take values between 1 and 9. The social orientation effect is significant at* $p<0.05$ *(F (2,215)=5.43).)*

discussion and critical examination of the traditional attraction-to-group formulation. However, in presenting an alternative perspective on group attraction in terms of self-categorization I have encompassed a range of other group phenomena. This, of course, is one of the strengths of the self-categorization perspective. Therefore, an assessment of the non-reductionist nature of the depersonalized attraction notion cannot be dissociated from an assessment of self-categorization and social identity theory as a whole. A recent forum for critical discussion of social identity theory and self-categorization theory is provided by Abrams and Hogg (1990a).

Turner and Oakes (1989) identify the crucial problem of individualism as being a failure to resolve the paradox that psychological processes are the province of individual minds, yet these minds are also produced by, and produce through interaction, emergent properties of societies that transcend individual minds. Individualistic theories are framed by the belief that 'the individual is the sole psychological and/or social reality, that the distinctive reality of the group or society is a fiction or a fallacy, that nothing "emerges" in social interaction' (Turner and Oakes, 1989, p. 238). Turner and Oakes argue that self-categorization theory is an example of the contrasting metatheory, interactionism, which explicitly recognizes the fundamental interdependence of individual (e.g. psychological process) and society (e.g. social process). One cannot be reduced to the other – they are dialectically related.

Doise (1986) differentiates between (I) intrapersonal, (II) interpersonal and situational, (III) positional, and (IV) ideological levels of explanation, and argues that complete explanations of social psychological phenomena need to articulate these four levels (see Chapter 4; see also Hewstone, 1989). Lorenzi-Cioldi and Doise (1990) have argued that self-categorization and social identity theories are located at Level I, and that they lack articulation with explanatory principles from other levels. This conclusion may, I suspect, be derived more from the intrapersonal cognitive appearance of self-categorization theory (e.g. Turner, 1985) than from an examination of the general social identity concept as a whole (e.g. Hogg and Abrams, 1988). Certainly, neither self-categorization nor social identity theory was ever intended to be so located. The general theory attributes certain generic forms of behaviour (e.g. ethnocentrism, perceptual homogeneity) to the operation of self-categorization (Level I) and social comparison (Level II?), and the situational and group-specific content of behaviour to situationally and historically conditioned subjective social beliefs to do with – for example – stereotypic dimensions, and relative status and prestige (Levels III and IV). (See discussion in Chapter 6 of measuring social identity.)

Recently, a number of people have questioned whether social identity and self-categorization theory pay sufficient attention to communication (e.g. Condor, 1990; Emler and Hopkins, 1990). It is argued that the shared representations underlying the social self-concept are constructed or refined through interindividual communication (cf. Owen's [1985] metaphor analysis of group cohesiveness, and Moscovici's [1961] theory of social representation, in Chapter 5); and, furthermore, that it is through communication and language that group behaviour is (usually) expressed. Without communication, social categories and group behaviour might very probably not exist at all. This is a valid point. However, the language, speech and communication aspect of the theory has been systematically researched since the mid 1970s, principally by Giles and Bourhis and their colleagues (e.g. Sachdev and Bourhis, 1990; see Chapter 8).

There is another criticism, which goes something like this. Social identity theory and self-categorization theory are reductionist because they reduce social processes to intrapsychic cognitive processes. Furthermore, the hypostatization of such processes introduces an element of inevitability and immutability into intergroup conflict, discrimination and prejudice, and thus ultimately contributes to a justification of a status quo in which dominant groups oppress subordinate groups. This sort of criticism surfaces with various emphases as part of the new discourse analysis approach in social psychology (e.g. Potter and Wetherell, 1987; see Chapter 4).

Apart from the fact that Henri Tajfel would turn in his grave if he were to hear such an interpretation of his ideas, this sort of criticism is unfounded – or, rather, it is founded upon certain misconceptions. First, any psychological theory has to deal with intrapsychic cognitive processes (Floyd Allport [1924] was quite correct in this respect at least!). The omission of such processes leaves one with sociological, physiological, or radical behaviourist theories. Second, cognitive processes can be conceptualized to operate in different ways to produce stasis or change: they are not by any means inevitably reductionist, nor do they inevitably reproduce and/or legitimate the status quo. Self-categorization, for example, is a process responsible for group, not interpersonal, behaviour, and it can produce social stasis or social change depending on the subjective belief structures and normative prescriptions associated with the salient identity. In other words, cognitive process is articulated with social process – the one is not reduced to the other. These arguments are dealt with in detail elsewhere (see Abrams and Hogg, 1990b; Hogg and McGarty, 1990; Chapter 4).

Conclusion

The aim of this chapter has been to evaluate the theoretical, empirical and metatheoretical status of a self-categorization perspective on group cohesiveness, in relation to the traditional social cohesion perspective. Conceptually, there appears to be a satisfying amount of consistency with ideas in relevant literature such as that dealing with social cognition and personal relationships. Furthermore, some of the core components of the social attraction argument have some indirect and direct empirical support – for example, there is some evidence for the personal/social attraction distinction, the relationship between social attraction and other group phenomena, and the depersonalized prototypical nature of group attraction. Further research is, of course, needed – not only to consolidate these findings, but to explore intergroup dimensions of social attraction, and the relationship between – and role of – mediating mechanisms (see end of Chapter 6).

In Chapter 8, the final chapter, I discuss ways in which a self-categorization perspective on group solidarity and cohesiveness may contribute new insights concerning some established group phenomena, and how it has a relevance beyond the small interactive groups to which the traditional group cohesiveness model is restricted. The idea is to illustrate the potential this new perspective may have to address a wide range of group-solidarity phenomena.

Chapter 8

Prospects and conclusions

In Chapter 2, I described the origins and development of the concept of group cohesiveness, and showed how it actually theorizes group solidarity in terms of interpersonal attraction based on goal-orientated mutual interdependence. This approach has produced a considerable literature, mainly prior to the late 1960s, documenting the antecedents and consequences of cohesiveness, and more recently a large number of cohesiveness scales (Chapter 3). There are, however, a number of well-documented theoretical and metatheoretical limitations of group cohesiveness that have, in association with historical trends in social psychology, contributed to its loss in popularity in mainstream social psychology (Chapter 4). Chapter 5 critically discusses explicit attempts that have been made to retheorize cohesiveness, as well as the potential relevance of social psychology research into other group processes, such as conformity.

Many of the concerns, themes and directions that emerge in Chapters 4 and 5 can be integrated and subsumed by a non-reductionist intergroup perspective on group processes. This perspective is formally expressed in social identity theory and self-categorization theory. Chapter 6 describes this approach and explains how it can theorize group attraction phenomena. Chapter 7 critically examines the theoretical, metatheoretical and empirical status of this approach to cohesiveness.

The utility of a self-categorization analysis of cohesiveness is further examined in this concluding chapter. The aim is to illustrate how a self-categorization analysis might open up new directions in research into established group phenomena. To this end, there is detailed critical discussion of some problematic areas of group cohesiveness research, specifically groupthink and group productivity/performance, which shows how an interpersonal attraction or attraction-to-group formulation may be partly responsible for the confusion, and how a reconceptualization in terms of self-categorization theory may help to identify a direction out.

One of the powerful features of a self-categorization perspective on cohesiveness is that it can deal equally well with small groups, large groups, transient groups, enduring groups, concentrated groups, dispersed groups, and so forth. For this reason, there is some discussion of this broader applicability of the concept – in the very different areas of social loafing and ethnolinguistic identity. The chapter closes with a few concluding comments about prospects for the future of group cohesiveness research.

Groupthink

Groupthink refers to deficient group decision-making processes that have a high probability of producing poor decisions with disastrous consequences. Janis (1972, 1982a) employed an archival method relying on retrospective accounts and content analysis to identify a constellation of features to be found in small decision-making groups that produce suboptimal decisions. He was particularly interested in suboptimal policy decisions with actual – or potential for – grave, widespread consequences. His analysis focused on US presidential decision-making groups involved in the 1961 Bay of Pigs fiasco, the 1950 escalation of the North Korean War, the defence of Pearl Harbor in 1941, and the escalation of the Vietnam War from 1964 to 1967. These allegedly deficient decisions were contrasted with instances of effective group decisions with favourable outcomes – e.g. the 1962 Cuban missile crisis (but see Lebow [1981] for critical discussion of the basis on which Janis decided which decisions were good and which were bad).

Janis defined groupthink as 'a mode of thinking that people engage in when they are deeply involved in a cohesive ingroup, when members' strivings for unanimity override their motivation to realistically appraise alternative courses of action' (1982a, p. 9). High group cohesiveness was seen as an important precondition of groupthink, and groupthink as an undesirable pitfall of such groups. Other important factors included insulation from other groups, directive leadership, and a lack of procedures for generating and appraising new options.

Some of the imprecision of Janis's original (1972) formulation (see Longley and Pruitt, 1980) were addressed by Janis and Mann (1977), who effectively redefined groupthink as concurrence-seeking behaviour, with the group leader given a major role: 'When a directive leader announces his preference on a policy issue . . . the members of a cohesive group will tend to accept his choice somewhat uncritically as if it were equivalent to a group norm' (Janis and Mann, 1977, p. 131).

In 1982 Janis published a second edition of his original book, in which the clearest and most complete exposition of the antecedents, symptoms and consequences of groupthink is to be found (see Figure 8.1). The principal antecedent is cohesiveness. Secondary conditions relate to structural faults in

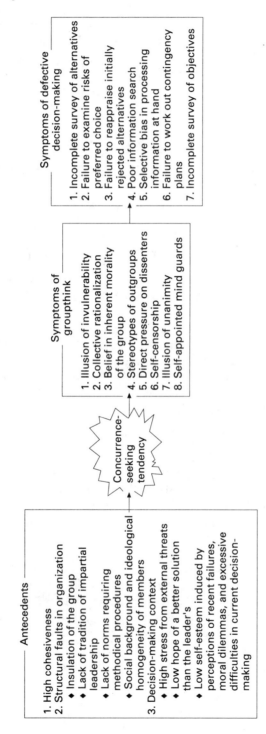

Figure 8.1 *Antecedents, symptoms and consequences of groupthink as concurrence-seeking. (This figure is adapted from I.L. Janis and L. Mann, Decision Making, © 1977 The Free Press, a division of Macmillan Inc., and I.L. Janis, Groupthink (2nd ed.), © 1982 Houghton Mifflin. Used with permission.)*

the organization: (1) insulation of the group; (2) lack of a tradition of impartial leadership; (3) lack of norms requiring methodological procedures; and (4) homogeneity of members' social background and ideology. Tertiary conditions relate to the decision-making context. These include (1) high stress from external threats; (2) low hope of a better solution than the leader's; and (3) low self-esteem temporarily induced by group members' perceptions of recent failures, moral dilemmas, and excessive difficulties in current decision-making.

These antecedents generate eight symptoms of groupthink: (1) illusion of invulnerability; (2) collective efforts to rationalize; (3) unquestioned belief in the group's inherent morality; (4) stereotyped views of enemy leaders as weak or stupid; (5) direct pressure on members who argue against the group's stereotypes; (6) self-censorship of deviations from group consensus; (7) shared illusion of unanimity; and (8) emergence of self-appointed mind guards to screen the group from adverse information.

These symptoms are associated with seven defects in the decision-making process: (1) discussion is limited to few alternatives; (2) originally preferred solutions are not reevaluated; (3) alternatives initially discarded are not reevaluated; (4) advice of experts is not sought; (5) where advice is presented, there is selective bias on the part of members; (6) members fail to consider how groups external to the focal group might react, and therefore fail to develop contingency plans; and (7) objectives are incompletely surveyed. Together, these defects produce suboptimal or defective decisions that may or may not have disastrous consequences.

Given certain background conditions, then, high cohesiveness appears to be the principal cause of groupthink. Janis identifies cohesiveness as the most prominent antecedent and, according to Longley and Pruitt (1980), adopts Festinger's (1950) attraction-to-group definition. However, a close reading of Janis suggests that the underlying conceptualization of cohesiveness may be in terms of interpersonal attraction. For example, he speaks of 'bonds of mutual friendship and loyalty . . . genuine friendship and mutual support' (1982a, p. 99), 'natural friends . . . too close, too personally fond of each other' (p. 101), 'relaxed friendly interchanges . . . informal social atmosphere . . . like old cronies' (p. 214), and 'intimate personal friends . . . friendly chatter, joking, and shared sentiments' (pp. 215–16). Indeed, as we shall see below, experimental research on groupthink has operationalized cohesiveness as friendship or interpersonal compatibility.

Groupthink research

There have been a number of descriptive studies of groupthink, including Manz and Sims's (1982) analysis of autonomous work groups, Hensley and Griffin's (1986) analysis of the Kent State Board of Trustees, Moorhead and

Montanari's (1986) analysis of simulated management groups, Esser and Lindoerfer's (1989) analysis of the space shuttle *Challenger* tragedy, Raven's (1974) analysis of the Watergate cover-up, Huseman and Driver's (1979) analysis of a price-fixing conspiracy, S. Smith's (1984) analysis of the Iran hostage rescue attempt, and Tetlock's (1979) rigorous reanalysis of the fiascoes originally analyzed by Janis (1972). The general model is supported to varying degrees, but the data do not allow a conclusive examination of the causal role of cohesiveness and concurrence-seeking. In one case, cohesiveness was found to be negatively related to groupthink (Moorhead and Montanari, 1986).

Published experimental studies are less plentiful but potentially more informative, as they can address the central issue of the role of group cohesiveness. These experiments establish background conditions for group-think, and then orthogonally manipulate cohesiveness and either a leadership variable (directiveness or need-for-power) or procedural directions for effective decision-making. Subjects generally participate in four-person thirty-minute group discussions that are tape-recorded for detection of symptoms of groupthink.

Studies that have manipulated cohesiveness in terms of friendship (i.e. by having groups of strangers or groups of acquaintances) found either no significant relationship between cohesiveness and groupthink (Flowers, 1977) or a significant negative relationship (Leana, 1985). In the latter experiment, the high-cohesiveness groups had actually functioned as a cohesive group for fifteen weeks before the experimental session. Leana summarizes: 'Teams whose members liked one another more, had experienced working together, and therefore had more opportunity to establish themselves as "concurrence seeking ingroups" were in fact more vigilant in their information gathering' (1985, p. 15), and were 'far less likely to engage in self-censorship of privately held information than were members of the non-cohesive teams' (*ibid.*, p. 16).

Fodor and Smith (1982) manipulated cohesiveness by creating an intergroup competition for a scarce reward (free theatre tickets), and found no significant relationship between cohesiveness and groupthink. The manipula-tion of cohesiveness in terms of 'alleged' compatibility and similarity that engenders liking reveals that high cohesiveness produces groupthink only where rapid concurrence is an explicit group objective (Courtright, 1978) or where no directions for effective group decision-making are given (Callaway and Esser, 1984). Callaway and Esser's experimental manipulation of cohesiveness was ineffective, so they reclassified their groups into low-, medium- or high-cohesiveness conditions on the basis of responses to the manipulation check. It is interesting to note that in the absence of explicit procedures for effective group decision-making, increased cohesiveness was not significantly associated with increased groupthink – that is, fewer statements of disagreement (see Figure 8.2).

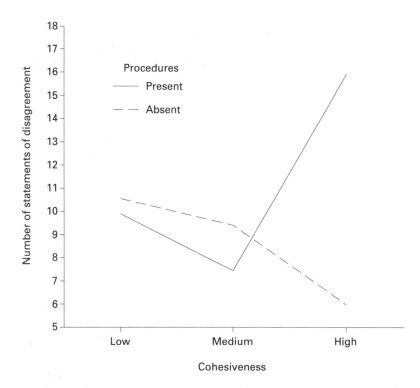

Figure 8.2 *Groupthink as a function of cohesiveness and the absence or presence of procedures for effective decision-making. (This figure is based on Figure 2 in Callaway and Esser (1984, p. 162). Reprinted by permission of the copyright holder, the Society for Personality Research Inc.)*

Taken together, these experiments do not provide convincing support for the alleged generative role of cohesiveness in groupthink. Its effect may depend on how it is operationalized, and whether there is a group norm that encourages or permits groupthink decision-making practices. The implication is that a revised explanation of groupthink needs to link, at a theoretical level, a reconceptualized 'group cohesiveness' with conformity to group norms.

Conceptual issues

Moorhead (1982) has noted that there is a link to be explored between cohesiveness, traditionally defined as 'bonds of friendship and mutual trust' (p. 436), and group norms, since 'highly cohesive groups are more effective at doing whatever the group is motivated to do than are less cohesive groups' (p. 435). The normative aspect is taken further by those who suggest that groupthink has many features of risky shift or group polarization (e.g. Myers and Lamm, 1975; Steiner, 1982; Whyte, 1989; see Chapter 6). For example, Thompson and Carsrud (1976) provide experimental data for 'an illusion of invulnerability, shared by most or all the members, which creates excessive optimism and encourages taking extreme risks' (p. 197). Groups that considered themselves to be highly efficient decision-makers made more risky decisions than control groups or groups that considered themselves to be relatively poor decision-makers. Janis (1972) remarked that groupthink was characterized by group members tending to 'show interest in facts and opinions that support their initially preferred policy and take up time in their meeting to discuss them, but . . . to ignore facts and opinions that do not support their initially preferred policy' (Janis, 1972, p. 10). That is, there is suppression of deviant thought, and a drive for concurrence in order to achieve mutual support and maintain self-esteem.

That cohesiveness itself needs to be reconceptualized has been suggested by a number of critics. For example, Longley and Pruitt (1980) and McCauley (1989) have noted the need for a more detailed specification of cohesiveness and its role in groupthink. In contrast, Janis has tended to move away from the problematic concept of cohesiveness. In the original groupthink hypothesis, he argues that the 'advantages of . . . a cohesive group are often lost when the leader and the members are subjected to stresses that generate a strong need for unanimity. The striving for concurrence fosters lack of vigilance, unwarranted optimism, sloganistic thinking, and reliance on shared rationalizations that bolster the least objectionable alternative' (Janis, 1985, p. 70). That is, stress experienced by the group produces enhanced concurrence-seeking, and thus groupthink.

Elsewhere there is clear evidence of a more marked change of direction in Janis's thinking: a change in emphasis from groupthink as a group process, to groupthink as an individualistic response to stress that is reinforced by the group. For example, 'symptoms of groupthink are behavioral consequences of a coping pattern of defensive avoidance, which is mutually supported by the group' (Janis, 1982b, pp. 481–2). Janis has shifted emphasis on to defensive avoidance as an individual response to stress. Decision-making stress produces individual coping patterns aimed at stress reduction. These coping strategies involve suboptimal decision-making procedures, and can therefore produce defective decisions. Groupthink is not an emergent property of group processes but an aggregation of suboptimal individual decision-making processes in response to individual decision-making stress. This direction has been taken by others: for example Callaway, Marriott and Esser (1985), Smith and White (1983), and Stewart (1988).

Self-categorization and groupthink

The reconceptualization of group cohesiveness in terms of self-categorization theory, presented in the previous chapters, allows a somewhat different revision of how groupthink may arise. To recapitulate: self-categorization theory argues that self-categorization in terms of a salient self-inclusive social category depersonalizes perception and behaviour in terms of the contextually relevant ingroup prototype (norm, stereotype). Ingroupers perceive themselves and other ingroupers in terms of the relevant ingroup prototype, like and hold attitudes about one another on the basis of their prototypicality, and act in terms of that prototype (i.e. conform to the ingroup norm, act stereotypically, behave prototypically). The content of the contextually relevant group prototype is determined by the salient intergroup context (i.e. the relative position of in- and outgroup on relevant comparison dimensions) such that the ingroup prototype minimizes intragroup differences and maximizes intergroup differences. Members of extreme groups will conform to an extremitized norm (group polarization), while members of moderate groups will conform to some non-extreme average group position (simple convergence on the mean). Group cohesiveness is not equated with interpersonal attraction; rather, group-based (prototypical) liking (social attraction) is theoretically distinct from friendship-based interpersonal liking (personal attraction). The latter has nothing to do with group processes, while the former is one of many consequences of group identification.

From this perspective, groupthink represents an unremarkable group phenomenon in which defective decision-making processes are adopted because group members identify (i.e. self-categorize) very strongly with a group that either has no procedures for effective decision-making, or has norms that explicitly encourage groupthink. Another possibility (particularly relevant, since groupthink scenarios frequently involve making decisions with risks attached) is that the group sees itself as extreme relative to other groups, and so produces a polarized norm. In any event, self-categorization produces conformity to these norms. The high level of 'cohesion' found in such groups is not a cause of groupthink, but a parallel effect of strong identification. So, cohesiveness operationalized as depersonalized social attraction will be strongly related to groupthink (provided the relevant norm is in place, or there is no counter-groupthink norm), whereas cohesiveness operationalized as interpersonal attraction or friendship will not. The experimental studies of groupthink mentioned above point tentatively in this direction.

An interesting alternative, however, is that groupthink is actually not a group phenomenon at all, but a relatively inevitable product of close and continuing interpersonal friendships. In this case, symptoms of groupthink should be detected in all decision-making aggregates only as a function of the degree of friendship, and will be quite independent of whether the aggregate constitutes a psychological group or not. The traditional theory of groupthink fails to distinguish between cohesiveness as group-based attraction and 'cohesiveness' as simply another word for interpersonal attraction/friendship. As a result, contradictory findings are inevitable and the theoretical relationship between group cohesiveness and groupthink is inevitably obscure.

Group productivity and performance ════════════

The concept of cohesiveness potentially has an important practical application in the areas of group productivity and performance (cf. Keller, 1986; Mudrack, 1989b). If cohesiveness is the defining feature of a group, then variations in the cohesiveness of small, interactive, task-orientated groups (particularly in work and sports contexts) might have a direct and predictable impact on the productivity or performance of such groups. Perhaps it is possible to increase the productivity of work groups in industrial settings, or the success of sports teams, by increasing their cohesiveness.

This question – the relationship between cohesiveness and group productivity/performance – has been the subject of an enormous amount of research over the years. In general this research, in dealing with interactive group tasks, has been distinct from research into audience and 'mere presence' effects (e.g. Geen and Gange, 1977), and social loafing (e.g. Latané, Williams and Harkins, 1979) – but see Harkins and Szymanski (1987). I shall say a few words about social loafing below.

Productivity and performance research

In their review of variables with antecedent or consequent relationships with group cohesiveness as interpersonal attraction, Lott and Lott (1965, pp. 296–8) cite 34 studies published between 1950 and 1962 that deal with group task productivity/performance as a consequence of cohesiveness (cf. Chapter 3). These studies employ a wide range of paradigms and a wide range of groups: carpenters, bricklayers, employment agency interviewers, surveyors, aircrews, combat squads, rifle teams, schoolchildren, women's residence units, summer camps, industrial work groups in supermarkets and shoe factories, and various laboratory groups. The findings are equivocal. Sometimes increased cohesiveness is associated with increased productivity and improved performance, sometimes there is no relationship, and sometimes there is a negative relationship. Lott and Lott feel that the findings are inconsistent because 'other variables such as the demands of the situation itself (instructions or job specifications), the standards of performance preferred by liked co-workers, and the degree to which sociability may interfere with the required behaviour for a particular job, may be highly significant' (1965, p. 298).

Stogdill (1972) reviewed 34 studies of the relationship between cohesiveness and productivity in a whole range of contexts. He found cohesive groups to be more productive in 12 studies, less productive in 11, and unrelated in 11. Mudrack (1989b) is critical of this work, because it fails to recognize that cohesiveness was measured in different ways in different studies. A comparison between studies therefore becomes meaningless, because different studies are effectively monitoring the effect of different variables on productivity.

Shaw's (1976, pp. 205–8) brief and selective discussion of cohesiveness and productivity (only 10 studies are discussed) deals with laboratory studies and field studies in military, industrial and classroom settings. In general, there is support for a positive relationship between cohesiveness (usually operationalized in terms of friendship choices) and productivity and quality of performance. It would appear that groups set goals specifying productivity or performance levels, and that cohesiveness influences how hard members work to achieve these goals. This is consistent with findings from Seashore's (1954) research on industrial work groups. It is also consistent with findings from a study of classroom groups by Shaw and Shaw (1962), in which more cohesive groups (better friends) set social activity as their goal and so appeared to suffer a decrement in the quality of their performance (i.e. learning).

Sports teams are generally unproblematic regarding their productivity or performance goals: to perform as well as possible in order to win. Presumably, then, research in this area should reliably produce a positive relationship between cohesiveness and performance. However, this is not the case. Some studies obtain a positive relationship, some no relationship, some a negative relationship, and some different relationships depending on the specific measures used (see Carron, 1980; Landers and Luschen, 1974; Martens and Peterson, 1971).

For example, Martens and Peterson (1971) administered an 8-item cohesiveness questionnaire to 1,200 male basketball players from 144 teams. The teams could be ranked as high, medium, or low performers on the basis of the number of games won during the season. They found that measures of cohesiveness monitoring interpersonal relationships (e.g. interpersonal attraction) did not distinguish between teams on the basis of performance, whereas measures monitoring subjective perceptions of the team's cohesiveness as a whole were related to performance. In another study, Landers and Luschen (1974) administered a 6-item cohesiveness questionnaire to more than 300 members of 52 four- to seven-member bowling teams. The 15 highest- and 15 lowest-scoring teams were compared; it was discovered that interpersonal attraction and friendship measures of cohesiveness were significantly negatively correlated with performance, while measures monitoring perceptions of team members' contributions to the teams' success were positively correlated with performance.

Conceptual issues

In order to explain these contradictory findings, researchers have drawn upon existent classificatory distinctions between different types of group task based on the nature of the interaction, means or goals invoked by the group task. For example, Landers and Luschen (1974) distinguish between team sports on the basis of how much interaction is required by the structure and demands of the sport. A distinction can be made between interactive and coactive sports: the former have a division of labour that requires coordination of distinct roles, while the latter have no (or very little) division of labour and thus do not require such coordination. Landers and Luschen argue that sports such as basketball, football and volleyball are highly interactive, while shooting and rowing are not. They go on to observe that studies of interactive sports reveal a positive cohesiveness-performance relationship, while studies of coactive sports do not.

Carron (1980) describes a similar model. It differs mainly in so far as it contains a somewhat more highly patterned classification which distinguishes between four types of task interdependence in sport: independence, coactive dependence, reactive–proactive dependence, and interactive dependence. Only the latter is considered a truly interdependent sport (e.g. basketball, hockey, soccer). Carron states that cohesiveness has a relationship with performance only in sports characterized by interactive interdependence, and then it 'contributes to improved coordination which, in turn, leads to improved performance' (1980, p. 248).

Most sports team studies of the cohesiveness–performance relationship are correlational, and so the causality question is left unanswered: does cohesiveness improve performance, does successful performance strengthen cohesiveness, do both occur, or are both correlated effects of some other factor? Although there have been attempts to tease out cause and effect (e.g. Landers, Wilkinson, Hatfield and Barber, 1982; Williams and Hacker, 1982), Levine and Moreland (1990) conclude from their review that the results are still inconclusive.

Let us recapitulate. Mudrack (1989b) concludes that forty years of research on the relationship between group productivity/team success and cohesiveness has left us little the wiser. The problem is that depending on how cohesiveness is measured, it can have a positive, negative, or non-significant relationship with productivity or success. Cohesiveness appears to be positively associated with group productivity or team success only where productivity or success is already an internalized norm of the relevant group (e.g. Greene, 1989; Griffin and Moorhead, 1986; Miesing and Preble, 1985; Schermerhorn, Hunt and Osborn, 1988); cohesiveness as interpersonal attraction or friendship does not reliably predict group/team effectiveness, productivity or success (e.g. Martens and Peterson, 1971; Peterson and Martens, 1973; see review by Nixon, 1977); and, in sports teams, cohesiveness may influence performance only if the sport is one requiring interactive dependence (e.g. Carron, 1980; Landers and Luschen, 1974). Martens and Peterson conclude that 'differences in interpersonal attraction among teams do not significantly affect team effectiveness' (1971, p. 57). For

Nixon, 'cohesiveness and interpersonal attraction are viewed as separate constructs' (1977, p. 19), and Williams and Hacker (1982) recommend abandoning interpersonal-attraction measures of group cohesiveness altogether.

Self-categorization and performance

From a social identity perspective, some comments can be made about this literature. Cohesiveness is operationalized in a number of different ways, but in general attraction-to-group and interpersonal attraction predominate. Attempts to deal with contradictory findings are promising when they point to the role of conformity to group norms concerning productivity and performance (e.g. Shaw, 1976). They are less promising when they brush aside problematic findings on the grounds that because they come from groups that are not characterized by interactive dependence, they are not valid, because such 'groups' are not actually groups at all (e.g. Carron, 1980)! This is a very convenient exercise in creative theorizing, but it is precisely the sort of solution that leads us straight back into the trap of reductionism (see Chapter 4). It is also patently inaccurate: non-interactive teams (e.g. swimming teams, athletic teams, or gymnastic teams in international contests) can, of course, be highly cohesive.

Instead, the relationship between cohesiveness and performance/productivity can be approached from self-categorization theory as follows. Task-orientated groups (the sort dealt with by research in this area) have specific goals relating to performance and productivity levels. These are cognitively represented by individual group members as prototypes. Identification with the group involves self-categorization that produces relatively prototype-consistent conduct. Self-categorization also produces the entire array of other behaviours associated with groups, including intragroup, or depersonalized social, attraction: that is, interindividual attraction based on perceived prototypicality rather than interpersonal friendship or idiosyncratic characteristics.

So, for example, we would expect to find a positive correlation between group-based liking and successful performance or elevated productivity only in groups defined by successful performance or high productivity norms. In groups defined by, for example, low productivity norms, a negative correlation would be expected between group-based liking and productivity. In groups where sociability is – or has become – the defining norm, there would be a positive correlation between group-based liking and sociability. In sports teams there would be a positive correlation between measures of group-based liking and performance (assuming that all sports teams exist to excel at performance, and to win), irrespective of the degree of interactive dependence.

From a social identity perspective, group processes can operate only with reference to an internalized group norm or goal, so productivity or success can be affected by cohesiveness only if they are the relevant norms.

Inter*personal* attraction or friendship, on the other hand, would be expected to have little or no relationship to *group* processes such as effectiveness in achieving consensual group goals. It would be affected only by opportunities to develop friendships. So it would not, perhaps, be surprising to discover that — quite independent of the group's performance or productivity norms — more interactive groups (this includes those where sociability is, or has become, the defining norm) would contain a greater number of friends than less interactive groups.

Measures of cohesiveness that focus on interpersonal relationships describe only personal relationships. They cast no light on group processes. The degree of interpersonal attraction and friendship is conceptually independent of the degree of group cohesiveness. In practice, however, cohesive small groups are also groups in which there is a great deal of opportunity for interpersonal interaction, so that friendships (but also interpersonal dislikes) are likely, in time, to arise.

An interesting social engineering implication of this analysis concerns recommendations about how to improve, for example, group productivity in the workplace. If we were to take the perspective of management, we would aim to arrange circumstances that encouraged group members to construct and internalize a group norm of high productivity and performance excellence. In principle, there would be no need to address interpersonal relationships. However, if the group task was one involving a great deal of face-to-face interaction, we might attempt to limit the development of friendship cliques (e.g. by staff rotation), as these might eventually produce a sociability norm to replace the desired productivity norm. At the other extreme, it should be recognized that people have a strong need to develop interpersonal relationships, and that work conditions devoid of such opportunities, particularly over an extended period of time, might be experienced by many as unsatisfying. An optimal balance would be sought between too much and too little opportunity to develop and sustain friendships.

Social loafing

Social loafing refers to a reduction in the effort individuals put into collective task performance in small groups (Latané *et al.*, 1979; see review by Harkins and Szymanski, 1987; Williams, Karau and Bourgeois, in press). Effort diminishes as a negatively accelerating power function of group size: that is to say, as group size increases, the addition of new members has an increasingly less significant impact on effort. So, for example, the reduction in individual effort as the consequence of a third person joining a two-person group is relatively large, while the impact of an additional member on a twenty-person group is minimal. The range within which group size seems to have a significant impact is about one to eight members.

Social loafing research generally adopts a paradigm in which individual or coactive performance is compared either with groups performing some sort of additive task (e.g. brainstorming – Harkins and Petty, 1982), or with the performance of 'pseudogroups', in which people are led to *believe* that they are performing collectively with varying numbers of others, but in fact circumstances are arranged so that they are performing individually (e.g. pulling a rope – Ingham, Levinger, Graves and Peckham, 1974). Using these sorts of paradigms, which are explicitly designed to monitor effort loss unconfounded with coordination loss, social loafing has been demonstrated on tasks involving physical effort (rope-pulling, clapping, pumping air, shouting) as well as cognitive effort (reacting to proposals, brainstorming and vigilance, solving mazes, evaluating essays), and in a wide variety of cultures (e.g. the USA, France, Poland, Japan, Taiwan, Thailand, India) (see Harkins and Szymanski, 1987).

Social loafing is usually explained in terms of social impact theory (e.g. Latané, 1981; Latané *et al.*, 1979). Very briefly, inaction is generally the safest course of social action for an individual, as it minimizes the possibility of unfavourable evaluation by others. However, individuals also have a strong sense of personal responsibility and social obligation. These two forces are in conflict. Generally, personal responsibility prevails; in groups, however, personal responsibility (and the obligation to do the best/most one can) can be shared among fellow group members (i.e. there is diffusion of responsibility), thus allowing individuals to pursue the less psychologically risky course of inaction. The social impact on the subject of the experimenter's instruction to clap, shout, brainstorm, or whatever (i.e. the social obligation to work as hard as possible) is reduced to the extent that it can be shared among a group of subjects. In this way there is reduced effort in groups, which is a function of the size of the group.

Diffusion of personal responsibility, and hence social loafing, is not an inevitable consequence of group performance. There are certain factors, apart from group size, that influence the tendency to loaf. For example, personal identifiability by the experimenter (Williams, Harkins and Latané, 1981), personal involvement in the task (Brickner, Harkins and Ostrom, 1986), partner effort (Jackson and Harkins, 1985), task attractiveness (Zaccaro, 1984), interdependence among group members (Worchel, Hart and Butemeyer, 1991), intergroup comparison (Harkins and Szymanski, 1989), high task meaningfulness in association with expectation of poor performance by co-workers (Williams and Karau, 1991), and group cohesiveness (as interpersonal friendship) (Williams, 1981) have all been shown to reduce loafing. Zaccaro's (1984) study is particularly interesting. He found that on attractive tasks (i.e tasks imbued with social relevance, and performed under intergroup competitive conditions) there was actually a significant *increment* in individual effort as a function of increasing group size (two- versus four-person): that is, being in a larger group increased individual effort.

Although social loafing is framed as an effect of group size, it is actually produced psychologically by lack of individual identifiability. Recently, Harkins and Szymanski (1987; Harkins, 1987) have suggested that this may cause loafing because it is associated with absence of evaluation by others. Another explanation is that there is a general belief that people loaf in groups, and therefore, when performing collectively, people do loaf (Jackson and Harkins, 1985). One problem with this explanation is that there is as yet no convincing evidence of the existence of a normative belief such as this. Social loafing appears to be mediated in some way or other by loss of or reduction in individual identifiability, and so may fall into the domain of effects of deindividuation (e.g. Diener, 1980), self-awareness (Wicklund, 1982), and so forth (see Chapter 5).

Self-categorization theory, however, suggests another possibility. To the extent that individuals categorize themselves in terms of the defining features of a specific group, they will exert effort to enact the normative (self-defining) behaviours of that group. Thus, quite irrespective of group size, people who identify strongly with a group will exert effort on behalf of that group. Social loafing will be negatively related to group identification, or to factors known to enhance the salience of a self-inclusive social category. If group membership is not valued or is unimportant, or the group is one with which the person does not identify, or from which the person is attempting to dis-identify, then factors rendering the group salient will quite probably reduce effort on behalf of the group: that is, social loafing will occur.

Perhaps this is why factors such as partner effort, task attractiveness, member interdependence, intergroup comparison, and personal involvement have been found to reduce loafing – or reverse it, in the case of Zaccaro's (1984) study. They render the self-inclusive task-defined group a more salient reference group. Worchel *et al.*'s (1991) study is particularly relevant. A dramatic reduction in social loafing was found under conditions of enhanced member interdependence and anticipated future interaction designed to make the group a more meaningful and coherent social entity. Most social loafing seems to occur where unrelated individuals, who are not *explicitly* categorized as a group (cf. minimal group studies – e.g. Billig and Tajfel, 1973), simply coact in an aggregate – psychologically, there is perhaps no group at all.

There have been only a few direct studies of the effects of group cohesiveness on social loafing. Gabrenya, Latané and Wang (1981) found that increasing group size increased loafing on a clapping and shouting task, but that there was generally greater effort in groups of strangers (low cohesiveness) than groups of friends (high cohesiveness). In contrast, Williams (1981) found that female typists randomly assigned to four-person groups (low cohesiveness) loafed in relation to individuals, while typists assigned to groups containing close friends (high cohesiveness) did not (there was even some evidence for increased typing speed). In another experiment, Karau and Williams (1992, Experiment 2) had members of mixed-sex dyads work coactively or collectively on an ideas-generation task. There was a general tendency for members of cohesive dyads (i.e. containing friends/couples) to work harder collectively than coactively, while members of low/non-cohesive dyads (i.e. containing strangers) loafed. These findings are contradictory: cohesiveness, as interpersonal attraction and friendship, increases loafing in the first study, and diminishes it in the other two. Clearly, further research is needed. From a social attraction perspective one might be able to hazard the prediction that social loafing would be relatively unaffected by cohesiveness operationalized in terms of friendship or interpersonal attraction, whereas it would be reduced by cohesiveness operationalized as depersonalized social attraction. This is clearly an interesting direction for future research.

Large-scale social categories

In many ways this chapter has been an extension of Chapter 7, in so far as it has assessed the theoretical potential of a self-categorization approach to cohesiveness. It differs from Chapter 7 in so far as the latter focuses very much on past and current research and theorizing, while this final chapter identifies some possible future directions: specifically in the area of groupthink, group productivity and performance, and social loafing.

One important advantage of conceptualizing group solidarity and cohesiveness in terms of self-categorization and social identity, rather than interpersonal processes (especially attraction), is that we are no longer restricted to small interactive groups. We can now quite sensibly discuss cohesiveness in all sorts of groups, ranging from small, interactive, task-orientated groups to large-scale social categories. The notion of depersonalized social attraction is equally at home in a discussion of – for example – committees, sports teams, organizational groups, nations, and ethnolinguistic groups.

Let us take ethnolinguistic groups as an example. These are large-scale social categories defined by language and culture – for example Greek Australians, French Canadians, the Welsh. There is now a whole body of literature, under the heading 'social psychology of language', which focuses on social psychological factors that influence language use by ethnolinguistic groups in multi-ethnic contexts (e.g. Giles, 1984; Giles and Johnson, 1981; Giles and St Clair, 1979; Sachdev and Bourhis, 1990; see Hogg and Abrams

[1988, pp. 186–206] for an overview). This literature adopts an intergroup perspective or a more specific social identity approach predicated on the belief that language is a stereotypic or normative (often defining) feature of ethnolinguistic groups. Language contains features that symbolize identity, and is thus a potent vehicle for communicating who one is. Factors that render the group salient operate in conjunction with social belief structures (called 'subjective vitality' in this literature: see Allard and Landry, in press; Bourhis, Giles and Rosenthal, 1981) to produce contextual or more enduring effects on language usage.

Some major concerns of this literature are language maintenance (e.g. Giles, 1978), speech accommodation (e.g. Giles, 1984), and second-language acquisition (e.g. Giles and Byrne, 1982). Very briefly, high subjective vitality refers not only to pride in and respect for the language of one's ethnolinguistic group, but also to a belief that the group and its language will thrive and prosper. In these circumstances people will often identify strongly with the group and express high levels of ethnolinguistic solidarity. A common consequence is language revival – the French-Canadian language revival is an excellent example (see overview by Sachdev and Bourhis, 1990). Immediate contextual factors that render ethnolinguistic identity salient will produce speech-style divergence from members of the dominant language group. This divergence represents self-enhancing positive ethnolinguistic distinctiveness, presumably produced by depersonalized ethnolinguistic perception. People are also rather unlikely to acquire native-like proficiency in the dominant group's language, as it may subtract from positive ethnolinguistic identity.

In contrast, low vitality is associated with marginalization and gradual withering of the ethnic language – over time, it might even disappear entirely (this has, for example, been the fate of many Aboriginal languages in Australia). People will tend to converge on the speech style of dominant group members, and will be highly motivated to acquire native-like proficiency in the dominant group's language.

These are all, quite obviously, group-solidarity phenomena. The solidarity and cohesiveness of ethnolinguistic groups appear to be mediated by self-categorization and self-evaluation processes that articulate with subjective beliefs concerning the nature of interethnic relations and the vitality of the ethnolinguistic group. It is difficult to see how a theory of cohesiveness and solidarity based on interpersonal processes, and largely seen to operate in terms of interpersonal attraction, can make much headway here. It is simply not very plausible to explain, for example, the recent French-language revival in Quebec in terms of interpersonal attraction and the development of friendship networks among many millions of French Canadians. This sort of analysis is completely upside down. Rather, positive attitude among specific French Canadians may, at least to some extent, be based on, and produced by, shared identity – but then, as this book has argued, it is a matter not of personalized inter*personal* attraction, but of depersonalized *social* attraction.

Conclusion

This book has been a critical review of origins, developments, findings, criticisms and reconceptualizations of the experimental social psychological concept of group cohesiveness. Since its formal introduction in the early 1950s as a core theoretical construct in the explanation of group behaviour, group cohesiveness has largely failed to live up to its theoretical expectations. The concept was very quickly and decisively simplified to refer to interpersonal processes – typically, interpersonal attraction – between individuals in small interactive aggregates. Since it was no longer a theory of group processes distinct from theories of interpersonal behaviour, group cohesiveness research and theorizing in mainstream social psychology lost popularity in the late 1960s. Conceptual controversies and criticisms remain largely unresolved, while social psychologists, mainly in applied domains, still employ the concept very much in its original, conceptually problematic, form.

The bulk of contemporary research concerns how to measure group cohesiveness. It focuses on the dimensional structure of cohesiveness, and on the derivation of scales. Recently, however, there have been a number of promising attempts to reconceptualize group cohesiveness – some of which are critical of its reductionist metatheory. Particularly promising among these is the social identity or self-categorization approach promoted in this book. This formulation treats attraction phenomena in groups as only one of an array of inter- and intragroup effects of self-categorization in terms of a shared group membership. Intermember attraction is not an interpersonal phenomenon – it is depersonalized liking for an individual group member, based on group prototypicality.

This is not to say that people in groups cannot become close personal friends or develop interpersonal relationships. On the contrary, common group membership, particularly membership of small, task-orientated, interactive groups, provides conditions which are generally conducive to positive inter*personal* relationships, although interpersonal rivalry and dislike may also arise. The crucial point is that inter*personal* liking and group cohesiveness are not the same thing. They are not interchangeable, nor does one produce the other. They are separate psychological phenomena, produced by entirely different psychological processes.

While the traditional group cohesiveness concept assigns liking a major descriptive and generative role, the self-categorization approach seems to be a great deal more cognitive (e.g. Turner, 1985), and the wider social identity theory seems more concerned with intergroup relations at the macrosocial level (e.g. Tajfel and Turner, 1979). Although both have spawned many publications concerning cognitive processes, social influence, conformity, stereotyping, strategies for social change, and so forth, there is notably less literature on attraction phenomena. One aim of this book has been to redress this apparent imbalance – formally to extend and develop self-categorization theory in the area of group attraction. I use the word 'apparent' because it would be a mistake to think that these theories do not place any conceptual importance on group attraction. On the contrary, it is — and has always been — considered to be just as significant an aspect of group behaviour as stereotyping, conformity, norm formation, discrimination, and so forth (e.g. Turner, 1982, 1984).

The depersonalized social attraction model of group cohesiveness presented here is, of course, only a start. A great deal more needs to be done. More questions are raised than answers given. For example, although there is some support for the idea of prototypical attraction, research still needs to be done to discover precisely how intergroup dimensions, macrosocial dimensions, and social belief structures influence social attraction within and between groups, and how specific mediating processes operate in conjunction with or opposition to one another (see the end of Chapter 6). In addition, the wider applicability of the social attraction idea to group processes needs to be pursued, perhaps in line with suggestions in this chapter.

At this point, perhaps the major advantage of a self-categorization or social identity analysis is that we are now asking questions about *group* solidarity and cohesiveness which are framed in such a way that they point towards the sort of research and thinking that will ultimately produce answers about *group* solidarity rather than interpersonal relationships. We may, finally, be asking the correct questions.

Bibliography

Abelson, R.P., Aronson, E., McGuire, W.J., Newcomb, T., Rosenberg, M.J. and Tannenbaum, P.H. (eds) (1968) *Theories of Cognitive Consistency: A sourcebook*, Chicago, IL: Rand McNally.

Abrams, D. (1990) 'How do group members regulate their behaviour? An integration of social identity and self-awareness theories', in D. Abrams and M.A. Hogg (eds), *Social Identity Theory: Constructive and critical advances* (pp. 89–112), Hemel Hempstead: Harvester Wheatsheaf/New York: Springer-Verlag.

Abrams, D. and Hogg, M.A. (eds) (1990a) *Social Identity Theory: Constructive and critical advances*, Hemel Hempstead: Harvester Wheatsheaf/New York: Springer-Verlag.

Abrams, D. and Hogg, M.A. (1990b) 'The social context of discourse: Let's not throw out the baby with the bath water', *Philosophical Psychology* 3, 219–25.

Abrams, D. and Hogg, M.A. (1990c) 'Social identification, self-categorization, and social influence', in W. Stroebe and M.R.C. Hewstone (eds), *European Review of Social Psychology* (vol. 1, pp. 195–228), Chichester: Wiley.

Abrams, D., Wetherell, M.S., Cochrane, S., Hogg, M.A. and Turner, J.C. (1990) 'Knowing what to think by knowing who you are: Self-categorization and the nature of norm formation, conformity and group polarization', *British Journal of Social Psychology* 29, 97–119.

Adorno, T.W., Frenkel-Brunswik, E., Levinson, D.J. and Sanford, R.M. (1950) *The Authoritarian Personality*, New York: Harper.

Allard, R. and Landry, R. (eds) (in press) *Ethnolinguistic Vitality*. Special issue of the *International Journal of the Sociology of Language*.

Allen, V.L. (1965) 'Situational factors in conformity', *Advances in Experimental Social Psychology* 2, 133–75.

Allen, V.L. (1975) 'Social support for non-conformity', *Advances in Experimental Social Psychology* 8, 1–43.

Allport, F.H. (1924) *Social Psychology*, Boston, MA: Houghton Mifflin.

Allport, F.H. (1962) 'A structuronomic conception of behavior: Individual and collective. I. Structural theory and the master problem of social psychology', *Journal of Abnormal and Social Psychology* 64, 3–30.

Allport, G.W. (1968) 'The historical background of modern social psychology', in G. Lindzey and E. Aronson (eds), *Handbook of Social Psychology* (2nd edn, vol. 1, pp. 1–80), Reading, MA: Addison-Wesley.

153

Anderson, A.B. (1975) 'Combined effects of interpersonal attraction and goal-path clarity on the cohesiveness of task-oriented groups', *Journal of Personality and Social Psychology* **31**, 68–75.

Andreyeva, G.M. and Gozman, L.J. (1981) 'Interpersonal relationships and social context', in S. Duck and R. Gilmour (eds), *Personal Relationships (vol. 1): Studying Personal Relationships* (pp. 47–66), London: Academic Press.

Asch, S.E. (1952) *Social Psychology*, Englewood Cliffs, NJ: Prentice Hall.

Ashmore, R.D. and Del Boca, F.K. (1981) 'Conceptual approaches to stereotypes and stereotyping', in D.L. Hamilton (ed.), *Cognitive Processes in Stereotyping and Intergroup Behavior* (pp. 1–35), Hillsdale, NJ: Erlbaum.

Atthowe, J.M. (1961) 'Interpersonal decision making: The resolution of a dyadic conflict', *Journal of Abnormal and Social Psychology* **62**, 114–19.

Augoustinos, M. and Innes, J.M. (1990) 'Towards an integration of social representations and social schema theory', *British Journal of Social Psychology* **29**, 213–31.

Back, K.W. (1951) 'Influence through social communication', *Journal of Abnormal and Social Psychology* **46**, 9–23.

Bakeman, R. and Beck, S. (1974) 'The size of informal groups in public', *Environment and Behavior* **6**, 378–90.

Bakeman, R. and Helmreich, R. (1975) 'Cohesiveness and performance: Covariation and causality in an undersea environment', *Journal of Experimental Social Psychology* **11**, 478–89.

Bales, R.F. (1950) *Interaction Process Analysis: A method for the study of small groups*, Reading, MA: Addison-Wesley.

Bass, B.M. (1960) *Leadership, Psychology, and Organizational Behavior*, New York: Harper and Row.

Bavelas, A. (1950) 'Communication in task groups', *Journal of the Acoustical Society of America* **22**, 725–30.

Bednar, R.L. and Kaul, T.J. (1978) 'Experiential group research: Current perspectives', in S.L. Garfield and A.E. Bergin (eds), *Handbook of Psychotherapy and Behavior Change: An empirical approach* (2nd edn, pp. 769–815), New York: Wiley.

Bednar, R.L., Weet, C., Evensen, P., Lanier, D. and Melnick, J. (1974) 'Empirical guidelines for group therapy: Pretraining, cohesion, and modeling', *Journal of Applied Behavioral Science* **10**, 149–65.

Benedict, R. (1935) *Patterns of Culture*, London: Routledge and Kegan Paul.

Berger, J., Fisek, M.H., Norman, R.Z. and Zelditch, M., Jr (1977) *Status Characteristics and Social Interaction*, New York: Elsevier.

Berkowitz, L. (1954) 'Group standards, cohesiveness, and productivity', *Human Relations* **7**, 509–19.

Berkowitz, L., Levy, B. and Harvey, A.R. (1957) 'Effects of performance evaluations on group integration and motivation', *Human Relations* **10**, 195–208.

Berkowitz, L. and Walster, E. (eds) (1976) *Equity Theory: Toward a general theory of social interaction* (vol. 9 of *Advances in Experimental Social Psychology*), New York: Academic Press.

Berscheid, E. (1985) 'Interpersonal attraction', in G. Lindzey and E. Aronson (eds), *Handbook of Social Psychology* (3rd edn, vol. 2, pp. 413–84), New York: Random House.

Billig, M. (1976) *Social Psychology and Intergroup Relations*, London: Academic Press.

Billig, M. and Tajfel, H. (1973) 'Social categorization and similarity in intergroup behaviour', *European Journal of Social Psychology* 3, 27–52.

Bion, W.R. (1961) *Experiences in Groups*, London: Tavistock.

Blumberg, H., Hare, A.P., Kent, V. and Davies, M. (eds) (1983) *Small Groups and Social Interaction*, New York: Wiley.

Bonacich, P. (1972) 'Norms and cohesion as adaptive responses to potential conflict: An experimental study', *Sociometry* 35, 357–75.

Bonner, H. (1959) *Group Dynamics: Principles and applications*, New York: Ronald Press.

Bourhis, R.Y., Giles, H. and Rosenthal, D. (1981) 'Notes on the construction of a "Subjective Vitality Questionnaire" for ethnolinguistic groups', *Journal of Multilingual and Multicultural Development* 2, 144–55.

Bovard, E.W. (1951) 'Group structure and perception', *Journal of Abnormal and Social Psychology* 46, 398–405.

Bovard, E.W. (1953) 'Conformity to social norms and attraction to the group', *Science* 118, 598–9.

Bowerman, C.E. and Day, B.A. (1956) 'A test of the theory of complementary needs as applied to couples during courtship', *American Sociological Review* 21, 602–5.

Boyanowsky, E.O. and Allen, V.I. (1973) 'Ingroup norms and self-identity as determinants of discriminatory behavior', *Journal of Personality and Social Psychology* 25, 408–18.

Brawley, L.R., Carron, A.V. and Widmeyer, W.N. (1987) 'Assessing the cohesion of teams: Validity of the Group Environment Questionnaire', *Journal of Sport Psychology* 9, 275–94.

Brawley, L.R., Carron, A.V. and Widmeyer, W.N. (1988) 'Exploring the relationship between cohesion and group resistance to disruption', *Journal of Sport and Exercise Psychology* 10, 199–213.

Brewer, M.B. (1981) 'Ethnocentrism and its role in interpersonal trust', in M.B. Brewer and B.E. Collins (eds), *Scientific Inquiry and the Social Sciences: A volume in honor of Donald T. Campbell* (pp. 245–360), San Francisco, CA: Jossey-Bass.

Brewer. M.B. (1988) 'A dual process model of impression formation', in T.K. Srull and R.S. Wyer (eds), *Advances in Social Cognition: A dual process model of impression formation* (vol. 1, pp. 1–36), Hillsdale, NJ: Erlbaum.

Brewer, M.B. (1991) 'The social self: On being the same and different at the same time', *Personality and Social Psychology Bulletin* 17, 475–82.

Brewer, M.B. and Campbell, D.T. (1976) *Ethnocentrism and Intergroup Attitudes: East African evidence*, New York: Sage.

Brewer, M.B. and Silver, M. (1978) 'Ingroup bias as a function of task characteristics', *European Journal of Social Psychology* 8, 393–400.

Brickner, M., Harkins, S.G. and Ostrom, T. (1986) 'Personal involvement: Thought provoking implications for social loafing', *Journal of Personality and Social Psychology* 51, 763–9.

Brinthaupt, T.M., Moreland, R.L. and Levine, J.M. (1991) 'Sources of optimism among prospective group members', *Personality and Social Psychology Bulletin* 17, 36–43.

Brown, R. (1965) *Social Psychology*, New York: The Free Press.

Brown, R.J. (1984) 'The role of similarity in intergroup relations', in H. Tajfel (ed.), *The Social Dimension: European developments in social psychology* (vol. 2, pp. 603–23), Cambridge: Cambridge University Press.

Brown, R.J. and Turner, J.C. (1981) 'Interpersonal and intergroup behaviour', in J.C. Turner and H. Giles (eds), *Intergroup Behaviour* (pp. 33–65), Oxford: Blackwell.

Bruner, J.S. (1957) 'On perceptual readiness', *Psychological Review* 64, 123–52.

Budge, S. (1981) 'Group cohesiveness reexamined', *Group* 5, 10–18.

Burnstein, E. and McRae, A. (1962) 'Some effects of shared threat and prejudice in racially mixed groups', *Journal of Abnormal and Social Psychology* 64, 257–63.

Burnstein, E. and Vinokur, A. (1977) 'Persuasive argumentation and social comparison as determinants of attitude polarization', *Journal of Experimental Social Psychology* 13, 315–32.

Byrne, D. (1971) *The Attraction Paradigm*, New York: Academic Press.

Byrne, D. and Wong, T.J. (1962) 'Racial prejudice, interpersonal attraction, and assumed dissimilarity of attitudes', *Journal of Abnormal and Social Psychology* 65, 246–52.

Callaway, M.R. and Esser, J.K. (1984) 'Groupthink: Effects of cohesiveness and problem-solving procedures on group decision making', *Social Behavior and Personality* 12, 157–64.

Callaway, M.R., Marriott, R.G. and Esser, J.K. (1985) 'Effects of dominance on group decision making: Towards a stress-reduction explanation of groupthink', *Journal of Personality and Social Psychology* 49, 949–52.

Campbell, D.T. (1958) 'Common fate, similarity and other indices of the status of aggregates of persons as social entities', *Behavioural Science* 3, 14–25.

Carron, A.V. (1980) *Social Psychology of Sport*, Ithaca, NY: Mouvement Publications.

Carron, A.V. (1982) 'Cohesiveness in sports groups: Interpretations and considerations', *Journal of Sport Psychology* 4, 123–38.

Carron, A.V. and Ball, J.R. (1977) 'Cause–effect characteristics of cohesiveness and participation motivation in intercollegiate hockey', *International Review of Sport Psychology* 12, 49–60.

Carron, A.V. and Chelladurai, P. (1981) 'The dynamics of group cohesion in sport', *Journal of Sport Psychology* 3, 123–9.

Carron, A.V., Widmeyer, W.N. and Brawley, L.R. (1985) 'The development of an instrument to assess cohesion in sports teams: The Group Environment Question-naire', *Journal of Sport Psychology* 7, 244–67.

Cartwright, D. (1968) 'The nature of group cohesiveness', in D. Cartwright and A. Zander (eds), *Group Dynamics: Research and theory* (3rd edn, pp. 91–109), London: Tavistock.

Cartwright, D. (1979) 'Contemporary social psychology in historical perspective', *Social Psychology Quarterly* 42, 82–93.

Cartwright, D. and Zander, A. (eds) (1953) *Group Dynamics: Research and theory*, Evanston, IL: Row, Peterson.

Cartwright, D. and Zander, A. (eds) (1960) *Group Dynamics: Research and theory* (2nd edn), Evanston, IL: Row, Peterson.

Cartwright, D. and Zander, A. (eds) (1968) *Group Dynamics: Research and theory* (3rd edn). London: Tavistock.

Carver, C.S. and Scheier, M.F. (1981) *Attention and Self-regulation: A control theory approach to human behavior*, New York: Springer-Verlag.

Cattell, R.B. (1951) 'Determining syntality dimension as a basis for morale and leadership measurement', in H. Guetzkow (ed.), *Groups, Leadership and Men: Research in human relations* (pp. 16–27), Pittsburgh, PA: Carnegie Press.

Charles, M.T. (1982) 'The Yellowstone Ranger: The social control and socialization of federal law enforcement officers', *Human Organization* 41, 216–26.

Cialdini, R.B., Borden, R., Thorne, A., Walker, M., Freeman, S. and Sloane, L.R. (1976) 'Basking in reflected glory: Three (football) field studies', *Journal of Personality and Social Psychology* 34, 366–75.

Clark, M.S. and Reis, H.T. (1988) 'Interpersonal processes in close relationships', *Annual Review of Psychology* 39, 609–972.

Coch, L. and French, J.R.P., Jr (1948) 'Overcoming resistance to change', *Human Relations* 1, 512–32.

Codol, J.-P. (1975) 'On the so-called "superior conformity of the self" behaviour: 20 experimental investigations', *European Journal of Social Psychology* 5, 457–501.

Cohen, A.I. (1981) 'Group cohesion and communal living', in H. Kellerman (ed.), *Group Cohesion: Theoretical and clinical perspectives* (pp. 375–91), New York: Grune and Stratton.

Cohen, A.R. (1958) 'Upward communication in experimentally created hierarchies', *Human Relations* 11, 41–53.

Condor, S. (1990) 'Social stereotypes and social identity', in D. Abrams and M.A. Hogg (eds), *Social Identity Theory: Constructive and critical advances* (pp. 230–49), Hemel Hempstead: Harvester Wheatsheaf/New York: Springer-Verlag.

Converse, P. and Campbell, A. (1968) 'Political standards in secondary groups', in D. Cartwright and A. Zander (eds), *Group Dynamics: Research and theory* (3rd edn, pp. 199–211), New York: Harper and Row.

Cook, S.W. (1978) 'Interpersonal and attitudinal outcomes in cooperating interracial groups', *Journal of Research and Development in Education* 12, 97–113.

Courtright, J.A. (1976) *Groupthink and Communication Process: An initial investigation*, unpublished doctoral dissertation: University of Iowa.

Courtright, J.A. (1978) 'A laboratory investigation of groupthink', *Communication Monographs* 45, 229–46.

Crosbie, P.V. (ed.) (1975) *Interaction in Small Groups*, New York: Macmillan.

Deutsch, M. (1949a) 'A theory of co-operation and competition', *Human Relations* 2, 129–52.

Deutsch, M. (1949b) 'An experimental study of the effects of co-operation and competition upon group processes', *Human Relations* 2, 199–232.

Deutsch, M. (1959) 'Some factors affecting membership motivation and achievement motivation in a group', *Human Relations* 12, 81–95.

Deutsch, M. (1968) 'Field theory in social psychology', in G. Lindzey and E. Aronson (eds), *The Handbook of Social Psychology*, Reading, MA: Addison-Wesley.

Deutsch, M. (1973) *The Resolution of Conflict*, New Haven, CT: Yale University Press.

Deutsch, M. and Gerard, H.B. (1955) 'A study of normative and informational influences upon individual judgement', *Journal of Abnormal and Social Psychology* 51, 629–36.

Deutsch, M. and Krauss, R.M. (1960) 'The effect of threat upon interpersonal bargaining', *Journal of Abnormal and Social Psychology* 61, 181–9.

Deutsch, M. and Krauss, R.M. (1965) *Theories in Social Psychology*, New York: Basic Books.

Diener, E., (1980) 'Deindividuation: The absence of self-awareness and self-regulation in group members', in P.B. Paulus (ed.), *Psychology of Group Influence* (pp. 209–42), Hillsdale, NJ: Erlbaum.

Dimock, H. (1941) *Rediscovering the Adolescent*, New York: Association Press.

Dion, K.L. (1973) 'Cohesiveness as a determinant of ingroup–outgroup bias', *Journal of Personality and Social Psychology* 28, 163–71.

Dion, K.L. (1979) 'Intergroup conflict and intragroup cohesiveness', in W.G. Austin and S. Worchel (eds), *The Social Psychology of Intergroup Relations* (pp.211–24), Monterey, CA: Brooks/Cole.

Dipboye, R.L. (1977) 'Alternative approaches to deindividuation', *Psychological Bulletin* 84, 1057–75.

Doise, W. (1978) *Groups and Individuals: Explanations in social psychology*, Cambridge: Cambridge University Press.

Doise, W. (1982) 'Report on the European Association of Experimental Social Psychology', *European Journal of Social Psychology* 12, 105–11.

Doise, W. (1986) *Levels of Explanation in Social Psychology*, Cambridge: Cambridge University Press.

Doise, W., Csepeli, G., Dann, H.-D., Gouge, C., Larsen, K. and Ostell, A. (1972) 'An experimental investigation into the formation of intergroup representations', *European Journal of Social Psychology* 2, 202–4.

Dollard, J., Doob, L.W., Miller, N.E., Mowrer, O.H. and Sears, R.R. (1939) *Frustration and Aggression*, New Haven, CT: Yale University Press.

Donnelly, P., Carron, A.V. and Chelladurai, P. (1978) *Group Cohesion and Sport*, Ottawa: C.A.H.P.E.R. Sociology and Sport Monograph Series.

Downing, J. (1958) 'Cohesiveness, perception and values', *Human Relations* 11, 157–66.

Drescher, S., Burlingame, G. and Fuhriman, A. (1985) 'Cohesion: An odyssey in empirical understanding', *Small Group Behaviour* 16, 3–30.

Duck, S.W. (1973a) 'Similarity and perceived similarity of personal constructs as influences on friendship choice', *British Journal of Social and Clinical Psychology* 12, 1–6.

Duck, S.W. (1973b) *Personal Relationships and Personal Constructs: A study of friendship formation*, London: Wiley.

Duck, S.W. (1977a) *The Study of Acquaintance*, Farnborough, Hants: Saxon House.

Duck, S.W. (ed.) (1977b) *Theory and Practice in Interpersonal Attraction*, London: Academic Press.

Duck, S.W (1977c) 'Inquiry, hypothesis and the quest for validation: Personal construct systems in the development of acquaintance', in S.W. Duck (ed.), *Theory and Practice in Interpersonal Attraction* (pp. 379–404), London: Academic Press.

Eder, D. (1988) 'Building cohesion through collaborative narration', *Social Psychology Quarterly* 51, 225–35.

Eiser, J.R. (1980) *Cognitive Social Psychology*, London: McGraw-Hill.

Eiser, J.R. and Stroebe, W. (1972) *Categorization and Social Judgement*, London: Academic Press.

Eisman, B. (1959) 'Some operational measures of cohesiveness and their interrelations', *Human Relations* 12, 183–9.

Emler, N. and Hopkins, N. (1990) 'Reputation, social identity and the self', in D. Abrams and M.A. Hogg (eds), *Social Identity Theory: Constructive and critical advances* (pp.113–30), Hemel Hempstead: Harvester Wheatsheaf/New York: Springer-Verlag.

Enoch, J.R. and McLemore, S.D. (1967) 'On the meaning of group cohesion', *Southwestern Social Science Quarterly* 48, 174–82.

Esser, J.K. and Lindoerfer, J.S. (1989) 'Groupthink and the space shuttle *Challenger* accident: Toward a quantitative case analysis', *Journal of Behavioral Decision Making* 2, 167–77.

Evans, N.J. and Jarvis, P.A. (1980). 'Group cohesion: A review and re-evaluation', *Small Group Behavior* 11, 359–70.

Evans, N.J. and Jarvis, P.A. (1986) 'The Group Attitude Scale: A measure of attraction to group', *Small Group Behavior* 17, 203–16.

Exline, R.V. (1957) 'Group climate as a factor in the relevance and accuracy of social perception', *Journal of Abnormal and Social Psychology* 55, 382–8.

Farr, R.M. and Moscovici, S. (eds) (1984) *Social Representations*, Cambridge: Cambridge University Press.

Feldman, R.A. (1968) 'Interrelationships among three bases of group integration', *Sociometry* 31, 30–46.

Feshbach, S. and Singer, R. (1957) 'The effects of personal and shared threats upon social prejudice', *Journal of Abnormal and Social Psychology* 54, 411–16.

Festinger, L. (1950) 'Informal social communication', *Psychological Review* 57, 271–82.

Festinger, L. (1953) 'Group attraction and membership', in D. Cartwright and A. Zander (eds), *Group Dynamics: Research and theory* (pp. 92–101), Evanston, IL: Row, Peterson.

Festinger, L. (1954) 'A theory of social comparison processes', *Human Relations* 7, 117–40.

Festinger, L. (1957) *The Theory of Cognitive Dissonance*, Stanford, CA: Stanford University Press.

Festinger, L. (1980) 'Looking backwards', in L. Festinger (ed.), *Retrospections on Social Psychology* (pp. 236–54), New York: Oxford University Press.

Festinger, L., Schachter, S. and Back, K. (1950) *Social pressures in informal groups*, New York: Harper and Row.

Fiedler, F.E. (1954) 'Assumed similarity measures as predictors of team effectiveness', *Journal of Abnormal and Social Psychology* 49, 381–8.

Fiedler, F.E. (1960) 'The leader's psychological distance and group effectiveness', in D. Cartwright and A. Zander (eds), *Group Dynamics: Research and theory* (2nd edn, pp. 586–606), Evanston, IL: Row, Peterson.

Fiedler, F.E. (1967) 'The effect of intergroup competition on group member adjustment', *Personnel Psychology* 20, 33–44.

Fisher, B.A. (1973) *Small Group Decision-making: Communication and the group process*, New York: McGraw-Hill.

Fisher, R.J. (1990) *The Social Psychology of Intergroup and International Conflict Resolution*, New York: Springer-Verlag.

Fiske, S.T. (1982) 'Schema-triggered affect: Applications to social perception', in M.S. Clark and S.T. Fiske (eds), *Affect and Cognition: The 17th annual Carnegie symposium on cognition* (pp. 55–78), Hillsdale, NJ: Erlbaum.

Fiske, S.T. (1988) 'Compare and contrast: Brewer's dual process model and Fiske *et al.*'s continuum model', in T.K. Srull and R.S. Wyer, Jr (eds), *Advances in Social Cognition* (vol. 1, pp. 65–76), Hillsdale, NJ: Erlbaum.

Fiske, S.T. and Neuberg, S.L. (1990) 'A continuum of impression formation, from category-based to individuating processes: Influences of information and motivation on attention and interpretation', in M.P. Zanna (ed.), *Advances in Experimental Social Psychology* (vol. 23, pp. 1–74). New York: Academic Press.

Fiske, S.T. and Taylor, S.E. (1991) *Social Cognition* (2nd edn), New York: McGraw-Hill.

Flowers, M.L. (1977) 'A laboratory test of some implications of Janis's groupthink hypothesis', *Journal of Personality and Social Psychology* 35, 888–96.

Fodor, E.M. and Smith, T. (1982) 'The power motive as an influence on group decision making', *Journal of Personality and Social Psychology* 42, 178–85.

Forsyth, D.R. (1983) *An Introduction to Group Dynamics*, Monterey, CA: Brooks/Cole.

Foucault, M. (1972) *The Archaeology of Knowledge*, London: Tavistock.

Frank, J.D. (1957) 'Some determinants, manifestations, and effects of cohesiveness in therapy groups', *International Journal of Group Psychotherapy* 7, 53–63.

French, J.R.P. (1941) 'The disruption and cohesion of groups', *Journal of Abnormal and Social Psychology* 36, 361–77.

French, J.R.P. and Raven, B.H. (1959) 'The bases of social power', in D. Cartwright (ed.), *Studies in Social Power* (pp. 118–49), Ann Arbor, MI: University of Michigan Press.

Freud, S. (1921) *Group Psychology and the Analysis of the Ego*, in J. Strachey (ed.) (1953–64) *Standard Edition of the Complete Psychological Works* (vol. 18), London: Hogarth Press.

Freud, S. (1922) *Group Psychology and the Analysis of the Ego*, London: Hogarth Press.

Gabrenya, W.K., Jr, Latané, B. and Wang, Y.E. (1981) 'Social loafing in cross-cultural perspective: Chinese in Taiwan', *Journal of Cross-Cultural Psychology* 14, 368–84.

Gaertner, S.L., Mann, J., Dovidio, J.F. and Murrell, A. (1989) 'Reducing intergroup bias: The benefits of recategorization', *Journal of Personality and Social Psychology* 57, 239–49.

Gage, N.L. and Exline, R.V. (1953) 'Social perception and effectiveness in discussion groups', *Human Relations* 6, 381–96.

Gal, R. (1986) 'Unit morale: From a theoretical puzzle to an empirical illustration: An Israeli example', *Journal of Applied Social Psychology* 16, 549–64.

Gal, R. and Manning, F.J. (1987) 'Morale and its components: A cross-national comparison', *Journal of Applied Social Psychology* 17, 369–91.

Garfinkel, H. (1967) *Studies in Ethnomethodology*, Englewood Cliffs, NJ: Prentice Hall.

Geen, R. and Gange, J. (1977) 'Drive theory of social facilitation: Twelve years of theory and research', *Psychological Bulletin* 84, 1267–88.

Gergen, K.J. (1973) 'Social psychology as history', *Journal of Personality and Social Psychology* 26, 309–20.

Gergen, K.J. and Gergen, M.M. (1981) *Social Psychology*, New York: Harcourt Brace Jovanovich.

Giles, H. (1978) 'Linguistic differentiation in ethnic groups', in H. Tajfel (ed.), *Differentiation between Social Groups* (pp. 361–93), London: Academic Press.

Giles, H. (ed.) (1984) 'The dynamics of speech accommodation. *International Journal of the Sociology of Language* 46, whole issue.

Giles, H. and Byrne, J.L. (1982) 'The intergroup model of second language acquisition', *Journal of Multilingual and Multicultural Development* 3, 17–40.

Giles, H. and Johnson, P. (1981) 'The role of language in ethnic group relations', in J.C. Turner and H. Giles (eds), *Intergroup Behaviour* (pp. 199–43), Oxford: Blackwell.

Giles, H. and St Clair, R.N. (eds) (1979) *Language and Social Psychology*, Oxford: Blackwell.

Goffman, E. (1959) *The Presentation of Self in Everyday Life*, Garden City, NY: Doubleday-Anchor.

Golembiewski, R.T. (1962) *The Small Group: An analysis of research concepts and operations*, Chicago: University of Chicago Press.

Goodacre, D.M. (1951) 'The use of a sociometric test as a predictor of combat unit effectiveness', *Sociometry* 14, 148–52.

Goodman, P.S., Ravlin, E. and Schminke, M. (1987) 'Understanding groups in organizations', in L.L. Cummings and B.M. Staw (eds), *Research in Organizational Behavior* (vol. 9, pp. 121–73), Greenwich, CT: JAI Press.

Greene, C.N. (1989) 'Cohesion and productivity in work groups', *Small Group Behavior* 20, 70–86.

Greenwald, A.G. (1982) 'Is anyone in charge? Personalysis vs. the principle of personal unity', in J. Suls (ed.), *Psychological Perspectives on the Self* (vol. 1, pp. 151–81), Hillsdale, NJ: Erlbaum.

Griffin, R.W. and Moorhead, G. (1986) *Organizational Behavior*, Dallas, TX: Houghton Mifflin.

Griffitt, W. (1974) 'Attitude similarity and attraction', in T.L. Huston (ed.), *Foundations of Interpersonal Attraction* (pp. 285–308), New York: Academic Books.

Gross, N. (1954) 'Primary functions of the small group', *American Journal of Sociology* 60, 24–30.

Gross, N. and Martin, W.E. (1952) 'On group cohesiveness', *American Journal of Sociology* 57, 546–64.

Gruber, J.J. and Gray, G.R. (1981) 'Factor patterns of variables influencing cohesiveness at various levels of basketball competition', *Research Quarterly for Exercise and Sport* 52, 19–30.

Gundlach, R.H. (1956) 'Effects of on-the-job experiences with negroes upon racial attitudes of white workers in union shops', *Psychological Reports* 2, 67–77.

Gusfield, J.R. (1975) *The Community: A critical response*, New York: Harper Colophon.

Hagstrom, W.O. and Selvin, H.C. (1965) 'The dimension of cohesiveness in small groups', *Sociometry* 28, 30–43.

Hare, A.P. (1962) *Handbook of Small Group Research*, New York: The Free Press.

Harkins, S.G. (1987) 'Social loafing and social facilitation', *Journal of Experimental Social Psychology* 23, 1–18.

Harkins, S.G. and Petty, R. (1982) 'Effects of task difficulty and task uniqueness on social loafing', *Journal of Personality and Social Psychology* 43, 1214–29.

Harkins, S.G. and Szymanski, K. (1987) 'Social loafing and social facilitation: New wine in old bottles', in C. Hendrick (ed.), *Review of Personality and Social Psychology: Group processes and intergroup relations* (vol. 9, pp. 167–88), Newbury Park, CA: Sage.

Harkins, S.G. and Szymanski, K. (1989) 'Social loafing and group evaluation', *Journal of Personality and Social Psychology* 56, 934–41.

Harré, R. (1977) 'The ethogenic approach: Theory and practice', *Advances in Experimental Social Psychology* 10, 283–314.

Harré, R. (1979) *Social Being: A theory for social psychology*, Oxford: Blackwell.

Harvey, J.H. and Smith, W.P. (1977) *Social Psychology: An attribution approach*, St Louis, LA: Mosby.

Harvey, J.H. and Weary, G. (1984) 'Current issues in attribution theory and research', *Annual Review of Psychology* 35, 427–59.

Heider, F. (1958) *The Psychology of Interpersonal Relations*, New York: Wiley.

Hensley, T.R. and Griffin, G.W. (1986) 'Victims of groupthink: The Kent State University Board of Trustees and the 1977 gymnasium controversy', *Journal of Conflict Resolution* 30, 497–531.

Hewstone, M.R.C. (ed.) (1983) *Attribution Theory: Social and functional extensions*, Oxford: Blackwell.

Hewstone, M.R.C. (1989) *Causal Attribution: From cognitive processes to collective beliefs*, Oxford: Blackwell.

Hewstone, M.R.C. and Brown, R.J. (eds) (1986) *Contact and Conflict in Intergroup Encounters*, Oxford: Blackwell.

Hinkle, S. and Brown, R.J. (1990) 'Intergroup comparisons and social identity: Some links and lacunae', in D. Abrams and M.A. Hogg (eds), *Social Identity Theory: Constructive and critical advances* (pp. 48–70), Hemel Hempstead: Harvester Wheatsheaf/New York: Springer-Verlag.

Hoffman, L.R. (1958) 'Similarity of personality: A basis for interpersonal attraction?', *Sociometry* 21, 300–8.

Hogg, M.A. (1983) *Investigations into the Social Psychology of Group Formation: A cognitive perspective*, unpublished doctoral dissertation, University of Bristol.

Hogg, M.A. (1985a) 'Masculine and feminine speech in dyads and groups: A study of speech style and gender salience', *Journal of Language and Social Psychology* 4, 99–112.

Hogg, M.A. (1985b) 'Cohesión de grupo', in C. Huici (ed.), *Estructura y procesos de grupo* (vol. 1, pp. 463–86), Madrid: Universidad de Educación a Distancia.

Hogg, M.A. (1987) 'Social identity and group cohesiveness', in J.C. Turner, M.A. Hogg, P.J. Oakes, S.D. Reicher and M.S. Wetherell, *Rediscovering the Social Group: A self-categorization theory* (pp. 89–116), Oxford and New York: Blackwell.

Hogg, M.A. (1990) *Groupthink: A critique from the perspective of social identity theory*, unpublished manuscript, University of Queensland.

Hogg, M.A. (in press) 'Group cohesiveness: A critical review and some new directions', in W. Stroebe and M. Hewstone (eds), *European Review of Social Psychology* (vol. 4), Chichester: Wiley.

Hogg, M.A. and Abrams, D. (1988) *Social Identifications: A social psychology of intergroup relations and group processes*, London and New York: Routledge.

Hogg, M.A. and Abrams, D. (1990) 'Social motivation, self-esteem and social identity', in D. Abrams and M.A. Hogg (eds), *Social Identity Theory: Constructive and critical advances* (pp. 28–47), Hemel Hempstead: Harvester Wheatsheaf.

Hogg, M.A., Cooper-Shaw, L. and Holzworth, D.W. (in press) 'Studies of group prototypicality and depersonalized attraction in small interactive groups', *Personality and Social Psychology Bulletin*.

Hogg, M.A. and Hardie, E.A. (1990) *Group Cohesiveness and Self-categorization: A study of lay explanations for depersonalized attraction*, unpublished manuscript, University of Queensland.

Hogg, M.A. and Hardie, E.A. (1991) 'Social attraction, personal attraction, and self-categorization: A field study', *Personality and Social Psychology Bulletin* 17, 175–80.

Hogg, M.A. and Hardie, E.A. (1992a) 'Prototypicality, conformity and depersonalized attraction: A self-categorization analysis of group cohesiveness', *British Journal of Social Psychology* 31, 41–56.

Hogg, M.A. and Hardie, E.A. (1992b) *Self-categorization and Depersonalized Attraction: Two experiments on the relationship between self-prototypicality and liking among group members*, unpublished manuscript, University of Queensland.

Hogg, M.A., Hardie, E.A. and Bailey, N. (1991) *Depersonalized Perception: A self-categorization analysis of group cohesiveness*, unpublished manuscript, University of Queensland.

Hogg, M.A., Hardie, E.A. and Reynolds, K.J. (1992) *Prototypical Similarity, Self-categorization, and Depersonalized Attraction: A perspective on group cohesiveness*, unpublished manuscript, University of Queensland.

Hogg, M.A. and McGarty, C. (1990) 'Self-categorization and social identity', in D. Abrams and M.A. Hogg (eds), *Social Identity Theory: Constructive and critical advances* (pp. 10–27), Hemel Hempstead: Harvester Wheatsheaf/New York: Springer-Verlag.

Hogg, M.A. and Turner, J.C. (1985a) 'Interpersonal attraction, social identification and psychological group formation', *European Journal of Social Psychology* 15, 51–66.

Hogg, M.A. and Turner, J.C. (1985b) 'When liking begets solidarity: An experiment on the role of interpersonal attraction in psychological group formation', *British Journal of Social Psychology* 24, 267–81.

Hogg, M.A. and Turner, J.C. (1987a) 'Social identity and conformity: A theory of referent informational influence', in W. Doise and S. Moscovici (eds), *Current Issues in European Social Psychology* (vol. 2, pp. 139–82), Cambridge: Cambridge University Press.

Hogg, M.A. and Turner, J.C. (1987b) 'Intergroup behaviour, self-stereotyping and the salience of social categories', *British Journal of Social Psychology*, 26, 325–40.

Hogg, M.A., Turner, J.C. and Davidson, B. (1990). 'Polarized norms and social frames of reference: A test of the self-categorization theory of group polarization', *Basic and Applied Social Psychology* 11, 77–100.

Hollingshead, A. (1949) *Elmstown's Youth*, New York: Wiley.

Homans, G.C. (1950) *The Human Group*, New York: Harcourt Brace Jovanovich.

Homans, G.C. (1961) *Social Behavior*, New York: Harcourt, Brace and World.

Hunt, J.McV. and Solomon, R.L. (1942) 'The stability and some correlates of group-status in a summer camp group of young boys', *American Journal of Psychology* 55, 33–45.

Huseman, R.C. and Driver, R.W. (1979) 'Groupthink: Implications for small group decision making in business', in R. Huseman and A. Carroll (eds), *Readings in Organizational Behavior* (pp. 100–10). Boston, MA: Allyn and Bacon.

Huston, T.L. (ed.) (1974) *Foundations of Interpersonal Attraction*, New York: Academic Press.

Huston, T.L. and Levinger, G. (1978) 'Interpersonal attraction and relationships', *Annual Review of Psychology* 29, 115–56.

Indik, B.P. (1965) 'Organizational size and member participation: Some empirical tests of alternative explanations', *Human Relations* 18, 339–50.

Ingham, A., Levinger, G., Graves, J. and Peckham, V. (1974) 'The Ringelmann effect: Studies of group size and group performance', *Journal of Experimental Social Psychology* 10, 371–84.

Ingraham, L.H. and Manning, F.J. (1981) 'Cohesion: Who needs it, what is it, and how do we get it to them?', *Military Review* 61, 2–12.

Isenberg, D.J. (1986) 'Group polarization: A critical review and meta–analysis', *Journal of Personality and Social Psychology* 50, 1141–51.

Israel, J. (1956) *Self-evaluation and Rejection in Groups*, Stockholm: Almqvist and Wiksell.

Israel, J. and Tajfel, H. (eds) (1972) *The Context of Social Psychology: A critical assessment*, London: Academic Press.

Jackson, J. and Harkins, S.G. (1985) 'Equity in effort: An explanation of the social loafing effect', *Journal of Personality and Social Psychology* 49, 1199–206.

Jackson, J.M. (1959) 'Reference group processes in a formal organization', *Sociometry* 22, 307–27.

James, J. (1951) 'A preliminary study of the size determinant in social group interaction', *American Sociological Review* 16, 474–7.

James, J. (1953) 'The distribution of free-forming small group size', *American Sociological Review* 18, 569–70.

Janis, I.L. (1972) *Victims of Groupthink: A psychological study of foreign policy decisions and fiascoes*, Boston, MA: Houghton Mifflin.

Janis, I.L. (1982a) *Groupthink: Psychological studies of policy decisions and fiascoes* (2nd edn), Boston, MA: Houghton Mifflin.

Janis, I.L. (1982b) 'Counteracting the adverse effects of concurrence-seeking in policy-planning groups: Theory and research perspectives', in H. Brandstätter, J.H. Davis and G. Stocker-Kreichgauer (eds), *Group Decision Making* (pp. 477–501)., New York: Academic Press.

Janis, I.L. (1985) 'International crisis management in the nuclear age', *Applied Social Psychology Annual* 6, 63–86.

Janis, I.L. and Mann, L. (1977). *Decision Making*, New York: The Free Press.

Jaspars, J.M.F. (1980) 'The coming of age of social psychology in Europe', *European Journal of Social Psychology* 10, 421–9.

Jaspars, J.M.F. (1986) 'Forum and focus: A personal view of European social psychology', *European Journal of Social Psychology* 16, 3–15.

Jellison, J. and Arkin, R. (1977) 'Social comparison of abilities: A self-presentation approach to decision making in groups', in J.M. Suls and R.L. Miller (eds), *Social Comparison Processes: Theoretical and empirical perspectives* (pp. 235–57), Washington, DC: Hemisphere.

Jennings, H.H. (1947a) 'Sociometric differentiation of the psychegroup and the sociogroup', *Sociometry* 10, 71–9.

Jennings, H.H. (1947b) 'Leadership and sociometric choice', *Sociometry* 10, 32–49.

Jennings, H.H. (1950) *Leadership and Isolation* (2nd edn), New York: Longmans Green.

Johnson, D.W. and Johnson, F.P. (1987) *Joining Together: Group theory and group skills* (3rd edn), Englewood Cliffs, NJ: Prentice Hall.

Johnston, L. and Hewstone, M. (1990) 'Intergroup contact: Social identity and social cognition', in D. Abrams and M.A. Hogg (eds), *Social Identity Theory: Constructive and critical advances* (pp. 185–210), Hemel Hempstead: Harvester Wheatsheaf/New York: Springer-Verlag.

Jones, E.E. and Davis, K.E. (1965) 'From acts to dispositions: The attribution process in person perception', *Advances in Experimental Social Psychology* 2, 219–66.

Jorgensen, D.O. and Dukes, F.O. (1976) 'Deindividuation as a function of density and group membership', *Journal of Personality and Social Psychology* 34, 24–9.

Julian, J.W., Bishop, D.W. and Fiedler, F.E. (1966) 'Quasi-therapeutic effects of intergroup competition', *Journal of Personality and Social Psychology* 3, 321–7.

Kandel, D.B. (1978) 'Similarity in real-life adolescent friendship pairs', *Journal of Personality and Social Psychology* 36, 306–12.

Kanter, R.M. (1968) 'Commitment and social organization: A study of commitment mechanisms in utopian communities', *American Sociological Review* 33, 499–517.

Kanter, R.M. (1972) *Commitment and Community: Communes and utopias in sociological perspective*, Cambridge, MA: Harvard University Press.

Karau, S.J. and Williams, K.D. (1992) *The Effects of Group Cohesiveness on Social Loafing and Social Compensation*, unpublished manuscript, Purdue University.

Keller, R.T. (1986) 'Predictions of the performance of project groups in R and D organisations', *Academy of Management Journal* 29, 715–26.

Kellerman, H. (ed.) (1981) *Group Cohesion*, New York: Grune and Stratton.

Kelley, H.H. (1951) 'Communication in experimentally created hierarchies. *Human Relations* 4, 39–56.

Kelley, H.H. (1952) 'Two functions of reference groups', in G.E. Swanson, T.M. Newcomb and E.L. Hartley (eds), *Readings in Social Psychology* (2nd edn, pp. 410–14), New York: Holt, Rinehart and Winston.

Kelley, H.H. (1967) 'Attribution theory in social psychology', in D. Levine (ed.), *Nebraska Symposium on Motivation* (pp. 192–238), Lincoln, NE: University of Nebraska Press.

Kelley, H.H. and Michela, J.L. (1980) 'Attribution theory and research', *Annual Review of Psychology* 31, 457–501.

Kelley, H.H. and Thibaut, J. (1954) 'Experimental studies of group problem solving and process', in G. Lindzey (ed.), *Handbook of Social Psychology* (pp. 735–85), Cambridge, MA: Addison-Wesley.

Kelley, H.H. and Thibaut, J. (1978) *Interpersonal Relations: A theory of interdependence*, New York: Wiley.

Kelly, G.A. (1955) *The Psychology of Personal Constructs*, New York: Norton.

Kelly, G.A. (1970) 'A brief introduction to personal construct theory', in D. Bannister (ed.), *Perspectives in Personal Construct Theory* (pp. 1–29), London: Academic Press.

Kelman, H.C. (1958) 'Compliance, identification and internalization: Three processes of opinion change', *Journal of Conflict Resolution* 2, 51–60.

Kelman, H.C. (1961) 'Processes of opinion change', *Public Opinion Quarterly* 25, 57–78.

Kiesler, C.A. and Kiesler, S.B. (1969) *Conformity*, Reading, MA: Addison-Wesley.

Kirshner, B.J., Dies, R.R. and Brown, R.A. (1978) 'Effects of experimental manipulation of self-disclosure on group cohesiveness', *Journal of Consulting and Clinical Psychology* 46, 1171–7.

Knowles, E.S. (1982) 'From individuals to group members: A dialectic for the social sciences', in W.J. Ickes and E.S. Knowles (eds), *Personality, Roles and Social Behavior* (pp. 1–32), New York: Springer-Verlag.

Knowles, E.S. and Brickner, M.A. (1981) 'Social cohesion effects on spatial cohesion', *Personality and Social Psychology Bulletin* 7, 309–13.

Krech, D. and Crutchfield, R.S. (1948) *Theory and Problems of Psychology*, New York: McGraw-Hill.

Kuhn, T.S. (1962) *The Structure of Scientific Revolutions*, Chicago, IL: University of Chicago Press.

Lakoff, G. and Johnson, M. (1980) *Metaphors We Live By*, Chicago, IL: University of Chicago Press.

Landers, D.M. and Luschen, G. (1974) 'Team performance outcome and the cohesiveness of competitive coacting groups', *International Review of Sports Sociology* 9, 57–71.

Landers, D.M., Wilkinson, M.O., Hatfield, B.D. and Barber, H. (1982) 'Causality and the cohesion–performance relationship', *Journal of Sport Psychology* 4, 170–83.

Landman, J. and Manis, M. (1983) 'Social cognition: Some historical and theoretical perspectives', *Advances in Experimental Social Psychology* 16, 49–123.

Latané, B. (1981) 'The psychology of social impact', *American Psychologist* 36, 343–56.

Latané, B. and Nida, S. (1980) 'Social impact theory and group influence: A social engineering perspective', in P.B. Paulus (ed.), *Psychology of Group Influence* (pp. 3–34), Hillsdale, NJ: Erlbaum.

Latané, B., Williams, K.D. and Harkins, S. (1979) 'Many hands make light the work:

The causes and consequences of social loafing', *Journal of Personality and Social Psychology* 37, 822–32.

Lauderdale, P., Smith-Cunnien, P., Parker, J. and Inverarity, J. (1984) 'External threat and the definition of deviance', *Journal of Personality and Social Psychology* 46, 1058–68.

Lazarsfield, P.F. and Merton, R.K. (1954) 'Friendship as social process: A substantive and methodological analysis', in M. Berger, T. Abel and C.H. Page (eds), *Freedom and Control in Modern Society* (pp. 18–66), New York: Van Nostrand.

Lea, M. (1991) *Friendships in Transition: Social attraction, value similarity, and the development of personal relationships*, unpublished manuscript, University of Manchester.

Lea, M. and Duck, S. (1982) 'A model for the role of similarity of values in friendship development', *British Journal of Social Psychology* 21, 301–10.

Leana, C.R. (1985) 'A partial test of Janis's groupthink model: Effects of group cohesiveness and leader behavior on defective decision making', *Journal of Management* 11, 5–17.

LeBon, G. (1908) *The Crowd: A study of the popular mind*, London: Unwin (first published in French in 1896).

LeBon, G. (1913) *The Psychology of Revolution*, New York: Putnam.

Lebow, R.N. (1981) *Between Peace and War*, Baltimore, MD: Johns Hopkins University Press.

Lenk, H. (1969) 'Top performance despite internal conflict: An antithesis to a functional proposition', in J.W. Loy and G.S. Kenyon (eds), *Sport, Culture and Society* (pp. 393–7), New York: Macmillan.

Lerner, M.J. and Becker, S. (1962) 'Interpersonal choice as a function of ascribed similarity and definition of the situation', *Human Relations* 15, 27–34.

Levine, J.M. and Moreland, R.L. (1985) 'Innovation and socialization in small groups', in S. Moscovici, G. Mugny and E. van Avermaet (eds), *Perspectives on Minority Influence* (pp. 143–69), Cambridge: Cambridge University Press.

Levine, J.M. and Moreland, R.L. (1990) 'Progress in small group research', *Annual Review of Psychology* 41, 585–634.

LeVine, R.A. and Campbell, D.T. (1972) *Ethnocentrism: Theories of conflict, ethnic attitudes and group behavior*, New York: Wiley.

Lewin, K. (1936) *Principles of Topological Psychology*, New York: McGraw-Hill.

Lewin, K. (1943) 'Psychology and the process of group living', *Journal of Social Psychology* 17, 119–29.

Lewin, K. (1948) *Resolving Social Conflicts*, New York: Harper and Bros.

Lewin, K. (1951) *Field Theory in Social Science*, New York: Harper.

Lewin, K. (1952) *Field Theory in Social Science*, London: Tavistock.

Libo, L.M. (1953) *Measuring Group Cohesiveness*, Ann Arbor, MI: Institute for Social Research, University of Michigan.

Lieberman, M.A., Yalom, I.D. and Miles, M.B. (1973) *Encounter Groups: First facts*, New York: Basic Books.

Lindzey, G. and Borgatta, E.F. (1954) 'Sociometric measurement', in G. Lindzey (ed.), *Handbook of Social Psychology* (pp. 405–48), Cambridge, MA: Addison-Wesley.

Lofland, J.F. (1981) 'Collective behavior: The elementary forms', in M. Rosenberg and R.H. Turner (eds), *Social Psychology: Sociological perspectives* (pp. 411–46), New York: Basic Books.

Longley, J. and Pruitt, D.G. (1980) 'Groupthink: A critique of Janis' theory', in L.

Wheeler (ed.), *Review of Personality and Social Psychology* (vol. 1, pp. 74–93), Beverly Hills, CA: Sage.

Lorenzi-Cioldi, F. and Doise, W. (1990) 'Levels of analysis and social identity', in D. Abrams and M.A. Hogg (eds), *Social Identity Theory: Constructive and critical advances* (pp. 71–88), Hemel Hempstead: Harvester Wheatsheaf/New York: Springer-Verlag.

Lott, A.J. and Lott, B.E. (1961) 'Group cohesiveness, communication level and conformity', *Journal of Abnormal and Social Psychology* 62, 408–12.

Lott, A.J. and Lott, B.E. (1965) 'Group cohesiveness as interpersonal attraction', *Psychological Bulletin* 64, 259–309.

Lott, B.E. (1961) 'Group cohesiveness: A learning phenomenon', *Journal of Social Psychology* 55, 275–86.

Lyndsay, J.S.B. (1972) 'On the number in a group', *Human Relations* 25, 47–64.

Lyndsay, J.S.B. (1976) 'On the number and size of sub-groups', *Human Relations* 29, 1103–14.

Mann, F. and Baumgartel, H. (1952) *Absences and Employee Attitudes in an Electric Power Company*, Ann Arbor, MI: Institute for Social Research.

Manning, F.J. and Fullerton, T.D. (1988) 'Health and well-being in highly cohesive units of the U.S. Army', *Journal of Applied Social Psychology* 18, 503–19.

Manz, C.C. and Sims, H.P. (1982) 'The potential for "groupthink" in autonomous work groups', *Human Relations* 35, 773–84.

Markus, H. and Zajonc, R.B. (1985) 'The cognitive perspective in social psychology', in G. Lindzey and E. Aronson (eds), *The Handbook of Social Psychology* (3rd edn, vol. 1, pp. 137–229), Reading, MA: Addison-Wesley.

Marlowe, D. and Gergen, K. (1969) 'Personality and social interaction', in G. Lindzey and E. Aronson (eds), *The Handbook of Social Psychology* (2nd edn, vol. 3, pp. 590–665), Reading, MA: Addison-Wesley.

Marques, J.M. (1990) 'The black-sheep effect: Out-group homogeneity in social comparison settings', in D. Abrams and M.A. Hogg (eds), *Social Identity Theory: Constructive and critical advances* (pp. 131–51), Hemel Hempstead: Harvester Wheatsheaf/New York: Springer-Verlag.

Marques, J.M.,and Yzerbyt, V.Y. (1988) 'The black sheep effect: Judgmental extremity towards ingroup members in inter- and intra-group situations', *European Journal of Social Psychology* 18, 287–92.

Marques, J.M., Yzerbyt, V.Y. and Leyens, J.-P. (1988) 'The black sheep effect: Extremity of judgements towards in-group members as a function of group identification', *European Journal of Social Psychology* 18, 1–16.

Marrow, A.J. (1969) *The Practical Theorist: The life and work of Kurt Lewin*, New York: Basic Books.

Marshall, J. and Heslin, R. (1975) 'Boys and girls together: Sexual composition and the effect of density and group size on cohesiveness', *Journal of Personality and Social Psychology* 31, 952–61.

Martens, R., Landers, D.M. and Loy, J. (1972) *Sports Cohesiveness Questionnaire*, unpublished manuscript, University of Illinois, Urbana.

Martens, R. and Peterson, J.A. (1971) 'Group cohesiveness as a determinant of success and member satisfaction in team performance', *International Review of Sports Sociology* 6, 49–61.

Marx, K. (1963) *Early Writings* (transl. and ed. T.B. Bottomore), New York: McGraw-Hill (first published in German in 1844).

McCarthy, B. (1981) 'Studying personal relationships', in S. Duck and R. Gilmour (eds), *Personal Relationships (vol. 1): Studying personal relationships* (pp. 23–46), London: Academic Press.

McCauley, C. (1989) 'The nature of social influence in groupthink: Compliance and internalization', *Journal of Personality and Social Psychology* 57, 250–60.

McDavid, J. and Harari, H. (1968) *Social Psychology: Individuals, groups, societies*, New York: Harper and Row.

McDougall, W. (1908) *An Introduction to Social Psychology*, London: Methuen.

McDougall, W. (1921) *The Group Mind*, London: Cambridge University Press.

McGarty, C. and Penny, R.E.C. (1988) 'Categorization, accentuation and social judgement', *British Journal of Social Psychology* 27, 147–57.

McGarty, C., Turner, J.C., Hogg, M.A., David, B. and Wetherell, M.S. (1992) 'Group polarization as conformity to the prototypical group member', *British Journal of Social Psychology* 31, 1–20.

McGrath, J.E. (1962) 'The influence of positive interpersonal relations on adjustment effectiveness in rifle teams', *Journal of Abnormal and Social Psychology* 65, 365–75.

McGrath, J.E. (1978) 'Small group research', *American Behavioral Scientist* 21, 651–74.

McGrath, J.E. and Kravitz, D.A. (1982) 'Group research', *Annual Review of Psychology* 33, 195–230.

McKeachie, W.J. (1954) 'Individual conformity to attitudes of classroom groups', *Journal of Abnormal and Social Psychology* 49, 282–9.

McMillan, D.W. and Chavis, D.M. (1986) 'Sense of community: A definition and theory', *Journal of Community Psychology* 14, 6–23.

Miesing, P. and Preble, J.F. (1985) 'Group processes and performance in a complex business simulation', *Small Group Behavior* 16, 325–38.

Mikula, G. (1984) 'Personal relationships: Remarks on the current state of research', *European Journal of Social Psychology* 14, 339–52.

Miller, N. and Brewer, M.B. (1984) *Groups in Contact: The psychology of desegregation*, New York: Academic Press.

Mills, T.M. (1967) *The Sociology of Small Groups*, Englewood Cliffs, NJ: Prentice Hall.

Minard, R.D. (1952) 'Race relations in the Pocahontas coalfield', *Journal of Social Issues* 8, 29–44.

Mobley, W.H., Griffeth, R.W., Hand, H.H. and Meglino, B.M. (1979) 'Review and conceptual analysis of employee turnover process', *Psychological Bulletin* 86, 493–522.

Moorhead, G. (1982) 'Groupthink: Hypothesis in need of testing', *Group and Organizational Studies* 7, 429–44.

Moorhead, G. and Montanari, J.R. (1986) 'An empirical investigation of the groupthink phenomenon', *Human Relations* 39, 399–410.

Moos, R.H., Insel, P.M. and Humphrey, B. (1974) *Preliminary Manual for Group Environment Scale*, Palo Alto, CA: Consulting Psychologists Press.

Moreland, R.L. (1985) 'Social categorization and the assimilation of "new" group members', *Journal of Personality and Social Psychology* 48, 1173–90.

Moreland, R.L. (1987) 'The formation of small groups', in C. Hendrick (ed.), *Review of Personality and Social Psychology: Group processes* (vol. 8, pp. 80–110), Newbury Park, CA: Sage.

Moreland, R.L. and Levine, J.M. (1982) 'Socialization in small groups: Temporal changes in individual–group relations', *Advances in Experimental Social Psychology* 15, 137–92.

Moreland, R.L. and Levine, J.M. (1984) 'Role transitions in small groups', in V. Allen and E. van de Vliert (eds), *Role Transitions: Explorations and explanations* (pp. 181–95), New York: Plenum.

Moreland, R.L. and Levine, J.M. (1989) 'Newcomers and oldtimers in small groups', in P.B. Paulus (ed.), *Psychology of Group Influence* (2nd edn, pp. 143–86), Hillsdale, NJ: Erlbaum.

Moreno, J.L. (1934) *Who Shall Survive?*, Washington, DC: Nervous and Mental Diseases Publishing Co.

Moreno, J.L. and Jennings, H.H. (1937) 'Statistics of social configurations', *Sociometry* 1, 342–74.

Moscovici, S. (1961) *La Psychanalyse: Son image et son public*, Paris: Presses Universitaires de France.

Moscovici, S. (1972) 'Society and theory in social psychology', in J. Israel and H. Tajfel (eds), *The Context of Social Psychology: A critical assessment* (pp. 17–68), New York: Academic Press.

Moscovici, S. (1976) *Social Influence and Social Change*, London: Academic Press.

Moscovici, S. (1981) 'On social representation', in J.P. Forgas (ed.), *Social Cognition: Perspectives on everyday understanding* (pp. 181–209), London: Academic Press.

Moscovici, S. and Zavalloni, M. (1969) 'The group as a polarizer of attitudes', *Journal of Personality and Social Psychology* 12, 125–35.

Motowidlo, S.J. and Borman, W.C. (1978) 'Relationships between military morale, motivation, satisfaction, and unit effectiveness', *Journal of Applied Psychology* 63, 47–52.

Mudrack, P.E. (1989a) 'Defining group cohesiveness: A legacy of confusion', *Small Group Behavior* 20, 37–49.

Mudrack, P.E. (1989b) 'Group cohesiveness and productivity: A closer look', *Human Relations* 42, 771–85.

Mugny, G. (1982) *The Power of Minorities*, London: Academic Press.

Myers, A. (1962) 'Team competition, success, and the adjustment of group members', *Journal of Abnormal and Social Psychology* 65, 325–32.

Myers, D.G. and Lamm, H. (1975) 'The polarizing effect of group discussion', *American Scientist* 63, 297–303.

Myers, D.G. and Lamm, H. (1976) 'The group polarization phenomenon', *Psychological Bulletin* 83, 602–27.

Neuberg, S.L. and Fiske, S.T. (1987) 'Motivational influences on impression formation: Outcome dependency, accuracy-driven attention, and individuating processes', *Journal of Personality and Social Psychology* 53, 431–44.

Newcomb, T.M. (1953) 'An approach to the study of communicative acts', *Psychological Review* 60, 393–404.

Newcomb, T.M. (1960) 'Varieties of interpersonal attraction', in D. Cartwright and A. Zander (eds), *Group Dynamics: Research and theory* (2nd edn, pp. 104–19), Evanston, IL: Row, Peterson.

Newcomb, T.M. (1961) *The Acquaintance Process*, New York: Holt, Rinehart and Winston.

Newcomb, T.M. (1968) 'Interpersonal balance', in R. Abelson, E. Aronson, W. McGuire, T. Newcomb, M. Rosenberg and P. Tannenbaum (eds), *Theories of Cognitive Consistency: A sourcebook* (pp. 28–51), Chicago, IL: Rand McNally.

Nixon, H.L. (1976) 'Team orientations, interpersonal relations, and team success', *Research Quarterly* 47, 429–33.

Nixon, H.L. (1977) 'Reinforcement effects of sports team success cohesiveness-related factors', *International Review of Sports Sociology* 12, 17–38.

Osgood, C.E. and Tannenbaum, P.H. (1955) 'The principle of congruity in the prediction of attitude change', *Psychological Review* 62, 42–55.

Owen, W.F. (1985) 'Metaphor analysis of cohesiveness in small discussion groups', *Small Group Behavior* 16, 415–24.

Paicheler, G. (1988) *The Psychology of Social Influence*, Cambridge: Cambridge University Press.

Parsons, T. and Shils, E.A. (eds) (1951) *Working Papers in the Theory of Action*, Cambridge: MA: Harvard University Press.

Pavelchak, M.A., Moreland, R.L. and Levine, J.M. (1986) 'Effects of prior group memberships on subsequent reconnaissance activities', *Journal of Personality and Social Psychology* 50, 56–66.

Pennington, D.F., Harary, F. and Bass, B.M. (1958) 'Some effects of decision and discussion on coalescence change and effectiveness', *Journal of Applied Psychology* 42, 404–8.

Pepitone, A. (1981) 'Lessons from the history of social psychology', *American Psychologist* 36, 972–85.

Pepitone, A. and Kleiner, R. (1957) 'The effects of threat and frustration on group cohesiveness', *Journal of Abnormal and Social Psychology* 54, 192–9.

Pepitone, A. and Reichling, G. (1955) 'Group cohesiveness and the expression of hostility', *Human Relations* 8, 327–37.

Pérez, J.A. and Mugny, G. (1990). 'Minority influence, manifest discrimination and latent influence', in D. Abrams and M.A. Hogg (eds), *Social Identity Theory: Constructive and critical advances* (pp. 152–68), Hemel Hempstead: Harvester Wheatsheaf/New York: Springer-Verlag.

Peterson, J.A. and Martens, R. (1973) 'Success and residential affiliation as determinants of team cohesiveness', *The Research Quarterly* 43, 325–32.

Piper, W.E., Marrache, M., LaCroix, R., Richardsen, M. and Jones, B.D. (1983) 'Cohesion as a basic bond in groups', *Human Relations* 36, 93–108.

Porter, L.W. and Lawler, E.E., III (1965) 'Properties of organization structure in relation to job attitudes and job behavior', *Psychological Bulletin* 64, 23–51.

Potter, J. and Litton, L. (1985). 'Some problems underlying the theory of social representation', *British Journal of Social Psychology* 24, 81–90.

Potter, J., Stringer, P. and Wetherell, M.S. (1984) *Social Texts and Context: Literature and social psychology*, London: Routledge and Kegan Paul.

Potter, J. and Wetherell, M.S. (1987) *Discourse and Social Psychology: Beyond attitudes and behaviour*, London: Sage.

Potter, J., Wetherell, M.S., Gill, R. and Edwards, D. (1990) 'Discourse: Noun, verb or social practice?', *Philosophical Psychology* 3, 205–17.

Prentice-Dunn, S. and Rogers, R.W. (1982) 'Effects of public and private self-awareness on deindividuation and aggression', *Journal of Personality and Social Psychology* 43, 503–13.

Radke, M. and Klisurich, D. (1947) 'Experiments in changing food habits', *Journal of the American Dietetic Association* 24, 403–9.

Ramuz-Nienhuis, W. and van Bergen, A. (1960) 'Relations between some components of attraction-to-group: A replication', *Human Relations* 13, 271–7.

Raven, B.H. (1974) 'The comparative analysis of power and power preference', in J.T. Tedeschi (ed.), *Perspectives on Social Power* (pp. 172–98), Chicago, IL: Aldine.

Raven, B.H. and Kruglanski, A. (1970) 'Conflict and power', in P. Swingle (ed.), *The Structure of Conflict* (pp. 69–109), New York: Academic Press.

Raven, B.H. and Rubin, J.Z. (1983) *Social Psychology* (2nd edn), New York: Wiley.

Reicher, S.D. (1982) 'The determination of collective behaviour', in H. Tajfel (ed.), *Social Identity and Intergroup Relations* (pp. 41–83), Cambridge: Cambridge University Press.

Reicher, S.D. (1984) 'Social influence in the crowd: Attitudinal and behavioural effects of deindividuation in conditions of high and low group salience', *British Journal of Social Psychology* 23, 341–50.

Reicher, S.D. (1987) 'Crowd behaviour as social action', in J.C. Turner, M.A. Hogg, P.J. Oakes, S.D. Reicher and M.S. Wetherell, *Rediscovering the Social Group: A self-categorization theory* (pp. 171–202), Oxford & New York: Blackwell.

Riecken, H.W. and Homans, G.C. (1954) 'Psychological aspects of social structure', in G. Lindzey (ed.), *Handbook of Social Psychology* (pp. 786–832), Cambridge, MA: Addison-Wesley.

Riger, S. and Lavrakas, P. (1981) 'Community ties: Patterns of attachment and social interaction in urban neighborhoods', *American Journal of Community Psychology* 9, 55–66.

Roark, A.E. and Sharah, H.S. (1989) 'Factors related to group cohesiveness', *Small Group Behavior* 20, 62–9.

Rosch, E. (1978) 'Principles of categorization', in E. Rosch and B.B. Lloyd (eds), *Cognition and Categorization* (pp. 27–48), Hillsdale, NJ: Erlbaum.

Roseborough, M. (1953) 'Experimental studies of small groups', *Psychological Bulletin* 50, 275–303.

Rosenfield, L.B. and Gilbert, J.R. (1989) 'The measurement of cohesion and its relationship to dimensions of self–disclosure in classroom settings', *Small Group Behavior* 20, 291–301.

Ross, L. (1977) 'The intuitive psychologist and his shortcomings', *Advances in Experimental Social Psychology* 10, 174–220.

Ross, M. and Fletcher, G.J.O. (1985) 'Attribution and social perception', in G. Lindzey and E. Aronson (eds), *Handbook of Social Psychology* (3rd edn, vol. 2, pp. 73–122), New York: Random House.

Rubin, Z. (1973) *Liking and Loving: An invitation to social psychology*, New York: Holt, Rinehart and Winston.

Sachdev, I. and Bourhis, R.Y. (1984) 'Minimal majorities and minorities', *European Journal of Social Psychology* 14, 35–52.

Sachdev, I. and Bourhis, R.Y. (1985) 'Social categorization and power differentials in group relations', *European Journal of Social Psychology* 15, 415–34.

Sachdev, I. and Bourhis, R.Y. (1987) 'Status differentials and intergroup behaviour', *European Journal of Social Psychology* 17, 277–93.

Sachdev, I. and Bourhis, R.Y. (1990) 'Language and social identification', in D. Abrams and M.A. Hogg (eds), *Social Identity Theory: Constructive and critical advances* (pp. 211–29), Hemel Hempstead: Harvester Wheatsheaf/New York: Springer-Verlag.

Sachdev, I. and Bourhis, R.Y. (1991) 'Power and status differentials in minority and majority group relations', *European Journal of Social Psychology* 21, 1–24.

Sakurai, M. (1975) 'Small group cohesiveness and detrimental conformity', *Sociometry* 38, 340–57.

Sampson E.E. (1977) 'Psychology and the American ideal', *Journal of Personality and Social Psychology* 35, 767–82.

Sampson, E.E. (1981) 'Cognitive psychology as ideology', *American Psychologist* 36, 730–43.

Sanders, G.S. and Baron, R.S. (1977) 'Is social comparison irrelevant for producing choice shifts?', *Journal of Experimental Social Psychology* 13, 303–14.

Schachter, S. (1951) 'Deviation, rejection, and communication', *Journal of Abnormal and Social Psychology* 46, 190–207.

Schachter, S. (1959) *The Psychology of Affiliation*, Stanford, CA: Stanford University Press.

Schachter, S., Ellertson, N., McBride, D. and Gregory, D. (1951) 'An experimental study of cohesiveness and productivity', *Human Relations* 4, 229–38.

Schaffer, L.S. (1978) 'On the current confusion of group-related behavior and collective behavior: A reaction to Buys', *Personality and Social Psychology Bulletin* 4, 564–7.

Scheier, M.F. and Carver, C.S. (1981) 'Private and public aspects of self', in L. Wheeler (ed.), *Review of Personality and Social Psychology* (vol. 2, pp. 189–216), London: Sage.

Schermerhorn, J.R., Jr, Hunt, J.G. and Osborn, R.N. (1988) *Managing Organizational Behavior*, New York: Wiley.

Schopler, J. and Bateson, N. (1962) 'A dependence interpretation of the effects of a severe initiation', *Journal of Personality* 30, 633–49.

Schriesheim, J.F. (1980) 'The social context of leader–subordinate relations: An investigation of the effects of group cohesiveness', *Journal of Applied Psychology* 65, 183–94.

Schutz, W.C. (1966) *The Interpersonal Underworld*, Palo Alto, CA: Science and Behavior Books.

Schwarzwald, J., Laor, T. and Hoffman, M. (1986) 'Impact of sociometric method and activity content on assessment of intergroup relations in the classroom', *British Journal of Educational Psychology* 56, 24–31.

Schwarzwald, J., Moisseiev, O. and Hoffman, M. (1986) 'Similarity versus social ambition effects in the assessment of interpersonal acceptance in the classroom', *Journal of Educational Psychology* 78, 184–9.

Scott, W.A. (1965) *Values and Organizations*, Chicago, IL: Rand McNally.

Scott, W.A. and Scott, R. (1981) 'Intercorrelations among structural properties of primary groups', *Journal of Personality and Social Psychology* 41, 279–92.

Seashore, S. (1954) *Group Cohesiveness in the Industrial Work Group*, Ann Arbor, MI: Institute for Social Research.

Secord, P.F. and Backman, C.W. (1964) *Social Psychology*, New York: McGraw–Hill.

Segal, M.W. (1979) 'Varieties of interpersonal attraction and their interrelationships in natural groups', *Social Psychology Quarterly* 42, 253–61.

Shaw, M.E. (1974) *An Overview of Small Group Behavior*, Morristown, NJ: General Learning Press.

Shaw, M.E. (1976) *Group Dynamics: The psychology of small group behavior* (2nd edn). New York: McGraw–Hill.

Shaw, M.E. (1981) *Group Dynamics* (3rd edn), New York: McGraw-Hill.

Shaw M.E. and Gilchrist, J.C. (1955) 'Repetitive task failure and sociometric choice', *Journal of Abnormal and Social Psychology* 50, 29–32.

Shaw, M.E. and Shaw, L.M. (1962) 'Some effects of sociometric grouping upon learning in a second grade classroom', *Journal of Social Psychology* 57, 453–8.

Sherif, M. (1936) *The Psychology of Social Norms*, New York: Harper and Bros.

Sherif, M. (1966) *In Common Predicament: Social psychology of intergroup conflict and cooperation*, Boston, MA: Houghton Mifflin.

Sherif, M. (1967) *Group Conflict and Cooperation*, London: Routledge and Kegan Paul.

Sherif, M. and Sherif, C.W. (1956) *An Outline of Social Psychology*, New York: Harper and Row.

Sherif, M. and Sherif, C.W. (1969) *Social Psychology*, New York: Harper and Row.

Smith, K.K. and White, G.L. (1983) 'Some alternatives to traditional social psychology of groups', *Personality and Social Psychology Bulletin* 9, 65–73.

Smith, M. (1945) 'Social situation, social behavior, and social group', *Psychological Review* 52, 224–9.

Smith, P.M. (1985) *Language, the Sexes and Society*, Oxford: Blackwell.

Smith, S. (1984) 'Groupthink and the hostage rescue mission', *British Journal of Political Science* 15, 117–26.

Sole, K., Marton, J. and Hornstein, H.A. (1975) 'Opinion similarity and helping: Three field experiments investigating the bases of promotive behavior', *Journal of Experimential Social Psychology* 11, 1–13.

Stagner, R. and Eflal, B. (1982) 'Internal union dynamics during a strike: A quasi-experimental study', *Journal of Applied Psychology* 67, 37–44.

Steers, R.M. (1977) 'Antecedents and outcomes of organizational commitment', *Administrative Science Quarterly* 22, 46–56.

Stein, A.A. (1976) 'Conflict and cohesion: A review of the literature', *Journal of Conflict Resolution* 20, 143–72.

Steiner, I.D. (1974) 'Whatever happened to the group in social psychology?', *Journal of Experimental Social Psychology* 10, 94–108.

Steiner, I.D. (1982) 'Heuristic models of groupthink', in N. Brandstätter, J.H. Davis and G. Stocker-Kreichgauer (eds), *Group Decision Making* (pp. 503–39), New York: Academic Press.

Steiner, I.D. (1983) 'Whatever happened to the touted revival of the group', in H. Blumberg, P. Hare, V. Kent and M. Davies (eds), *Small Groups and Social Interaction* (vol. 2, pp. 539–48), New York: Wiley.

Steiner, I.D. (1986) 'Paradigms and groups', *Advances in Experimental Social Psychology* 19, 251–89.

Stewart, R.A. (1988) 'Habitability and behavioral issues of space flight', *Small Group Behavior* 19, 434–51.

Stockton, R. and Hulse, D. (1981) 'Developing cohesion in small groups: Theory and research', *Journal for Specialists in Group Work* 6, 188–94.

Stogdill, R.M. (1959) *Individual Behavior and Group Achievement: A theory, the experimental evidence*, New York: Oxford University Press.

Stogdill, R.M. (1972) 'Group productivity, drive, and cohesiveness', *Organizational Behavior and Human Performance* 8, 26–53

Stokes, J.P. (1983) 'Toward an understanding of cohesion in personal change groups', *International Journal of Group Psychotherapy* 33(4), 449–67.

Stokes, J.P., Fuehrer, A. and Childs, L. (1983) 'Group members' self-disclosures: Relation to perceived cohesion', *Small Group Behavior* 14, 63–76.

Suls, J.M. and Miller, R.L. (eds) (1977) *Social Comparison Processes: Theoretical and empirical perspectives*, Washington, DC: Hemisphere.

Sumner, W.G. (1906) *Folkways*, Boston, MA: Ginn.

Tagiuri, R. (1958) 'Social preference and its perception', in R. Tagiuri and L. Petrullo (eds), *Person Perception and Interpersonal Behavior* (pp. 316–36), Stanford, CA: Stanford University Press.

Tajfel, H. (1957) 'Value and the perceptual judgment of magnitude', *Psychological Review* 64, 192–204.

Tajfel, H. (1959) 'Quantitative judgement in social perception', *British Journal of Psychology* 50, 16–29.

Tajfel, H. (1963) 'Stereotypes', *Race* 5, 3–14.

Tajfel, H. (1969a) 'Social and cultural factors in perception', in G. Lindzey and E. Aronson (eds), *Handbook of Social Psychology* (vol. 3, pp. 315–94), Reading, MA: Addison-Wesley.

Tajfel, H. (1969b). 'Cognitive aspects of prejudice', *Journal of Social Issues*, 25, 79–97.

Tajfel, H. (1972a) 'Experiments in a vacuum', in J. Israel and H. Tajfel (eds), *The Context of Social Psychology: A critical assessment* (pp. 69–119), London: Academic Press.

Tajfel, H. (1972b) 'Some developments in European social psychology', *European Journal of Social Psychology* 2, 307–22.

Tajfel, H. (1972c) 'Social categorization.' English manuscript of 'La catégorisation sociale', in S. Moscovici (ed.), *Introduction à la Psychologie Sociale* (vol. 1, pp. 272–302), Paris: Larousse.

Tajfel, H. (1973) 'The roots of prejudice: Cognitive aspects', in P. Watson (ed.), *Psychology and Race* (pp. 76–95), Harmondsworth: Penguin.

Tajfel, H. (1974) *Intergroup Behaviour, Social Comparison and Social Change*, unpublished Katz–Newcomb lectures at University of Michigan, Ann Arbor, MI.

Tajfel, H. (ed.) (1978) *Differentiation between Social Groups*, London: Academic Press.

Tajfel, H. (1981a) *Human Groups and Social Categories: Studies in social psychology*, Cambridge: Cambridge University Press.

Tajfel, H. (1981b) "Social stereotypes and social groups', in J.C. Turner and H. Giles (eds), *Intergroup Behaviour* (pp. 144–67), Oxford: Blackwell; and in H. Tajfel (1981) *Human Groups and Social Categories: Studies in social psychology* (pp. 143–61), Cambridge: Cambridge University Press.

Tajfel, H. (ed.) (1982a) *Social Identity and Intergroup Relations*, Cambridge: Cambridge University Press.

Tajfel, H. (1982b) 'Social psychology of intergroup relations', *Annual Review of Psychology* 33, 1–39.

Tajfel, H. (ed.) (1984) *The Social Dimension: European developments in social psychology*, Cambridge: Cambridge University Press.

Tajfel, H. and Turner, J.C. (1979) 'An integrative theory of intergroup conflict', in W.G. Austin and S. Worchel (eds), *The Social Psychology of Intergroup Relations* (pp. 33–47), Monterey, CA: Brooks-Cole.

Tajfel, H. and Wilkes, A.L. (1963) 'Classification and quantitative judgement', *British Journal of Psychology* 54, 101–14.

Taylor, D.M. and Brown, R.J. (1979) 'Towards a more social social psychology?', *British Journal of Social and Clinical Psychology* 18, 173–9.

Terborg, J.R., Castore, C. and DeNinno, J.A. (1976) 'A longitudinal field investigation of the impact of group composition on group performance and cohesion', *Journal of Personality and Social Psychology* 34, 782–90.

Tetlock, P.E. (1979) 'Identifying victims of groupthink from public statements of decision makers', *Journal of Personality and Social Psychology* 37, 1314–24.

Theodorson, G.A. (1957) 'The relationship between leadership and popularity roles in small groups', *American Sociological Review* 22, 58–67.

Thibaut, J.W. (1950) 'An experimental study of the cohesiveness of underprivileged groups', *Human Relations* 3, 251–78.

Thibaut, J.W. and Kelley, H.H. (1959) *The Social Psychology of Groups*, New York: Wiley.

Thompson, J.E. and Carsrud, A.L. (1976) 'The effects of experimentally induced illusions of invulnerability and vulnerability on decisional risk taking in trials', *Journal of Social Psychology* 100, 263–7.

Tickle-Degen, L. and Rosenthal, R. (1987) 'Group rapport and nonverbal behaviour', in C. Hendrick (ed.), *Group Processes and Intergroup Relations* (pp. 113–36), Newbury Park, CA: Sage.

Triandis, H. (1977) *Interpersonal Behavior*, Monterey, CA: Brooks-Cole.

Turner, J.C. (1981) 'The experimental social psychology of intergroup behaviour', in J.C. Turner and H. Giles (eds), *Intergroup Behaviour* (pp. 66–101), Oxford: Blackwell.

Turner, J.C. (1982) 'Towards a cognitive redefinition of the social group', in H. Tajfel (ed.), *Social Identity and Intergroup Relations* (pp. 15–40), Cambridge: Cambridge University Press.

Turner, J.C. (1984) 'Social identification and psychological group formation', in H. Tajfel (ed.), *The Social Dimension: European developments in social psychology* (vol. 2, pp. 518–38), Cambridge: Cambridge University Press.

Turner, J.C. (1985) 'Social categorization and the self-concept: A social cognitive theory of group behaviour', in E.J. Lawler (ed.), *Advances in Group Processes: Theory and research* (vol. 2, pp. 77–122), Greenwich, CT: JAI Press.

Turner, J.C. (1991) *Social Influence*, Milton Keynes: Open University Press

Turner, J.C. and Giles, H. (eds) (1981) *Intergroup Behaviour*, Oxford: Blackwell.

Turner, J.C., Hogg, M.A., Oakes, P.J., Reicher, S.D. and Wetherell, M.S. (1987) *Rediscovering the Social Group: A self-categorization theory*, Oxford and New York: Blackwell.

Turner, J.C., Hogg, M.A., Turner, P.J. and Smith, P.M. (1984) 'Failure and defeat as determinants of group cohesiveness', *British Journal of Social Psychology* 23, 97–111.

Turner, J.C. and Oakes, P.J. (1986) 'The significance of the social identity concept for social psychology with reference to individualism, interactionism and social influence', *British Journal of Social Psychology* 25, 237–52.

Turner, J.C. and Oakes, P.J. (1989) 'Self-categorization theory and social influence', in P.B. Paulus (ed.), *The Psychology of Group Influence* (2nd edn, pp. 233–75), Hillsdale, NJ: Erlbaum.

Turner, J.C., Sachdev, I. and Hogg, M.A. (1983) 'Social categorization, interpersonal attraction and group formation', *British Journal of Social Psychology* 22, 227–39.

Turner, J.C., Wetherell, M.S. and Hogg, M.A. (1989) 'Referent informational influence and group polarization', *British Journal of Social Psychology* 28, 135–47.

Turner, R.H. (1964) 'Collective behavior', in R.E.L. Faris (ed.), *Handbook of Modern Sociology* (pp. 382–425), Chicago, IL: Rand McNally.

van Bergen, A. and Koekebakker, J. (1959) 'Group cohesiveness in laboratory experiments', *Acta Psychologica* 16, 81–98.

van Knippenberg, A.D.F. (1984) 'Intergroup differences in group perceptions', in H. Tajfel (ed.), *The Social Dimension: European developments in social psychology* (vol. 2, pp. 560–78), Cambridge: Cambridge University Press.

Veit, H. (1970) 'Some remarks upon the elementary interpersonal relations within ball game teams', .in G.S. Kenyon (ed.), *Contemporary Psychology of Sport* (pp. 355–62), Chicago, IL: Athletic Institute.

Vinokur, A. and Burnstein, E. (1974) 'The effects of partially shared persuasive arguments on group-induced shifts: A problem-solving approach', *Journal of Personality and Social Psychology* 29, 305–15.

Wang, R.S. (1977) 'External hostility and internal conflict: Group cohesion theory in international politics', *Dissertation Abstracts International* 37, 7954A.

Watson, G. and Johnson, D. (1972) *Social Psychology: Issues and insights*, Philadelphia, PA: J.B. Lippincott.

Wegner, D.M., Guiliano, T. and Hertel, P.T. (1984) 'Cognitive interdependence in close relationships', in W.J. Ickes (ed.), *Compatible and Incompatible Relationships* (pp. 253–76), New York: Springer-Verlag.

Weiner, B. (1986) *An Attributional Theory of Motivation and Emotion*, New York: Springer-Verlag.

Wetherell, M.S. (1987) 'Social identity and group polarization', in J.C. Turner, M.A. Hogg, P.J. Oakes, S.D. Reicher and M.S. Wetherell, *Rediscovering the Social Group: A self-categorization theory* (pp. 142–70), Oxford and New York: Blackwell.

Wheeless, L.R., Wheeless, V.E. and Dickson-Markman, F. (1982) 'The relations among social and task perceptions in small groups', *Small Group Behavior* 13, 373–84.

Whyte, G. (1989) 'Groupthink reconsidered', *Academy of Management Review* 14, 40–56.

Wicklund, R.A. (1982) 'How society uses self-awareness', in J. Suls (ed.), *Psychological Perspectives on the Self* (vol. 1, pp. 209–30), Hillsdale, NJ: Erlbaum.

Widmeyer, W.N., Brawley, L.R. and Carron, A.V. (1985) *The Measurement of Cohesion in Sports Teams: The group environment questionnaire*, London, Ontario: Sports Dynamics.

Wilder, D.A. (1977) 'Perception of groups, size of opposition and social influence', *Journal of Experimental Social Psychology* 13, 253–68.

Williams, J.M. and Hacker, C.M. (1982) 'Causal relationships among cohesion, satisfaction, and performance in women's intercollegiate hockey teams', *Journal of Sport Psychology* 4, 324–37.

Williams, K.D. (1981) *The Effects of Group Cohesiveness on Social Loafing*, paper presented at the annual meeting of the Midwestern Psychological Association, Detroit.

Williams, K.D., Harkins, S.G. and Latané, B. (1981) 'Identifiability as a deterrent to social loafing: Two cheering experiments', *Journal of Personality and Social Psychology* 40, 303–11.

Williams, K.D. and Karau, S.J. (1991) 'Social loafing and social compensation: The effects of expectations of co-worker performance', *Journal of Personality and Social Psychology* 61, 570–81.

Williams, K.D., Karau, S.J. and Bourgeois, M.J. (in press) 'Working on collective tasks: Social loafing and social compensation', in M.A. Hogg and D. Abrams (eds), *Group Motivation: Social psychological perspectives*, Hemel Hempstead: Harvester Wheatsheaf.

Wolf, S. (1979) 'Behavioral style and group cohesiveness as sources of minority influence', *European Journal of Social Psychology* 9, 381–96.

Worchel, S., Hart, D. and Butemeyer, J. (1991) *Is Social Loafing a Group Phenomenon? The effect of membership interdependence on work output*, unpublished manuscript, Texas A & M University.

Wright, T.L. and Duncan, D. (1986) 'Attraction to group, group cohesiveness and individual outcome: A study of training groups', *Small Group Behavior* 17, 487–92.

Yalom, I.D., Houts, P.S., Zimerberg, S.M. and Rand, K.H. (1966) 'Prediction of improvement in group therapy', *Archives of General Psychiatry* 17, 159–68.

Yalom, I.D. and Rand, K.H. (1966) 'Compatibility and cohesiveness in therapy groups', *Archives of General Psychiatry* 15, 267–75.

Yukelson, D., Weinberg, R. and Jackson, A. (1984) 'A multidimensional group cohesion instrument for intercollegiate basketball teams', *Journal of Sport Psychology* 6, 103–17.

Zaccaro, S.J. (1984) 'Social loafing: The role of task attractiveness', *Personality and Social Psychology Bulletin* 10, 99–106.

Zaccaro, S.J. and McCoy, M.C. (1988) 'The effects of task and interpersonal cohesiveness on performance of a disjunctive group task', *Journal of Applied Social Psychology* 18, 837–51.

Zander, A. (1979) 'The psychology of group processes', *Annual Review of Psychology* 30, 417–51.

Zander, A., Stotland, E. and Wolfe, D. (1960) 'Unity of group, identification with group, and self esteem of members', *Journal of Personality* 28, 463–78.

Zimbardo, P.G. (1970) 'The human choice: Individuation, reason and order vs. deindividuation, impulse and chaos', in W.J. Arnold and D. Levine (eds), *Nebraska Symposium on Motivation 1969* (pp. 237–307), Lincoln, NE: University of Nebraska Press.

Subject index

178

Author index

Abelson, R.P. 18, 52
Abrams, D.A. x, 5, 17, 24–6, 61, 63, 76, 81,
    83–6, 89, 92, 95–7, 99, 131–3, 149
Adorno, T.W. 13
Allard, R. 150
Allen, V.L. 66, 95, 125
Allport, F.H. 3, 16–17, 19, 24, 54, 63, 133
Allport, G.W. 54
Anderson, A.B. 41–2, 56–7, 70, 112
Andreyeva, G.M. 116
Arkin, R. 81, 83, 96
Aronson, E. 18, 52
Asch, S. 17, 82
Ashmore, R.D. 95
Atthowe, J.M. 42
Augoustinos, M. 76

Back, K. 6, 17, 19–23, 42, 56, 59, 120
Backman, C.W. 28
Bailey, N. 126–7
Bakeman, R. 54, 125
Bales, R.F. 4, 64
Ball, J.R. 48, 57
Barber, H. 144
Baron, R.S. 81, 83, 96
Bass, B.M. 4, 6
Bateson, N. 38
Baumgartel, H, 42
Bavelas, A. 66
Beck, S. 54, 125
Becker, S. 37
Bednar, R.L. 24, 49, 52, 57–8
Benedict, R. 121
Berger, J. 67
Berkowitz, L. 23, 26, 28, 37
Berscheid, E. 112
Billig, M. 5, 8, 13, 58, 61, 74, 98, 117, 121,
    148
Bion, W.R. 13–14
Bishop, D.W. 117

Blumberg, H. 7
Bonacich, P. 125
Bonner, H. 4, 23
Borden, R. 41–2, 56
Borgatta, E.F. 51
Borman, W.C. 51
Bourgeois, M.J. 146
Bourhis, R.Y. 92, 98, 104, 117, 121, 132, 149–50
Bovard, E.W. 39, 42, 57
Bowerman, C.E. 37
Boyanowsky, E.O. 124
Brawley, L.R. 22, 44–6, 49, 56–7
Brewer, M.B. 33, 90, 93, 114–17, 120
Brickner, M. 23, 120, 147
Brinthaupt, T.M. 79
Brown, R. 112
Brown, R.A. 41
Brown, R.J. 33, 37, 61, 92, 120
Bruner, J.S. 94
Budge, S. 23, 73
Burlingame, G. 7, 24, 40, 42, 56
Burnstein, E. 37, 81, 83, 96, 124
Butemeyer, J. 147–8
Byrne, D. 29, 36–7, 39, 107, 113, 120, 127
Byrne, J.L. 150

Callaway, M.R. 138–40
Campbell, A. 42
Campbell, D.T. 11, 17, 35, 90, 94, 107,
    116–17
Carron, A.V. 7, 18, 22–3, 40, 44–6, 48–9, 52,
    56–8, 76, 111, 143–5
Carsrud, A.L. 140
Cartwright, D. 6–7, 18, 22–4, 28, 32, 51, 53,
    61
Carver, C.S. 84–5
Castore, C. 42, 56
Cattell, R.B. 4
Charles, M.T. 120
Chavis, D.M. 76–7, 111

180